MW01107179

Hugh B. Cave, 1930.

Cave of a Thousand Tales:

The Life and Times of Pulp Author Hugh B. Cave

Milt Thomas

Arkham House Publishers
2004

ISBN 0-87054-183-8

First Edition

CONTENTS

To my wife Sandra, whose encouragement and support has made all things possible; Philip Rahman and Dwayne Olson for their guidance; Tom Roberts for his knowledge of Hugh Cave works.

INTRODUCTION

WHEN I FIRST MET HUGH B. CAVE, HE HANDED me his business card, which read, "Hugh B. Cave, Writer." It wasn't embellished with fancy logos, awards or titles—simply, "Writer." He had just come from garage sale-ing with the lovely woman in his life, Peggie—not from a book signing, or from giving a lecture, or a photo op with other big name writers—just a garage sale.

That is the essence of Hugh B. Cave. He is a humble man, shy and without pretense. "A writer writes," is how he describes what he does, but few writers have ever accomplished what he has in his 76-year career, a career that is still a work in progress.

Hugh B. Cave is considered an icon to those who know him —pulp fiction fans, publishers, editors, and other writers. It is difficult to imagine any American over the age of 40 who has not read something by Hugh Cave. For instance, his short-short story, "Two Were Left," has been published 76 times since 1942, primarily in scholastic magazines and textbooks. You probably read it yourself in school.

However, Hugh Cave did not earn a reputation for writing one story published 76 times. He earned it first as one of our premier pulp fiction writers, then as a mainstay of the slick magazine fiction era, and finally, as a novelist. He would establish a well-deserved reputation in each of those fields, writing over 1,000 short stories and more than 40 books, works that have been published in 27 foreign countries.

For those too young to remember, pulp magazines were the immensely popular publications that dominated newsstands before World War II. For five or ten cents each, the reader could select from more than 100 different titles like *Action Stories, Argosy, Dime Detective, Modern Romances, Strange Tales* and *Western Story.* Their popularity waned with World War II paper shortages and the advent of popular radio, then television.

As a pulp fiction writer, Cave's contemporaries included Robert Bloch (*Psycho*), Ray Bradbury, Edgar Rice Burroughs, John Dickson Carr, Erle Stanley Gardner, Dashiell Hammett, L. Ron Hubbard, MacKinley Kantor, Louis L'Amour, H. P. Lovecraft, John D. MacDonald, Clarence E. Mulford (Hopalong Cassidy), and Tennessee Williams.

Hugh Cave never achieved the celebrity status eventually accorded some of his pulp contemporaries; however, he was certainly one of the most prolific of his day. He wrote more than 800 stories in 90 popular fiction magazines during pulp fiction's best years, from 1929–1942. His stories included every genre from romance to western to horror. He was so prolific, he used more than a dozen pen names. You could find as many as four Hugh Cave stories in one issue, under the pseudonyms Justin Case, C.H. Barnett, Allen Beck, and Geoffrey Vace, to name a few. During the depths of the Great Depression, when college graduates scraped by on $18 per week, Cave the writer made $5,000 a year, much of it earned at the going rate of a penny per word.

But his reputation wasn't built on the number of stories he wrote. Popular fiction was truly "popular" back then, before radio and TV. Cave's South Pacific adventure stories, especially those surrounding a British outpost in Borneo called Tsiang House, earned a huge following among readers. His detective stories were in such demand, he hardly wrote anything else in the mid-to-late 1930's. He became best known for his "weird menace" tales. Cave wrote them back before the days of slash and gore, when a writer conveyed real terror to a reader through tense dialogue and well-turned phrases.

Pulps all but disappeared after the war, and if he had never written another word, his legacy was secure. But "Hugh B. Cave, Writer," went wherever he found an opportunity to write.

During World War II, as pulp magazines were fading into

history, he moved into the more lucrative slick paper magazines. There, Hugh Cave adapted to a totally different market and style, connecting him with an eager new audience of fans. Cave published 350 fiction and non-fiction pieces, including 43 stories in The *Saturday Evening Post* alone. ("The Mission" is still considered one of that magazine's most popular short stories of all time.)

The war also provided him with an opportunity to write full-length books about real-life soldier-heroes. With his success, he branched out into travel and fiction. Since then, he has authored more than 40 books, fiction and non-fiction, four of them best sellers. *Haiti: High Road to Adventure* remained in print for 16 years, considered by many to be the authoritative book on that troubled country. *Four Paths to Paradise* revealed Jamaica in much the same way, earning him similar recognition. *The Cross on the Drum,* Cave's novel set in a country remarkably similar to Haiti, was the recommended selection for two national book clubs in its day. *Long Were the Nights,* one of his true stories about bravery during World War II, remained on the *Herald Tribune* bestseller list for six months. He wrote a string of supernatural thrillers in the 1980's, and continues writing them. In July, 2001, his paperback novel, *The Evil Returns,* was released nationally on his 91st birthday.

Yes, Hugh B. Cave is a master at his craft. He is one of the last survivors from a generation whose written words helped millions survive the Great Depression and World War II. He has thrilled, scared, educated and comforted three generations of readers, stirred their imaginations and warmed their hearts. Anyone who loves books, who writes for a living, or hopes to do so, must pay homage to this man. Moreover, the fact he is alive to talk about it —and *still* writing for publication—is a hook to make for a compelling story.

"Hugh B. Cave, Writer." It is such a bland description for someone who has lived his life in front of a keyboard, most of those years using a manual typewriter. The wellspring of his creativity was not a keyboard though; it was his mind. That mind transported him to places most people can only imagine. It was just a matter of time before his body would follow.

This is where his story becomes an inspiration—to me, to his fans, and to anyone who seeks the meaning of life itself. Hugh Cave lived—and lives—to write. Yet, while his existence hangs on the very words he writes, he has also *experienced* a life of adventure, mystery, tragedy and romance that could be grist for an exciting story even if he had never put pen to paper.

"Hugh B. Cave, War Correspondent." After writing a series of successful books about American war heroes, Cave was invited to serve as a correspondent in the South Pacific Theater. He took part in the last major amphibious assault of the war. There he found himself under fire as the troops landed, later ambushed by snipers, and then living under the most hostile circumstances imaginable. All this occurred in Borneo and New Guinea, locales for some of his most famous pulp adventure stories of the 1930's. Now he was experiencing adventures rather than imagining what they might be like.

"Hugh B. Cave, Anthropologist." He went on to spend five years in Haiti, exploring the entire rugged country on foot and horseback. He learned to speak Creole, and his humble manner endeared him to the people. Cave became an acknowledged expert on Haitian culture, including the mysterious practice of voodoo. He was probably the first white man ever awarded full access to the most secret ceremonies. Haiti became the setting for many of his most successful novels. He fled the country during a revolution that brought Papa "Doc" Duvalier to power.

"Hugh B. Cave, Coffee Baron." Jamaica became the next stop on his journey through life. There he purchased a "ruinate," 200-year old plantation, then learned how to plant, grow and harvest coffee. Hugh Cave ended up producing what is still regarded today as the world's best coffee. He also single-handedly started the Jamaican timber industry. His 15-year plantation adventure ended at a dark time in Jamaican history, when a Marxist-leaning government chased away foreigners. His plantation overlooked a secret base where Fidel Castro and his troops came and went from Jamaica.

Unfortunately, where there's a yin, there's a yang. With all these accomplishments, Cave suffered his share of failure and tragedy. He endured the death of his son, a loveless and lonely marriage, the tragic fire that destroyed his life's work, and financial setbacks surely devastating to most people. He narrowly escaped death himself on at least four occasions. Yet through it all, from the mountain tops to the chasms, he always maintained his humility, his zest for life—and his love affair with the written word.

Ironically, his humility may be responsible for keeping him under the radar screen of public consciousness. He is known and idolized by his fans around the world, but Hugh B. Cave is not a household name. If he had developed a talent for self-promotion, this book might be a capstone, not an introduction.

Fortunately, his body of work will always be here for us to enjoy. Just go to your local bookstore and ask for themed short story collections about vampires, ghosts or ghouls. You will find many of them include at least one Hugh Cave classic. Or log on to the Internet and search "Hugh Cave." At this date, the search engine, Google.com, lists 12,700 references to Hugh B. Cave, and the leading Internet bookseller, *amazon.com,* offers 29 Hugh Cave selections.

You can even find Hugh Cave stories in that last repository of literary history, the neighborhood garage sale. Cave himself recovered many of his published works lost in the previously mentioned tragic fire by rooting through old books and magazines at garage sales. It was after attending one such sale, that I first met him.

Today he is enjoying a level of popularity which rivals his pulp days, thanks to collectors and anthologists. However, if you want to know the man behind the legend—the Cave of a Thousand Tales—you can find it all right here.

FOREWORD

I FIRST MET HUGH CAVE AND PEGGIE IN 1987 AT A restaurant where they were dining with mutual friends, Cricket and Jere Pechstein. We didn't see much of each other after that, but when Hugh and Peg moved out to Washington state the following year, I sent him birthday cards and an occasional manuscript. I was a fledgling writer after a 20-year career in the music industry and he gave me some very sound advice. ('Just keep writing and read the work of other writers.')

It was after their return to Sebastian, Florida in 1994, that I began to see him regularly. By then, I was writing full-time—14,000 words a month for publication—and had just finished a business book. Always on the lookout for human interest stories, I wrote a feature about Hugh Cave for one of my magazine markets.

Hugh called after reading the article and showered me with praise. Those who know Hugh Cave, know he is generous in praising others. So, I asked his permission to write a book. He answered, "I would be honored," his reply again, typically Cave. I knew that Audrey Parente had written a short biography, *Pulp Man's Odyssey* (Starmont House, 1988), but after interviewing him for my 800-word article, I felt he had a story to tell about living that could inspire people and read like a novel.

On April 13, 1995, I drove to the Cave household for my first of 20 interviews over the next six months, accumulating 40 hours of taped conversations with Hugh and Peggie. Since that time, I visited with Hugh and Peg numerous times, and rarely did a visit go by without some new tidbit of information popping up.

So why is this book only now being published? As John Lennon once wrote, "Life is what happens when you're making other plans." I didn't know it at the time, but my full-time writer's life was about to change. Just as I completed the Cave interviews, a key employee of the local Chamber of Commerce resigned and as a board member, I volunteered to assume that position for 90 days until they found a replacement. The 90 days ended up being five years, consuming all my time and energy. I'm one of those clearly demarcated right brain-left brain people; when I am active in one hemisphere, I can't seem to function in the other. My writing dropped off almost entirely during that time.

I continued to visit Hugh and Peggie though. Finally, Hugh said to me, "you know Milt, I'm almost 90 years old and I don't know how much longer I can wait for this book of yours."

I had an enjoyable five years at the Chamber, but after Hugh's comment and some introspection about life's priorities, I resigned my position and called Hugh to tell him. I could hear his smile of relief.

Fortunately, I had transcribed all the taped interviews back in 1995. During those interviews, we skipped around quite a bit, and we often revisited the same material, but when we did, new gems would emerge which Hugh had not thought about for years. After our interviews were complete, I then organized all the transcribed material into chronological order. The stage was now set for me to write the book.

Several points to note. I have written this biography within the context of our interview sessions. Hugh's comments are all in quotes, while mine are generally written from a first person perspective to make it less confusing. I have also taken the liberty of expanding on some of the earlier incidents in his life where he may not remember much detail. In other words, certain passages have been fictionalized to give the reader a more intimate feel for some of the events in his early years. I did this with his knowledge to convey how these events may have influenced him at the time and shaped his later life and work. Those passages are in italics so they are easy to identify.

This book is also written as a personal history of the man, and as such, does not go into depth about the pulp market. While his fan base today is focused in the pulp era, his life and career went far beyond that period. However, pulp fans will find plenty of new information here to build a more complete picture of this living legend from that golden age of popular American fiction.

I have put together a listing of Hugh Cave works in the back of the book. While I did extensive checking and cross-checking, most of the information comes from Hugh himself. A number of people have found Hugh Cave pulp stories, particularly pulp fans and especially Tom Roberts, noted pulp artist, collector and publisher of Black Dog Books. Hopefully, as this book makes the rounds, more people will come out of the woodwork with names and even copies of stories listed here as "Title Unknown." The reason these gaps and omissions exist is due to the fire at his home in 1967 that destroyed all carbon copies, magazines and sales records he had kept from the pulp era.

I met, talked with, or e-mailed Hugh Cave regularly throughout the course of writing this book. It isn't often a writer has the opportunity to speak with his subject 50 or 60 years after events occurred. I took full advantage of that opportunity so this portrayal is as true to life as possible.

Finally, you should understand that Hugh Cave is a very humble and honorable soul, so there were incidents in his life that he asked me not to put in print. I complied with his wishes, although I felt some of his concerns were unfounded and might have added even more dimension to his character. Other than those few instances though, this book describes Hugh Cave's life as accurately as possible from his point of view. I feel his story is exciting as a life well lived and an inspiration, not only to writers or would-be writers, but to all those readers who wish their lives were different and love reading about people who changed theirs. In that respect, *Cave of a Thousand Tales* is also a self-help book.

About five years ago, I met a magazine editor on a writer's junket to Grenada in the West Indies. He asked what I was currently working on and I gave him a brief overview of Hugh Cave's life and works. Afterwards, I mentioned that I planned to get together with Hugh after this trip, and the editor looked at me, astonished, and said, "You mean this man is still alive!"

He certainly is, and after you finish this book, you will know what "alive" really means.

Milt Thomas

Cave of a Thousand Tales:

The Life and Times of Pulp Author Hugh B. Cave

PART ONE: BEGINNINGS

Chapter 1: Meeting the Master

THE PHONE RANG UNTIL A RECORDED MESSAGE greeted me that you might expect to hear on one of those great 1940's radio mysteries. A voice, shapeless, in measured syllables, spoke the dreaded words: "We're not home now," then added, "just leave a message and someone—or someTHING—will get back to you."

Someone *and* something did get back to me. The some*one* was Hugh B. Cave, master of menace, purveyor of popular fiction, literary icon to the writers, editors, publishers and fans—past and present—who have known him.

He returned my call promptly and seemed happy to hear from me. I interpreted his demeanor as typical of a lonely old man willing to invite even the most obnoxious telemarketer into his home for companionship. I would be more off target than an Iraqi missile.

The some*thing* did not become apparent until we started our weekly interview sessions, and it did not frighten me—it inspired me.

Hugh Cave and Peggie—the woman who figures prominently in his life story—live today in Sebastian, Florida. Sebastian is a tiny, peaceful, old-time fishing village, nestled on the Indian River lagoon, about a two hour drive from Disney World and well within the embrace of moderating Atlantic Ocean breezes.

Sebastian is a retiree's dream—small and friendly, free of crime, congestion and other big city ills. The weather is sunny and warm all year, ideal for golf, boating or just sitting out in the back yard sipping prune juice. It was especially beautiful that day in April 1995 when I met Hugh B. Cave for our first interview.

Hugh and Peggie make their home in a small, ranch-style house in a neighborhood of small ranch-style homes, hardly the setting you might expect for someone who has written so many great adventure, mystery and horror stories.

However, this is typical of the contradiction that is Hugh Cave. Outwardly, a quiet, humble man; on the inside, a mind on fire. It rages with images of life as a vividly colored tapestry, undaunted by age. Fortunately for us, we have access to that wonderful side of him we cannot see. It is recorded in the volumes of work he has produced over a career spanning 76-plus years.

Our first meeting occurred in a restaurant several years earlier. My introduction to Cave was uneventful; we chatted with each other across our respective tables. He gave me his "Hugh B. Cave, Writer" business card. I did not give it much thought then. For all I knew, he had retired long ago from some mundane job and now filled his hours with self-indulgent musings about a little life lost.

I stood at his door and rang the bell, notebook in hand, tape recorder under my arm. I glanced over at a blue-haired lady tinkering in her flowerbed next door, turning dirt in slow motion. If I end up like her, I thought, please shoot me.

I heard someone coming to answer the door, spry footsteps on a tile floor, stark contrast to that lady plodding away in her garden.

The door opened and there stood the Master himself, Hugh Cave, all 85 years of him, slightly hunched over, gaunt, and bald as a newborn. He smiled, a lifetime of wrinkles etched on his face. "Good to see you, Milt."

As I followed him to the kitchen, I began to fear this venture might be a mistake. My experience with 85-year olds told me that conducting a coherent interview would be difficult, not to say an entire book's worth of interviews. Living in Florida, I had grown accustomed to cranky seniors who drove five miles per hour in the passing lane and elevated complaining into an art form.

However, Cave's youthful gait encouraged me. It was as though he had switched souls with a 19-year old boy who now inhabited his ancient body. I thought of suggesting that as a story line to him. On second thought, he had probably already used it.

Cave turned his head to speak and his body followed, a common trait in elderly people with limited mobility. "Would you like some coffee?"

"Sure."

He looked his age—the stooped posture, the gaunt, pale features—yet he exuded this underlying energy about him—quick movement, alert eyes, and command of his actions. I felt more optimistic.

"Why don't we sit in my office," Cave suggested.

I followed him into a converted bedroom, furnished with two chairs and a desk, on which sat a Gateway computer, scanner and laser printer. Cave motioned for me to sit, then pulled up a chair in front of his computer.

"I wish we had one of these in the pulp days," he said, gesturing toward the computer. "Back then I was cranking out 30–40,000 words a month on a second-hand typewriter. Everything was carbon copied and very flammable."

I grunted in agreement as I looked around the room, impressed further that he had adapted so well to modern technology.

The wall behind his computer was filled with people photos, some yellowed with age, some recent. An original oil painting hung nestled among the photos. It was clearly not the work of a beginner.

"Who's the artist?" I asked.

"Oh, I did that when I lived in Haiti. I always loved to paint and I had plenty of subjects down there, believe me. Sold a few, gave away most of them. You start shedding possessions as you get older."

The other three walls were lined with built-in shelves, stocked from floor to ceiling with books, magazines and recorded music tapes. I looked over the numerous books, which all had one thing in common—every one of them was authored by or written about Hugh B. Cave.

"I don't have copies of everything I've written, unfortunately," he said. "Back in 1967 we had a fire in the shed where I stored the old magazines. All my work from the pulp days went up in smoke."

He spoke dispassionately about something that would have

devastated me. This equanimity served him well through his life, it turned out.

I fumbled with my tape recorder as he sat silently and watched —no, studied—my every move. It was a look I would observe frequently in our months together, as though a video camera whirred in his head, recording every sight and sound for use in some future story.

"Where should we start?" he asked.

Hell if I know, I thought, finally engaging the tape recorder. I ignored him, busying myself with my writer's trappings while I tried to summon up an impressive answer to his question. I positioned the microphone close to him, cleared my throat of self-doubt, then spoke.

I asked how he would start if he were interviewing Hugh Cave back in the pulp days.

Cave gave a dismissing chuckle. "I never had to interview anyone; whatever I needed to fill the page was up here."

He tapped the side of his shiny head with a crooked finger, then looked at me, video camera whirring.

I turned away toward his book and magazine collection, asking if they had been saved from the fire.

"No, most were written afterwards. I have rediscovered some of my older works though, at garage sales, believe it or not. People are always discarding things; you can't imagine how many pulp magazines I've found for next to nothing."

He seemed proud of his accomplishment. I could only feel sad that this man must search for his life's work on bargain tables in nameless garages.

I asked how he managed to be so consistently productive throughout his career.

"It isn't difficult. Writers write just like golfers play golf and welders weld. Writing is what I do, Milt. I get up in the morning and can't wait until I get in here to boot up this computer. Right now I'm working on material for another hardcover collection of my stories."

(He would have three collections of his work published during the next year, many more in subsequent years.)

"Back in the pulp days, I thought nothing of sitting at my manual typewriter for 18 hours a day. It was my life and I loved it. I never suffered from writer's block. I couldn't—I liked to eat too much. During the Depression, when publishers only paid a penny or two a word, you had to write quite a few words to pay rent and buy groceries."

However, I told him, it took more than that to account for his prolific career—was it schooling? Parental encouragement? A good gene pool?

"All the above, I suppose. However, if I had to choose one thing to account for my creative output, I guess it would be reading."

I rebutted that many people read while few have published over 1,000 stories.

"I'm not talking about reading, like a daily newspaper or four novels a year. I mean having my nose buried in a book every chance I could get. My fondest childhood memories centered on reading adventure tales so exciting, I lost myself somewhere between the pages, totally oblivious to my surroundings. That's where I lived.

"Of course, I don't know that I would have developed such a love of reading if television had been around in those days. But TV isn't the only culprit; I think parents must shoulder at least some of the blame. We learn from our parents. If Mom and Dad are busy or tired, they tell their kids to watch TV. Then they reward kids for 'being good' by allowing them to watch more television. Imagine rewarding children for sitting quietly in front of a screen and staring at it? Then, as if this isn't enough damage, when evening rolls around, what do the parents do—they watch TV *with* the kids!

"Now, as I told you, reading has always been a great passion of mine, and my mother was responsible for it," he said proudly. "She started reading to me and my brothers long before we had any memory of it. Then, as we grew older, she encouraged us to read on our own."

Cave smiled fondly at the thought of his mother. "She always encouraged us—in *anything* we did."

Then he continued, "But reading is also something uniquely *human*, right? Just think about it. Only we humans have the ability to look at a page with symbols on it, understand those symbols, and translate them into images so intense they become reality. What greater affirmation of humanity do we have?"

I still couldn't see the connection between great readers and great writers.

"Milt, if you are looking for some magic author potion here, I think you will be disappointed."

I said I wasn't looking for the potion, just a list of ingredients. We both laughed.

"All right, let's try coming up with a list," said Cave. He seemed completely absorbed in the effort. "Reading is first, maybe even the most important ingredient. But reading is really a passive activity, whereas writing is an active one. So maybe another ingredient is whatever bridges the gap between active and passive."

You mean like playing tennis rather than watching it on TV? I suggested.

"Yes."

Well, I wondered, if your mother encouraged your reading by being an avid reader, how did she encourage your proactivity?

"By example, I suppose; she and my father both had that effect. It probably had something to do with the world in which they grew up."

Chapter 2: Beginnings

Cave's mother, Edith Mary Barnett (pronounced Barn-it) was born in Bombay, India, on August 9, 1870, the youngest of seven children. Her father—Hugh Cave's grandfather—George Barnett, was Lord Mayor of Bombay back when India was the crown jewel of the British Empire. He moved there from England to help build the Great Indian Peninsula Railway (which would make for a fateful coincidence in Cave's life 100 years later). He was offered knighthood for his accomplishments in that effort, but refused, preferring instead the title, C.I.E. (Companion of the Indian Empire). Queen Victoria granted his wish and bestowed the title on him personally at a Buckingham Palace ceremony.

Edith shared a wonderful childhood with her sisters and loving parents, cushioned by the privileges of rank, with exotic, fabled India as a playground. Their large, rambling, oceanfront home, known as "Breach Candy," had terraces in front, peacocks in the gardens and a rear compound with quarters for their 20-odd servants. The estate bustled with brightly dressed attendants and a constant stream of interesting, important visitors.

The Prince of Wales was one. He became a regular guest at their home and visited often when in the country to hunt tigers. While staying at the house, he spent evenings entertaining Edith and her sisters, dancing with each of them to music on the Victrola. He eventually went on to become King Edward VII. Those were good times.

Edith returned to England when she was only nine years old and attended a private school in Croydon. After graduating at age 19, she pursued a course in nursing, completing it in three years. This was before the days of Registered Nurses, so she graduated with the title, "Sister Edith Mary Barnett, Trained Nurse." Her father returned from India to attend the ceremony.

After graduation, she accepted a nursing position in the city of Coventry. There she first met Thomas Edward Cave, an accountant by trade with a promising career. He was a dashing young man, two years her junior, tall and handsome, sporting a David Niven-type mustache. She was petite, very attractive and full of life.

He fell for her immediately, but timing was not on their side. Edith was drawn to other priorities. Filled with visions of saving the world, she responded immediately when her government put out a call for nurses to serve with the British Army in South Africa. Conditions were deteriorating and an armed conflict was imminent. It became known as the Boer War.

For a young girl raised in exotic India, Sister Edith Mary Barnett would not be denied this opportunity to serve in such a faraway place. So she bid her good-byes and left on the long voyage to South Africa, accompanied by her sister, Dora, also a nurse, both filled with anticipation and purpose.

One of those she left behind was Thomas Edward Cave of Coventry. He missed her terribly from the start. So after several months of careful consideration, he made a decision. Thomas gave up his promising job and career, booking passage to South Africa at his own expense.

"You can imagine Edith's surprise," said Cave. "When one day Thomas showed up. She had grown lonely in this desolate, war-torn land, without family or friends, thousands of miles from home. So when he proposed marriage, she offered little resistance. They were wed on December 19, 1898 in CapeTown."

He reflected a moment. "I never really knew that much about my father. He wasn't the type who talked about himself, and what little I did know about him came from my mother. I know he was born in Coventry in 1872, but that's about all.

"You know, Milt, I have many photos of my mother, including some of her as a young woman. She was very pretty then. But sadly, I have none of my father, at any age. To tell you the truth, I can't even remember what he looked like."

He said it without hesitation, not making any attempt to conjure up his father's image, as if he had tried to do so recently—possibly often—but failed.

"They were married just as the Boer War began. I know life proved difficult for them because my mother told me—just like she told me everything else I know about their lives, beyond what part of it I shared with them, of course."

Edith worked hard tending to the sick and wounded. She continued working well into her first pregnancy in 1900. Then she and Thomas, who had joined the Army Service Corps as a paymaster, traveled by refugee train for a week to reach his new post. It was the same CapeTown-to-Johannesburg train that Gandhi had been thrown off just seven years earlier. On the trip, Edith became ill and started bleeding. As soon as they reached Johannesburg, she was rushed to the hospital, but not in time to save her child. The baby boy was stillborn.

"He is buried there, somewhere in South Africa," Cave said grimly. "I have a photo of the gravesite."

He quickly left the subject. "Here, I have something to show you."

Cave stood up and reached for several old photo albums on a shelf. He thumbed through one of them until he came to the book and page he wanted, then placed the album in my lap, pointing at a photo. "That's her," he said, "my mother, Edith."

The grainy, yellowed print revealed an attractive young woman with softly sculpted features and brilliant, silky hair, apparently blond.

"No, she wasn't blond; her hair was pure white, just like the fresh-fallen snow."

I looked up at him for an explanation.

"It had always been chestnut brown until that terrifying incident in South Africa, long before I was born. She and Dad were just married, living on an army post. Mother was returning home from her job at the hospital one day, walking along the dirt path that led to their quarters. . . ."

Every step was an effort for Edith, a slightly built, thin woman. Her legs were swollen from a long day running between the makeshift operating room and an overcrowded, understaffed field hospital next door. A steady stream of wounded British soldiers arrived from the front, on stretchers or in their comrades' arms.

The sound of battle was a safe distance away from medical personnel, but all too close for these dazed and bloody combatants.

Both facilities were set up under tan canvas tents, with side flaps raised to let in what little breeze existed on the hot, tinder dry veldt. The smell of death was pervasive. Hordes of flies swarmed over both tents, settling on discarded, blood-soaked rags and clothing, or directly on soldiers' wounds.

The metal operating table—it was really more of a gurney—stood on wheels with rocks wedged behind them to hold the table in place. A bloodstained sheet lay draped over it. The sheets were changed between patients, but quickly bloodied up from gaping, often mortal wounds of soldiers placed there in a desperate attempt to save them. They were all so young, full of life just hours earlier. Now their life trickled out of them into the fabric of a spreading red stain.

Edith tried to stop the bleeding, often helplessly pressing her small, porcelain-like hand over a flowing wound. Sometimes she could only stroke the dirty, blanched brow of a soldier as he slipped into lifelessness.

When it all became too much for her normally bedrock constitution, she simply walked next door to the field hospital. There she always found a soldier recovering from his wounds who wanted to make simple conversation. Edith was the only woman on staff and relished these opportunities to temporarily blot out the screams and groans next door.

At the end of every ten-hour shift, which she spent almost entirely on her feet, Edith would walk the rocky path that meandered a mile over barren terrain to reach the married officer's barracks. Her black, lace-top shoes were badly scuffed and well worn, but at least they held together. She had purchased them in London before coming to South Africa and they reminded her of civilized life back home. Edith promised herself that she would wear them until this terrible war ended, then she would leave them here along with all this misery and buy new ones back home in celebration of her return to civilization.

Rows of drab, wood and canvas cottage-tents called marquees were all now visible as she neared the end of her daily trek. Life was not easy for the Brits, set against a backdrop of dust storms, torrential rains, swarms of mosquitoes and howling jackals.

Today Edith was so exhausted, her legs began to cramp up. She stopped once, reaching down to massage her calf muscles until the cramps went away. Then she continued, shielding her eyes from the bright sun as she looked for Thomas. He would normally be sitting outside their primitive home, on a canvas folding chair, smoking his pipe.

Edith saw him and waved furiously. As she approached, about 200 feet away, Thomas suddenly stood upright. He held the pipe down at his side. She was close enough to see the disturbed look on his face as he dropped the pipe, turned and ran inside.

Edith thought it odd but stopped walking as her leg again went into a cramp. Thomas came back out with his Enfield rifle. She reached down and massaged her calf muscle, but kept her eyes fixed on Thomas as he raised the rifle to his shoulder and took aim. He was aiming at her.

She let go of her leg and began to stand upright as she heard him yell, "Get down!"

Edith quickly fell to her knees, just as a shot rang out. She felt a sudden rush of air and "phfffft" as the bullet flew past her making a thud in the dirt. Horrified and confused, she turned to look behind her. There stood a six-foot black mamba, one of the world's deadliest snakes, known as "the snake that walks on its tail" for how it stalks game with its body upright, ready to strike. A second shot rang out, a second bullet whizzed past Edith. This time, the snake's head jerked backwards.

"Mother fainted straight away," said Cave. "With all the horror she faced every day, you might expect she could withstand anything. But Mother had this mortal fear of snakes. Most people only see harmless garden snakes that slither in the grass; they are rarely six feet long, and you never see one standing on its tail poised to kill."

Edith lay unconscious for more than 24 hours. When she awoke, Thomas was right there, sitting at the edge of her metal frame bed. He leaned over and embraced her. His voice choked with uncharacteristic emotion, Thomas cried, "Thank God you are all right."

She brought her arm up and patted him on the back, just as she often did for her poor, wounded soldiers. Thomas then sat up, eyes a bit moist. He cleared his throat. "I was so afraid that dreadful snake would bite you," he finally said.

Only then did Edith recall the black mamba. After being surrounded by dying men at the hospital every day, she quickly realized how close she had come to death herself. She lay silently, looking at him. Something in his expression though, was not quite right. "What is it, darling?" she asked.

He shook his head, then stood. "Would you like some tea?" he asked.

"Not now, darling. Please tell me; something's the matter, isn't it?"

He closed his eyes momentarily. "No, I'm just happy you are alive."

Thomas turned and walked away softly, the wood plank floor echoing under him with each step. He was always uncomfortable in emotional situations. Edith stared at his back as he went outside, sat in his canvas chair and looked off toward the distant hills.

Feeling much better and swept with an urge to use the toilet, Edith rose from her bed. She felt somewhat shaky as she walked toward the wash basin. It sat on a cabinet, over which hung a mirror nailed into the rough wood wall.

She poured water into the basin from a large, milk-colored glass pitcher and leaned over, splashing her face. The water refreshed her in the stifling summer heat. A hand towel lay draped over one side of the makeshift cabinet. Edith picked it up to dry her face. Then she looked in the mirror and gasped.

"Her expression of shock brought Thomas back from the verandah. He must have been listening for this moment." Cave paused, as if purposely adding to his story's drama.

So what was it, I asked impatiently, a little annoyed at being suddenly yanked away from South Africa so many years ago.

"Her hair," he answered. "It had turned overnight from a beautiful chestnut brown—to pure white."

I told him that was impossible.

"I know it's hard to believe," Cave answered, "but there are documented cases. My mother wasn't one to make up stories, either, so I believe her. How else could you explain a 29-year-old woman whose hair suddenly turns pure white?"

I recalled a girlfriend of mine in high school whose hair turned gray before her 21st birthday. It did not happen overnight though —and she did not have a son who was a master storyteller, either.

"Anyway," Cave continued, "her hair remained pure white until the day she died in 1950."

I did not comment, but looked again at young Edith's photo. There she was, in the springtime of her life, with such a beautiful face—framed with silky, snow-white hair.

"The Boer War ended in 1902," continued Cave, "soon after Edith's father, George Barnett, died. Her parents had moved back to Surrey, England after 40 years in India and even named their new home "Breach Candy."

"That same year, on September 23, Edith gave birth to a second son, Thomas Barnett Cave. About a year after Tom was born, my family left South Africa and returned to England. Dad bought Ways Green House in Chester, in the sub-district of Over, which still stands today, I think, in use as a hostel.

"Dad became a grain merchant, buying and selling crops, rather successful too, I understand. My brother Geoffrey Barnett Cave was born in May, 1906 and four years later, on July 11, 1910, I came along."

I asked if the "B" in Hugh B. Cave also stands for Barnett.

"Yes; Mother wanted us all to honor her father's good name."

Was your first name in the family, too? I asked.

"No, but I told you Mother was an avid reader. We always had books around the house and I grew up reading them all. Writing was in her blood, too. She had a brother who was published. Mother said she named me after one of her favorite authors, Hugh Walpole. Her favorite work was his novel *Fortitude,* about a young man's struggle to become a writer. She named my brother Geoffrey after Jeffrey Farnol, giving the name what she called 'a proper English spelling.' Farnol wrote some great novels too, among them *The Broad Highway, Black Bartlemy's Treasure*—a great pirate's yarn—and *Martin Connisby's Vengeance,* all of which I eagerly read as a kid. My brother Tom, of course, was named after our father."

Cave smiled thoughtfully. "My mother once lived next door to Kipling; I think it was in India. Thank God she didn't name me Rudyard Cave; I would have sounded like some underground tourist attraction in West Virginia!"

His eyebrows raised and he let out a laugh, youthful in its intensity. "Actually, everyone called me HughB, I guess because mine was the only one syllable first name in the family."

It seemed clear to me now that his taste for adventure didn't come exclusively from reading books.

"That's true. Although my parents didn't talk much about their own lives, what I learned was enough to fuel my imagination and create in me a desire to live as they did. My mother had relatives in Australia, a new frontier back then. I never met them but she had some great stories about life on the Outback."

My recorder shut off abruptly and I turned over the tape. Cave asked if I wished more coffee, then went to fetch it. I picked up his old photo album and re-examined Edith Mary Barnett Cave's picture. She certainly was attractive. I could imagine her in the arms of a dashing young British Army paymaster, with shells exploding all around them as soldiers scurried for cover. But the snake? I don't know . . .

Chapter 3: Coming to America

"Mother did more than encourage me to read. She created in me an appreciation—and a respect—for the written word."

I pointed out that even casual readers have their favorite writers.

"Yes, but I am talking about appreciation for the *act* of writing. Mother had favorite passages she would read over and over because they were just the right combination of words, phrases and thoughts. That respect is so often missing in today's writing. I can't believe some of the crap getting published these days. It seems like every other word is filthy. In my day, we didn't use language like that. What we called horror in those days sent chills up and down your spine without the slash and gore you find in novels today. And sex scenes. We were suggestive, true, but these days it's nothing more than pornography. I'm no prude, but writing today simply lacks the integrity that existed in my generation. There is a certain beauty in being able to express yourself while at the same time showing respect for the reader."

I offered that today's writing merely reflects society. With so many more demands on people's attention, everything from books to movies and even music often shock you just to get noticed.

"Well, some day, when our society has decayed and fallen, historians will look for symptoms that may have foretold our demise. They will find one of them in literature's loss of integrity."

He waved it off. "Enough of that. Now, let's see, where were we? Oh, yes. Back in England. I have some vague recollections of our house in Chester. I seem to remember being pulled around the yard in a cart by two great Danes. And we owned a Shetland pony.

"However, my father wasn't one who stayed put for long. Maybe it was the same wanderlust that sent him to South Africa after Mother. He had quite an adventurous streak and in spite of his apparent success, he felt the need at some point to explore new worlds.

"I'm not sure why he chose America. He was so thoroughly British that it must have been difficult for him to accept the American way of life. All I know is, he somehow lined up a job as an accountant with Ford Motor Company in Boston. I don't know what kind of money that job paid, but it surely wasn't what he probably earned as a grain merchant.

"My father left for America alone to first determine whether it was a suitable place to raise his family. Apparently the country met his requirements, so he found us a home, then sent for Mother and we three boys. I really don't remember what went through our minds at the time. Kids that age—Tom was 13, Geoff was eight and I was four—are pretty adaptable. I don't think it would have been an adventure to our mother, though—selling her home, moving to a strange land, uncertain about the future, and caring for three rambunctious boys. If she felt unhappy, we certainly had no knowledge of it. Anyway, moving itself wasn't a problem, so far as I know, but the transatlantic trip, according to my mother, was quite traumatic. Indeed, my first big adventure nearly became my last."

They left Liverpool, England in June 1914. The threat of war hung over Europe, yet most people did not seem to notice, or care for that matter. War was something that happened in faraway places, fought by anonymous people.

Edith knew differently. She had seen the personal side of war and wanted no part of it. That was probably one reason she agreed to leave. The horror she had experienced would be brought home to her countrymen in less than a year. Also within a year, another passenger liner named the Lusitania, making this identical Transatlantic route, would be torpedoed en route with 1,200 passengers losing their lives.

The H.M.S. Caronia, a Cunard liner like the Lusitania, had been commissioned nine years earlier and remained one of the fleet's standouts. It was best known in those days for being one of the ships that responded to the doomed Titanic's futile call for help. All space for this trip had been booked, which meant more than 3,000 passengers were boarding along with the Caves, jostling for position in long, snaking lines. It was an unusually hot summer day and Edith could not wait to leave port. She knew from her long journeys between England and South Africa years before, that everything would cool down once they were at sea.

The ship left port only two hours late. Passengers filled the decks, waving to crowds lined up at the dock's edge. It was a festive air, foghorns blowing, bells ringing, people in brightly colored vacation clothes laughing and singing.

The three Cave boys were eager to explore this giant floating city as it glided silently away from shore, belching columns of black smoke into the pale blue summer sky. Edith tried to share her boys' excitement while suppressing her own apprehension. Although she had certainly traveled to faraway places before, she felt this might be her last departure from England. The possibility of never seeing her friends and family again left Edith depressed.

And what of the New World? America seemed so uncivilized compared to England or even British Colonial India. What if something ever happened to Thomas, leaving her and the boys alone in a strange new land.

All these concerns served to temper the excitement that surrounded her. However, by evening on the first day, everyone's emotions had mellowed, passengers and crew alike, as they settled into their shipboard routines.

To save money, Edith had booked an inside cabin. Thomas left her barely enough to cover all their moving and transportation expenses. The tiny cabin seemed even smaller without a window for daylight and fresh air. Her three boys unwillingly shared bunk beds while Edith slept on a mattress laid directly on the floor.

The ship's dining room was always crowded, with clinking glasses, rattling silver and ever-louder conversation bouncing off bare polished mahogany walls. Everyone seemed friendly though, with food palatable enough to keep Edith focused on the moment. Her boys' excitement about their great sea adventure finally prevailed over concerns about leaving Mother England.

Everything went smoothly until late the third day, when a severe squall pummeled the liner. Two days of calm seas left them ill-prepared for the nausea-inducing waves and fierce winds. Edith and her boys took turns vomiting in their room until she finally decided it would be wiser to get fresh air on deck, no matter how inclement the weather.

Tom, Geoff and HughB were awestruck at the sight of those huge ground swells, the size of mountains in their eyes. Edith also knew how dangerous those waves were as they crashed over the deck and tossed the ship around like a bathtub toy.

"Mother, can we please walk along the deck?" shouted Geoff over a thunderous surf.

"No; it's too dangerous!" Edith answered after quickly surveying the landscape. Other passengers were on deck, but few children.

"Please?" Geoff pleaded.

"I'll watch after him, Mother," offered Tom.

"All right, Tom," Edith relented, thankful for any reprieve from their suffering. "But you must take Geoff's hand, and both of you hold on to the railing. HughB stays here with me."

Geoff squealed with delight as he and Tom inched away from their mother, clinging to the chain link railing that snaked around the deck's perimeter a few short feet from water's edge. The chain had been set up especially for bad weather so passengers could move about the ship. Any potential danger on deck was more than offset by the potential for disgruntled passengers forcibly confined to the ship's interior.

HughB cried out, pleading to join his brothers, but Edith gripped his hand tightly as she focused on Tom and Geoff working their way along the railing. Her fears for their safety were somewhat mollified because Tom was a responsible boy for his age. He seemed to instinctively mature the day his father left for America two months earlier. Besides, plenty of other adults were on deck if an emergency arose.

That emergency did not take long to materialize. The ship's bow dipped into one wave as another came crashing down over the deck. Several people screamed, and for a moment, Edith lost sight of her two boys. When the water and mist subsided, she saw them both clinging to the chain railing, looking a bit dazed.

"Come back, Tom! Right this minute!" She screamed, waving her arms.

As she let go of HughB's hand to wave, he saw the opportunity to run toward his brothers. Just then a second monstrous wave hit the deck. Edith screamed as sheets of angry, cold water sprayed her and knocked down little HughB.

The deck then pitched upward, sending the wave's frothy residue cascading overboard, pulling HughB with it. Edith screamed, "My son! My son!" She lunged toward him and fell face down on the deck.

HughB's tiny body gathered speed until it abruptly slammed into a lifeboat stanchion. Edith kept her eyes focused on him and screamed, "HughB, darling, grab the chain!"

He looked and tried to grab the chain link railing, but it lay just beyond his reach. He started crying as the salt water gathered momentum around him and began to burn his eyes. Then, from out of nowhere, a stranger's strong arm grabbed HughB around the waist and yanked him to a standing position.

Edith ran over, crying hysterically as she wrapped her arms around HughB, clutching him to her water-soaked breast. Tom and Geoff joined them and tried to comfort their mother.

"Damn you, Thomas Cave!" She screamed, waving a fist to the heavens. "Damn you to hell!"

Young Tom whimpered, "What did I do, Mother?"

She wrapped her arm around him. "Nothing, my sweet Tom; nothing at all."

"When we arrived in Boston it was sunny and hot just like the day we left England. Dad greeted us at the pier, and according to my brothers, was more animated than they had ever seen him before or since.

"We left our trunks at the dock to be picked up later, then went by taxi to our new home in Allston. It would be the first of eight homes over the next eight years."

Eight homes in eight years?

"For some reason Dad had this need to move around. Every one of those eight homes was a rental, too. I don't know why he was that way and neither did my mother. But Dad ran the household and everyone just followed his lead. The only common thread among our homes was their proximity to his office in Boston. We always lived within commuting distance by streetcar, which is how we got around in those days.

"We first lived in Allston, then moved to Granville Road in Cambridge, near Harvard University."

He thought a moment. "We moved to our third home within two years of arriving. It was at 4 Elm Street in Winchester, Mass. My first vivid memories are of that home. I started in the first grade when we moved there. Mother grew gooseberries in our backyard. She would send me to a grocery store at the end of our street to buy bread. World War I battleships were pictured on the wrapper of each loaf. I collected them, pinned them on my bedroom wall. I remember being conscious of the war. We had a Chinese laundry on our street, too. They washed everything by hand and ironed it right there. I always got a lychee nut when I picked up our clothes.

"I have many warm memories of our time in Winchester. Two neighbor ladies used to give me cocoa or candy in the evenings after dinner. Then I sat between them and they would read the Thornton W. Burgess bedtime story that appeared every day in the newspaper—stories like Reddy Fox and Jimmy Skunk. I always looked forward to them. I also remember walking in the woods, hiking to the Fells, fishing in a small lake for crappies and bluegills. We made our own fishing poles. Geoff and I would collect bloodsuckers in a jar for bait and study them at home. I think we even sold some to the hospital."

Cave let out a nostalgic laugh. "Medicine has certainly changed since then."

I noticed that Cave didn't seem to speak very well of his father, so I asked why.

He paused thoughtfully, then in a voice not much more than a whisper, said, "I'm not sure how I felt about my father. He was . . . okay in my early childhood years, before . . ."

Before what?

"I'll get to that later," Cave quickly responded, his voice stronger.

"The next year—let's see, it was 1917—we moved to Brighton, 148 Washington Street. It was across from the Passionate Fathers Monastery. I remember a quarry in the neighborhood. Geoff and I had an underground hut that we dug out, put on a roof and held club meetings with some other neighborhood kids, you know, Tom Sawyer stuff. As kids, Geoff and I were virtually inseparable, but Tom, who was almost eight years older than me, had very different interests. Mother was the center of our universe though, always encouraging, always loving. She was so different from our father."

We sat quietly for a few moments.

"You were asking me what sparked my desire to become a writer. I remember one incident as a young boy that I think ended up in one of my stories."

It was well into October and autumn was gaining momentum. The late afternoon sun had begun its retreat from the deep blue, cloudless skies and winter's bite filled the air. With each gentle, nippy breeze, faded leaves drifted to the ground. HughB and Geoff shuffled their feet through nature's fallen debris, the only sound on an otherwise pastoral afternoon. They wore down-filled jackets, completely unbuttoned, and they each had a knit cap stuffed in one pocket, gloves in the other. Their red cheeks and ice-cold fingers would certainly prompt a reprimand from Mother when they got home from this day of fishing.

The Cave household sat at one end of these woods, their school at the other. Walking home in the afternoon, they could choose from a wide selection of routes, each yielding one of earth's treasures—a brightly colored leaf, a pine cone, a bird feather—to be picked up and carried with them. Sometimes Mother allowed them to keep what they found, but usually she made them throw it back.

Their favorite spot was a fairly large pond where they often went fishing. On this late October day, on their way home from one of their fishing trips, they followed a previously undiscovered path in the woods to come upon an old house and barn.

The wooden frame house looked a little creepy, captured in the afternoon sun's dying rays and surrounded by thick, silent woods. It was a small house, tall and narrow, with a slab of decaying lumber nailed at an awkward angle across the front door. Nearly all the windows were broken, target practice for other young boys walking home, no doubt. A battered screen dangled from one window, scraping the house with each breeze.

Ten-year old Geoff stood facing the house, HughB, age six, a few steps behind. Geoff bent over to pick up a small stone. He looked at HughB, who nodded. Geoff aimed for the front window and threw the stone. It sailed through a jagged hole in the glass, then bounced and rattled around inside. Silence returned. No sign of life.

As they moved a few steps closer, the woods around them seemed to close in as well. It was much too quiet and still.

HughB pulled at Geoff's jacket. "What," Geoff whispered sharply.

HughB pointed towards the barn. It was small too, narrow and tall like the house, but with more weather-worn siding. Entire planks were missing so you could see inside. An open door beckoned them.

They walked tentatively towards the barn, with Geoff nervously glancing back at the silent house. Together, Geoff and HughB walked through the open barn door, then stood firm, surveying their discovery. A single stall, once occupied by a horse, was lined with dry, stale hay that permeated the musty air. At first glance, little seemed worth investigating. Trespassers over the years must have taken for themselves whatever valuables once existed there.

They walked around, then crawled into dark recesses, searching for any overlooked treasure. Geoff had the nagging feeling they were being watched. It was probably that fear-tinged excitement of being somewhere and doing something forbidden.

Suddenly a noise came from the house next door. Something had fallen. Then they heard scratching sounds. HughB looked to Geoff, his eyes pleading for an explanation.

"Just the wind," said Geoff, feigning assurance.

Then came a loud crash. HughB screeched, Geoff jumped.

They stooped down, just out of sight, and peered through a missing plank over to the house.

"I saw something!" Geoff exclaimed in a breathy whisper.

"I want to go home," HughB pleaded.

Geoff grabbed HughB's arm. They both watched silently, then heard footsteps echoing throughout the house. They seemed to move towards the front door. Both boys held their collective breath, eyes riveted at the front of the house, waiting to see what would appear.

"Look, a cat!" Said HughB, all excited.

"No, silly; it's a raccoon," answered Geoff.

Relieved—or maybe disappointed—they went back to searching the barn. After a few minutes HughB announced, "Look what I found." He held up a rust-covered hammer, hardly recognizable with its broken handle.

Just at that moment, they both heard a noise coming from the surrounding woods. This time it was not a small animal—these were the unmistakable sounds of human footsteps. And judging from the noise they made trudging through that thick carpet of fallen leaves, the footsteps belonged to adults.

"Let's get out of here!" Geoff shrieked.

HughB had already bolted, but Geoff quickly passed him.

They both ran full throttle, HughB struggling to keep up, for almost a mile, then slowed down as they approached their neighborhood. When their house came into view, they were walking at a normal pace. By the time they walked through their kitchen door, Geoff and HughB had both caught their breath.

Edith was preparing dinner. She turned and looked at her boys, cheeks blazing red, caps and gloves stuffed in their jacket pockets. She shook her head.

Then she noticed HughB clutching something in his hand.

"What do you have there, HughB?" She said in her proper English accent.

HughB looked down, then back at her. "It's an old hammer."

"I can see that. Where did you get it?"

HughB and Geoff looked at each other.

"I found it."

She turned fully towards them. "Where did you find it?"

Geoff spoke. "It was in an old abandoned barn, back in the woods. Nobody lives there anymore."

She put her hands on her hips and glared down at tiny HughB. "Young man; you take that hammer back where you found it right this minute!"

HughB looked in horror at Geoff, then back to his mother. "But . . ."

"Do you hear me? Right this minute!"

Then she turned at Geoff. "And you go with him."

"What?!"

"You heard me. Do it. NOW!"

The back door slammed shut and she could hear HughB crying as her two boys headed back to the woods.

Cave laughed. "Fear of punishment may have motivated me as I left our house, but fear of being discovered by who knows what, overcame me as I neared the barn. I remember being scared to death. I ran inside the barn, threw the hammer down about where I had found it, then ran out like hell! For weeks afterwards, I had nightmares about what could have happened to me in that old barn.

"You know, Milt, the most believable stories are often drawn from a writer's experiences. It doesn't have to be anything earth-shaking either. Do you watch *Seinfeld* on TV?"

Occasionally, I answered, finding it hard to believe Cave watched "Seinfeld."

"Whoever writes that show simply takes everyday, common events, the small details of life, and makes great comedy from them. Those same details make great stories."

I asked Cave since he loved to read, what books influenced him the most as a child.

"I loved reading Edgar Rice Burrough's *Tarzan* series, Rudyard Kipling short stories, H. Rider Haggard books, Sir Arthur Conan Doyle, Robert Louis Stevenson, Ambrose Bierce, *King Solomon's Mines. River of Darkness* by William Murray Graydon was probably my favorite; it made a big impression on me. I read everything I could get my hands on about the South Seas—Borneo,

Australia, and the South Pacific where I later went as a war correspondent. My mother's sisters were in Australia and I loved reading letters from them. One of them died and left me a donkey, but I never saw it.

"I also read Joseph Conrad's *Heart of Darkness* many times. William Seabrook's, *The Magic Island,* kindled my interest in Haiti, an interest that later became a passion. It also turned out that much of the detail in *The Magic Island* was just plain wrong, although he is credited with introducing the word 'zombie' to U.S. readers. Today you can't get away with fudging the facts; we live in a much smaller world and the truth is easier to discover. Why, the Internet alone accesses more information than the best public library did back in those days.

"I loved to read ghost stories as a child. On winter days, it got dark around 4:30–5:00 in the afternoon, which created a perpetually scary atmosphere. Nothing scary happens in broad daylight. Later on, in the 1940's, a short story writer named John Russell would have the same impact on me as those earlier writers. I even tried to copy his style of writing."

It seemed to me that Hugh Cave had a typical childhood.

"For a while it was very typical. As a family, we spent our evenings sitting around the dining room table playing hearts, old maid or poker for matches. We would all listen to recordings. I remember our first hand-cranked Victrola, and our first recording, 'Razors in the Air,' later sung by the Kingston Trio. We had every new recording—Paul Whiteman, Fred Waring and His Pennsylvanians, Bing Crosby and the Rhythm Boys, Fats Waller, George Olson . . . oh, the list was long indeed."

Cave chuckled. "Paul Whiteman had a song called 'Looking for the Ogo Pogo'; we had a kitten and named it Ogo Pogo.

"Geoff and I used to walk to the music store in Brookline Village with just enough money for a couple of records. You could sample a record in those days before buying it, and we listened to all the latest stuff before spending our money. We always had the latest model phonograph, starting with the early wind-up kind, to modern electric ones that could play a whole stack of records. Dad didn't care for music by American artists, though, not even "Rhapsody in Blue," if you can believe that.

"We had a piano, too. Mother would play while Dad stood by her and sang. He loved to sing, especially classical or church music. We were all fond of Beethoven, Haydn and the other classical composers. Geoff and I sang in a choir considered one of the country's best men and boys' choirs. Anyway, Dad would belt out Handel's Messiah, or musical versions of Kipling poems like 'Danny Deever' and 'The Road to Mandalay.' "

Cave smiled affectionately at the memory. "He used to sing so loud you could hear him clear down the block. He wrote some music too, church hymns as I recall."

Cave paused again, deep in thought. I gulped down some coffee, watching him closely.

"I guess he wasn't so bad in those days. Dad was never what one would call a jolly fellow. He was always rather solemn and serious—aloof, perhaps."

Cave reflected more, searching his memory. "I seem to remember Dad as a tall, dark-haired, slender man. He wore what I thought of as a typical Englishman's mustache, but I also recall him as clean-shaven. Perhaps the mustache was a temporary thing.

"I certainly don't remember him as a warm, loving man, though. I don't think he ever hugged or kissed me, for instance. But Dad was dependable, and I was never afraid of him, at least not in those days."

Cave looked at me, a vague pleading in his eyes. "It's funny; he had an office downtown, on Boylston Street, but I don't think I ever went there. I don't remember ever knowing anything about his job or the people who worked with him. Dad never talked about his childhood, or the years he spent in South Africa. Everything I ever knew about him I learned from my mother. He wasn't the type to play ball with us boys, or go skating with us. No, he never did things like that. But he did show interest in my homework, especially anything written, like a book report or composition."

Cave smiled again. "Dad had a vegetable garden out back and he spent a lot of time tending it during the spring and summer months. We lived in Brighton at the time, which in those years was out in the country. There was a horse farm across the street from us, next to Passionate Father's Monastery. I took my wagon over to the horse farm and brought it back full of manure for his garden. Dad would pay me ten cents for each load. The only time I ever broke a bone was at that horse farm. I was 'tightrope walking' on the fence there, fell and broke my arm."

He paused. "Come to think of it, Dad did take me to Boston once. We went in on the streetcar. He bought me some new clothes. I think I was seven or eight at the time. Then we went to the Copley Plaza Hotel for lunch, near Emmanuel Episcopal Church where Geoff and I sang in the choir. It was a very fancy place—I had never been in a restaurant like it. I ordered steak with mushrooms for lunch. It was the first time I had ever eaten mushrooms.

"He was a good Dad then," Cave conceded, "but that was before the accident."

Chapter 4: The Accident

"It was in the fall of 1919. I was nine years old and had just been promoted into the fifth grade after a month or two in fourth grade. I guess that wasn't too unusual back then. I must have been a pretty fair student. My oldest brother Tom was already out of school and had decided to pursue a life at sea. The old adventure bug had bitten all of us boys. Tom was fascinated by anything electronic, which was an utterly new field at the time. He spent hours tinkering with radios and other gadgetry. He was also a Charles Lindbergh fan; had photos of him all over his wall. Tom decided to become a ship's radio operator. He never even finished high school because for a long time he was simply bored with it.

"Geoff and I were both singing in the choir during this time; I remember that. When we came home from school in the afternoons we would play with friends, or help Mother, or work in Dad's vegetable garden. We always looked forward to dinnertime, even though Mother was a terrible cook. The English aren't known for their cooking, you know. She was proud of baking cakes that truthfully, if you dropped one, would probably break the floor."

Cave reared his head and let out a hearty laugh.

"We ate porridge for breakfast almost every morning. On Sunday we had a 'joint' or roast. We'd eat leftovers served cold for the next few days. She cooked cauliflower and other vegetables to death. But she did make good tapioca and bread pudding.

"Saturdays, Geoff and I went down to Billy Woods' Theater in Brighton. On the way, we would stop by this shop run by a tiny Italian lady. She was less than five feet tall and always wore a black dress. Inside the front door to her shop, she had a barrel of sour pickles. They cost five cents each and the movies cost a dime. We would sit in the theater, eating those pickles and watching Tom Mix or William S. Hart westerns. I'm sure people sat around us and wondered where the strong smell came from. We also went to

Norumbega Park together. It was like Coney Island and not far from where we lived. Geoff took me there on the handlebars of his bike.

"I had a really good friend during this time, too. His name was Paul Levaque—he was French or French Canadian—and he lived next door. We used to sit on the porch watching cars go by and writing down the make of each car as it went by. The idea was to make a list of all the autos. I was a great one for making lists of just about anything.

"Yes," Cave recalled, "things were good at this time in my life." He grew somber. "But that would soon change."

Thomas E. Cave never relinquished his British passport, nor did he apply for U.S. citizenship. He considered himself an English aristocrat even though he came from more humble origins. Thomas envied his late father-in-law's status, a C.I.E. who received that honor from Queen Victoria herself. In his household though, Thomas Cave represented everything British, which meant to him all that was good in this world. The first time he ever left British soil was when he followed Edith to South Africa. He was proud to serve in South Africa. It was, after all, a British colony, and South Africans, whatever their race or national origin, were British subjects.

His decision to leave England for America was a relatively easy one. He had absorbed some losses in the grain markets and prospects were cloudy, at least in the near future. America, a former British colony, seemed to be a land of unending opportunity and Europeans by the millions were emigrating there. He, as a loyal British subject, certainly deserved the right to take advantage of this opportunity created by his nation.

A job with the Ford Motor Company is what brought him here, but after a year Thomas decided to go into business for himself as a public accountant. He opened an office on Boylston Street in Boston. It was small but the rent affordable. He saw no reason to purchase a car since the city's electric streetcar system provided adequate transportation. Of course, it paled by comparison to public transportation back home, as did everything else American.

Thomas worked long hours. He claimed no professional designation at the end of his name, nor did he have any intention of paying the price necessary to earn one. He simply resigned himself to charging lower fees from more clients and working longer hours.

His goal was to reap the financial benefits of this opportunity in America, then return to his beloved England. That's why he did not buy a car, why he only rented furnished homes, and why he worked long hours.

His streetcar station was at the bottom of a steep hill on Commonwealth Avenue, only a half-mile from their Brighton home. His office was even closer to the station downtown.

One day in late fall 1919, Thomas decided to leave work early because a friend bought a new car and offered Thomas a ride. He drove Thomas to his regular Brighton streetcar station.

"Thanks for the lift, James. It is quite a handsome car."

"Would you like me to pick you up in the morning then?"

Before answering, Thomas glanced quickly up the hill to see a streetcar coming toward the station. "Yes, that would be a pleasant change from the overcrowded streetcar."

"I will collect you at eight, how is that?"

The shiny new car pulled away and Thomas waved. He stopped at the newsstand to buy an afternoon paper, glancing up again at the streetcar as it continued down the hill towards its regular stop. Thomas did not know, however, as he paid for his paper, that the streetcar had lost its brakes.

The conductor repeatedly rang his warning bell, but Thomas did not hear it above the din of busy street noise. Thomas scanned the front page as he walked, looking down and unaware as people started running clear of the tracks. Nor did he see the streetcar conductor's horror-stricken face. He did hear an unusually loud, grinding sound, and finally looked up from his paper.

But it was too late. The streetcar bore down on him, out of control. Thomas had no time to react.

Cave spoke solemnly. "He could do nothing but accept the inevitable—and that brief moment changed our lives forever."

He paused, picked up his coffee cup, took a swallow and set it back down, all in one rote motion, his eyes focused five feet in front of him.

An ambulance arrived within minutes. Two men with a stretcher wormed their way through the somber crowd. They knelt down by Thomas's crumpled, unconscious body. One man checked Thomas for vital signs. Then they lifted him carefully, battered and bleeding, onto the stretcher. The police tried to clear a path. A stocky, freckle-faced Irishman named Callahan, admonished the crowd in his thick Irish brogue, "Please step back now, folks. Let these fellas do their job and take this poor gentleman to the hospital."

Callahan knew Thomas Cave. He also knew Edith and the boys. He had visited their home on Washington Street. He would be the one to tell them about this terrible accident.

Geoff and Hugh were out in the backyard. Young Tom no longer lived at home; he had already gone to sea as an apprentice radio operator. The boys were playing catch when they heard a scream coming from the house. Geoff and Hugh looked at each other, then ran for the back door.

I asked if his father survived.

"Yes, but the impact broke just about every bone in his body. He didn't regain consciousness for a week. Then he spent months recovering in a hospital bed; months more at home. Over time, he recovered physically—but emotionally, the accident left him a different man."

It had been three months since Thomas came home from the hospital. Edith fixed dinner each night for Geoff and Hugh, then prepared a tray and brought it in to their father. He spent nearly all his time in the bedroom alone—Edith had taken over Tom's bedroom, moving Hugh and Geoff back in together.

After dinner, Edith, Hugh and Geoff sometimes sat together reading to themselves. More often though, the boys ended up in their room. The family no longer enjoyed song sessions together or match stick poker sitting around the dining room table, because the noise disturbed their father. Dad's vegetable garden, once his pride and joy, now lay barren and weed-choked.

At first, after regaining consciousness, Thomas Cave remembered nothing—who or where he was, family, friends—nothing. Gradually his memory returned, but even three months later, he remembered no details of that tragic accident.

The most radical change in his behavior from pre-accident days though, had the greatest emotional effect on his family. He had ceased to be a husband and father. Thomas Cave was nothing but a shell. While he recognized Edith and the boys, clearly the emotional bond holding them together as a family, no longer existed. He lived with them as though they were mere acquaintances. Not only that, he assumed an unnerving demeanor around them.

* * *

One evening, Hugh sat in the living room, reading a book. Although they lived in the same house, he had not seen his father for three days. Dad always kept the bedroom door shut tight. To young Hugh, now nine years old, that door also shut him out from his life before the accident, a life he sorely missed.

Hugh immersed himself even more into his reading; it helped to shut out the pain of real life. He lived now between those pages, side-by-side with the characters. When they were in Borneo's jungles, he was there too, feeling the heat, the mosquitoes, the danger.

On this night though, something tugged at Hugh's consciousness. As he and his characters crawled through the thick, bug-infested jungle, he felt a presence out there somewhere beyond the printed page. None of the book's characters referred to this presence. Why didn't they sense it as he did?

Hugh looked up from his book to see a countenance far more terrifying than anything in Borneo. There stood his father, holding open the bedroom door, his clothing rumpled, hair disheveled, face ashen. Black circles underlined his eyes as though painted there for some jungle death ritual.

His father's eyes upset Hugh the most. They were dull and empty, staring right through him. Hugh shuddered. The man he once loved as his father, stood there, a soul-less zombie, a creature more worthy of fiction than reality.

Hugh stared right back at the creature, because he knew it wasn't really staring at him. Hugh had come to know that look all too well. Tears began to form as he watched this empty shell of the man he once admired.

Then his father turned away and slipped back into the bedroom, quietly shutting the door behind him. Hugh looked sadly at the barrier that now separated him from his carefree, loving childhood.

Cave spoke of this time with the same intensity he must have felt when it happened. "Not only did we lose our father, but in his place we were left with a stranger. Every aspect of our lives changed. I retreated to my room most of the time and immersed myself into a life of fantasy, reading, writing little stories, sketching and painting."

I asked if this incident had ever found its way into any of his stories.

"I never even tried. It was just too painful, especially with what happened afterward."

* * *

The Cave family fell on hard times. At first, they lived off the money Thomas had saved for his triumphant return to England. When that ran out, Edith began taking jobs as a visiting nurse. By now, Geoff held a full-time job, Hugh worked before and after school, and Tom sent home whatever cash he could spare. Together, they paid the bills and survived.

In 1921, they moved to less expensive quarters, an apartment in Back Bay, near Fenway Park. Edith wore herself out physically and emotionally. She worked all day, then came home to fix dinner for the boys and her husband. He never lifted a finger to help, even after he was physically capable.

Gradually, Thomas started back to work. His business had all but disappeared in the months following the accident. He began taking on clients again, completely rebuilding the practice within a year.

While his physical condition improved, it became increasingly clear to the family that his emotional health was beyond repair. Thomas would come home after work, just like the old days. However, when the boys tried to tell him about their school day, he showed no interest. He never attended any of Hugh's school activities. Eventually they just stopped trying to involve him.

Edith, however, never missed any of Hugh's school functions. She always had friends stopping by, too, whereas Thomas no longer brought friends or business associates home. Thomas and Edith had no friends together. Thomas would simply come home from work, eat dinner and then disappear into his room, shutting the door behind him.

At first, Edith would see the boys to bed, then retire to Tom's old room and weep quietly. As time wore on, she wept less, until she stopped weeping altogether and accepted her life alone. The relationship between Thomas and Edith that blossomed on the battlefields of South Africa, had become history, just like the war itself.

If Thomas behaved like nothing more than a boarder, he eventually became a disgruntled boarder. Back when he first came home from the hospital, Thomas precipitated some ugly scenes by suggesting that Edith had been unfaithful to him during his absence. It was not true, of course. No one demonstrated more dedication than Edith did to her husband and family. She had never failed to give the love, support and encouragement her boys needed, all the while enduring the loss of her spouse. Thomas's accusations of unfaithfulness became more frequent and strident with time. Finally, they crossed the line from verbal to physical.

Hugh, now 15 years old and an 11th grader, walked into the house one evening to the wrenching sound of his father's accusing voice. It was not the first time his father screamed at his mother. She had cautioned Hugh against interfering when his father became agitated. The accident, now years in the past, caused him to be this way, she told Hugh, and he did not mean the horrible things he said to her.

Hugh avoided the kitchen where his parents quarreled and sat in the living room. Although Hugh had resigned himself to his father's outbursts, this one seemed different. Mother was pleading with Dad to stop. Her voice quivered, his screams became more furious.

Hugh feared his father, but felt he could no longer endure the abuse. It was time to stand up and defend the mother he loved so dearly. Heart pounding, he jumped out of his chair and rushed to the kitchen. He was horrified to see his mother pinned in front of the stove, cowering, those delicate porcelain-colored hands covering her face. The man who was once his father leaned into her, fist clenched, poised to strike at any moment.

Hugh ran over and wedged himself between them, facing his father, back to his mother. With an angry, tremulant voice, he shouted, "Don't you dare hit my mother!"

Stunned, Thomas abruptly stepped back and retracted his fist. Edith, tears streaming down her face, leaned against Hugh's back and hugged his shoulders. She sobbed deeply.

Hugh continued to glare at his father until he backed off completely.

Silent in defeat, Thomas turned away, walked out of the kitchen and into his bedroom, closing the door softly behind him.

I asked if there were any more confrontations after that.

"He was quite humble for a week or two, barely speaking to any of us. Then one day he simply walked out and never came back."

Where did he go?

"Mother told me he went to Sweden."

Sweden? Why? I asked.

"That's where his secretary came from. They had apparently been carrying on an affair for some time. He finally left us for her."

Did your mother know or suspect anything?

"She never said, but we had a clue back when I was too young to recognize it. Once, when my brother Tom was home for a visit, he had apparently gone to Dad's office, where he met her. Tom told us she was quite attractive, in her early 20's like him.

"The next thing I know, he and Dad had this terrible argument. It seems that Tom had asked her out on a date. When Dad found out he exploded, forbidding Tom to go near her again. At the time he said something like it wasn't good business for family to fraternize with employees.

"I think Mother must have known what was going on, although she never said anything. After all the heartbreak and suffering she had to endure, it was a terrible way for their once loving marriage to end."

Tears formed in Cave's eyes. "You know, it would have been better for all of us if he just died that day when the streetcar struck him. At least we would have had insurance money to live on and loving memories of our life with him."

I asked if they had any contact with his father after that.

"We never heard from him; not a call, not a letter—nothing. It was as if he never existed. I really missed having a father in those years after the accident. Even if he wasn't the most affectionate person, he was an anchor in our lives."

What about your mother?

"She seemed relieved once he left, although she never talked about her feelings toward him. I can only imagine Mother was devastated, losing that dashing young man she married in South Africa, the man who shared her vision for life, whose children she bore. After the accident, it must have been dreadful. She had to look at the face she loved for so many years, now the face of a stranger.

"She didn't have time to dwell on it though, not with two boys to raise. After the accident she held our family together by taking visiting nurse jobs. Sometimes she would be gone for several days. But Mother was a rugged soul. And we all pitched in to help. I worked before and after school every day and all day Saturday making deliveries on my bike for Delano's, a local clothing and dry goods store. In the morning, I went there before school to start the furnace, shovel snow off the sidewalks and sweep floors. It was tough during the winter, riding my bike several miles in the rain or snow and getting to work before daylight. I'll never forget how cold I felt trying to stoke up that furnace so it would be warm when the employees arrived for work. Then I would go back after school and make deliveries. My mother and I also hand painted greeting cards for money. I stopped by the Brookline Greeting Card Company after school and brought them home along with a sample for us to copy.

"I had choir rehearsal three times a week, too, twice on Sunday, a five mile bike trip each way. Actually, I got paid for it. We lived in Brookline by then and I rode my bike to Emmanual Church near Boston Commons on Newbury Street. Along the way, I might find chunks of rubber on the street, like retreads off a semi and sometimes off cars. I carried a big bag on my handlebars and picked up rubber to sell as scrap.

"We all wanted to help Mother in her time of need. Even Tom was writing more often and coming home whenever he had time off. After Dad left, we all pulled together and those years were filled with some of my fondest memories."

He sighed deeply.

"Mother and Dad were so different. He was never an affectionate man and didn't seem interested in our daily lives, so from that standpoint, he wasn't much different after the accident. I don't ever recall him showing affection for my mother, either, although I do believe they loved each other.

"But Mother—she was very demonstrative with her love for us, always affectionate, always encouraging. I will forever cherish the time I had with her.

"I especially remember one summer she and I were alone together for a few weeks at a resort hotel on the ocean in, I think, Ounquit, Maine. Everyone at this hotel seemed fond of Mother and we had a grand time together. I was just a kid at the time, something like seven or eight years old."

I asked him again if he had any contact with his father after that.

"I seem to remember him coming around once a few years later and Mother turned him away, but I never saw him again as a child. I did see him some years later, though."

Chapter 5: A Stranger Calls

"About ten years passed; I think I was 24. I had become a full-time writer, making an admirable living at it, I might add. I lived alone, in a studio apartment in Pawtucket, Rhode Island, near the woman who would become my wife. I was writing 25–30,000 words a month for publication and had to, because back then during the heyday of the pulps, a writer only earned one to three cents a word. To make a living in this field, you had to spend nine or more hours a day creating stories and sending them out to publishers."

Hugh banged away at his typewriter on a cold and snowy evening. It was exceptionally quiet; everyone stayed home on a night like this. A few cars did drive by in near silence, their sound muffled by the snow. Hugh's apartment building was never noisy except for an occasional child's cry, burst of laughter or a domestic argument. Not tonight though. When the temperature outside dipped below twenty, people huddled to conserve heat. The only sound to be heard was an occasional ping in the radiator as it struggled to keep the building's inhabitants warm.

Hugh was deeply engrossed in a mystery story taking place on a night just like this. The eerie quiet inspired him, even though his body ached for sleep. In his story, someone was about to commit a murder and Hugh could feel the tension as he typed away. Writing such tales was, for Hugh, the same as reading them. In his mind, he became part of the story itself. Hugh imagined a knock at the victim's door. A second knock brought him back to the reality of his quiet apartment.

Hugh's writing schedule left little time for friends or socializing, and with the miserable weather outside, he could not imagine who might be calling.

Hugh opened the door and at first didn't recognize the man in the dimly lit hallway. He had gained some weight, and Hugh noticed lines in his face that were not there before. He was shorter than Hugh remembered him, too.

"Mind if I come in," said Thomas Edward Cave.

Without saying a word, Hugh moved aside to let him enter. His father walked past him, removing hat, scarf and overcoat in one motion, then sat in the only upholstered chair. Hugh, still speechless, closed the door and walked over to sit down at the desk next to him. His mind raced with questions and emotions pent up for years.

They stared at each other a few moments. Thomas sat, legs crossed, coat and scarf lodged in the crook of his arm, fingers gripping the rim of his hat. Hugh propped his elbows on the arms of his chair, hands together with fingers resting under his chin. The only clue that betrayed his father's outer calmness was the way he gripped the rim of his hat.

"I've read some of your work," he said. "Quite good, actually. You must get that from your mother's side of the family. Her brother was a writer, you know."

"Yes, I know," Hugh finally answered, while continuing to stare.

"How is your mother?" Thomas asked, clearing his throat, somewhat tentative for the first time.

"She's fine," Hugh answered, wanting to follow with, "Where the hell have you been all these years!"

"Good, I'm happy for her. And how are your brothers?"

"They are fine, too. And what . . ."

"Thomas smiled knowingly. "Oh yes, and what am I up to these days?"

"No . . . what are you doing here?" Hugh said it without a smile, but pleased that his father misjudged the question.

Thomas coughed nervously. "As I say, I have read some of your stories and thought it might be nice to pay you a visit, catch up a bit."

"Would you like to catch up a bit from my last story or from the last time you saw me?" Hugh's mouth and mind were beginning to work past the emotional blockade.

When his father ran off to Sweden, Hugh had just published his first story. Since then, he had published 140 more. He had also graduated from high school, met his future wife, seen both of his brothers married and weathered the worst of the Depression. In Hugh's mind, the years of unshared memories formed a gulf between them they could not breach, or even approach.

"Actually, I was curious about your Tsiang House stories," his father said, ignoring Hugh's retort.

Hugh had published a series of popular pulp stories set in a British South Seas military post called Tsiang House.

In one respect, his father had not changed. He never talked about himself, his past or his feelings about anything. To Hugh, his father was a one-dimensional, cardboard character. If it were not for his mother, Hugh probably would never have known about his father's family and background or how his parents met before South Africa. If it were up to his father, Hugh probably wouldn't have known his parents lived in South Africa. Hugh did not intend to open up now.

"Those stories are written with an accuracy that could only

come from someone who has lived there," Thomas continued. "Have you actually been to the South Pacific?"

"Yes," Hugh decided to lie. "I went on a tramp steamer after high school; Tom arranged it for me. He is an expert ship radio operator, you know."

"Really?" He said, gushing with pride. "He has always shown interest in it, hasn't he."

They went on for about twenty minutes, Thomas asking questions about Hugh's stories and Hugh giving answers as fictitious as the stories themselves. Hugh never once asked a question of his father even though there was so much he desperately wanted to know.

Then suddenly Thomas looked at his watch. "Oh, dear, I really must be going."

He stood up and reached out to shake Hugh's hand. "I'm glad we had this chance to chat."

Hugh looked at his father's outstretched arm and absently accepted his hand. It was one of the few times in his life Hugh recalled having any kind of physical contact with the man.

"Maybe we can do this again," he said as he donned his overcoat, scarf and hat.

Hugh did not respond, nor did he smile.

"Well then, I'm off."

With that, he opened the door and walked out. Hugh watched his father go down the hallway. Then he disappeared down the stairs, never once looking back.

Hugh continued to listen as the footsteps grew fainter. He heard the front door of his building open briefly, just enough to let in the sound of a passing car. The door shut quickly behind him, leaving Hugh again in a coccoon of silence.

"That was the last time I ever saw my father," said Cave, his voice cracking slightly. "He had some nerve walking into my life like that after so many years. As far as I was concerned, he had no right to know anything about us and I wasn't about to tell him."

I nodded in agreement, which, I assumed, is what Cave wanted of me. Then I asked if his father made contact with Cave's brothers or mother.

"Not then, not ever."

Do you know what happened to him afterwards?

"Even that is strange. Some years later, an English aunt wrote to my mother, saying he had returned to Coventry, his hometown.

According to her letter, he was killed in one of those horrible bombing raids during the Nazi Blitz in 1941."

How did you take the news?

"Not hard, really. Except for his brief visit in 1934, which left me emotionally puzzled for months afterwards, I had successfully shut him out of my life. As far as I was concerned, my real father was killed by that streetcar years earlier."

I suggested that knowing he died in the war probably provided Cave with some closure. It seemed, after all, a fitting end based on how he lived his life early on.

"I suppose; and maybe I accepted that as a way to preserve my earlier positive memories of him. But however I dealt with his loss, he still found a way to come back again to haunt me."

What do you mean? I asked him.

"Years later, I think it was 1964 or '65, I was living in Jamaica. My wife and I owned a coffee plantation up in the Blue Mountains, kind of an isolated place. We had no telephones, so our only communication with the outside world came by way of a small, provincial post office three miles away.

"One day a young boy ran up to the house waving a telegram. It was actually a handwritten message on a piece of pink paper. It wasn't unusual for me to receive messages that way, especially when an editor was looking for a story from me or confirming the purchase of one. Anyway, the telegram truly upset me. It came from a medical center in Boston. They had tracked me down through a publisher. The message read that my father, Thomas E. Cave, had just died and the hospital needed my permission to conduct an autopsy. Would I please send a return telegram with the requested permission.

"My first reaction was, how could this be my father? My father, after all, had died during the Blitz back in 1941. If this man truly was my father, then he was more than 90 years old. I was quite distraught and asked my wife what I should do about it. I finally answered the telegram, saying I could neither give nor withhold permission because as far as I was concerned, my father had died in the war."

What happened then?

"I never heard another word, nor did I try to contact the man who sent me that telegram."

Cave reflected a moment, then shook his head. He spoke somberly. "I feel bad whenever I think about it. I should have done more to follow up."

His eyes glistened as he looked at me. I felt as though he sought forgiveness.

I looked at my watch, announced that it was time to go, and turned off the tape recorder.

We walked to the front door in silence, just as Cave and his father did the last time they saw each other. He opened the door as I reached out to shake his hand.

I thanked him and said I would call in a few days to schedule our next session. I searched his face unsuccessfully for clues as to whether he even wanted a next session.

"Certainly," he said, suddenly coming to life. "I'll look forward to it."

As I climbed into my car and started the engine, I looked up to see Cave standing in his doorway, his eyes squinting in the mid-day sun, a smile on his face. Unlike that fateful meeting with his father back in 1934, I knew we would see each other again.

Chapter 6: Tom the Enigma

Cave had not said much about his oldest brother Tom. Was there a reason?

"Remember, Geoff and I were only four years apart, but Tom was almost eight years older. When you are a kid, eight years is like a lifetime. I don't really remember that much about Tom, even after becoming an adult. Geoff and I were close up until the time he died seven years ago. But Tom was different from the rest of us —always secretive. He wasn't home much as a kid, and when he was, Tom kept to himself, building something or fooling around with a radio.

"He loved anything to do with science and the radio fascinated him. He built crystal radios from kits and sat for hours listening, logging different stations he picked up on the air.

"Tom was about 13 when we came to the states and had the benefit of schooling in England. He even studied calculus by the time he started school here. At his grade level the kids were just beginning algebra, so Tom became bored and lost interest in his classwork. He wanted to go to radio school instead, so our parents let him drop out of public school to do it.

"Tom wasn't around at the time of Dad's accident in 1919; he was already out to sea as a merchant ship's radio operator. He had traveled around the world by the time I graduated from high school and began looking for a job. I remember he was once on a tanker that went to South America. He caught malaria and ended up in the hospital. His ship went on without him but disappeared on her way back to the U.S. Weeks later they found the body of a crew member floating on debris from the ship, but nothing else. The malaria saved Tom's life. It's funny, but I had a similar experience during the war, missing a flight due to illness and finding out the plane was shot down with no survivors."

Your father's wanderlust bug bit Tom then, too?

"Except Tom took it a bit further. He ended up as manager of the Chatham-Cape Cod ship-to-shore radio station. Then something strange happened. Soon after World War II started, he mysteriously disappeared. We never heard a word from him; his wife didn't even know where he was, other than to tell her he was 'working for the government.'

"Then one day—it was in 1942 and I was married by then, living in Rhode Island—I heard a car pull into my driveway. I went to look out the living room window and didn't recognize the car. The driver's door opened and out stepped Tom.

Hugh had not seen Tom for almost three years. He rushed outside to greet his brother, they hugged and then walked back in the house. Tom kissed Margaret on the cheek and Hugh's three-year-old son, Ken, on the forehead. Margaret asked if he wanted some coffee.

"No thanks, Margaret, I can't stay long."

Hugh slumped in disappointment, not seeing or talking with Tom for so long and his mind brimming with questions. An awkward tension built of long absences always hung over them when Tom came around. His secretive ways and short visits did not help.

"So what brings you here?" Hugh asked, prepared for Tom's typically cryptic response.

"I'm working for the government now, Hugh."

"Oh, I thought you already worked for them," Hugh asked.

"That was the state of Massachusetts; this is the U.S. government."

Hugh felt embarrassed that he did not really know where his brother worked or precisely what he did.

Either Tom didn't detect Hugh's discomfort or chose to ignore it. He leaned forward in his chair. "Hugh, you still do a lot of fishing, don't you?"

"Sure, but I can't believe you stopped off to go fishing with me?"

"Where do you usually go fishing?"

"Out in the south counties; there's great fly fishing there."

"Good," he replied. "I understand that the highest point in Rhode Island is down there. Is that true?"

"Uh-huh," Hugh answered, not sure where this conversation was leading.

"Can you show me where it is on a map?"

Hugh nodded and went to his office, returning with the map. They went to the dining room table, where he unfolded the map of Rhode Island. "Here's what you're looking for," said Hugh, tapping on the lower left hand corner of the map.

"Good. Can I borrow this?" Tom asked.

"Take it," said Hugh, knowing there was no point in asking him why he needed it.

They chatted small talk for a few more minutes, then Tom said good-bye. He walked briskly out to his car, waved, and drove off, never looking back.

Hugh looked at Margaret, who shrugged her shoulders and walked back to the kitchen. "Some family you have there," she sneered.

I first learned about Margaret, or "Meg" as he sometimes referred to her, during my second interview with Cave. She is not to be confused with Peg. Cave married Margaret in 1935 after years of on again-off again courtship. They lived together until separating in 1975 after 40 mostly unhappy years. Cave did not meet Peg, the love of his life, until he was 68 years old.

Cave continued. "I didn't really expect to see Tom again anytime soon, but he surprised me by turning up three days later. He pulled into the driveway, and just like the first time, I went out to greet him."

"Let's go for a walk," said Tom, without even a hello.

They walked briskly through the backyard, down by Gorton Pond and across an open field, into a wooded area where they were totally alone.

"Hugh, what I am about to tell you is top secret, but I know you have security clearance."

Hugh was writing a book about a heroic PT boat crew and had gained security clearance to spend time with the crew members who were stationed at a secret PT boat base. Hugh had not told Tom about any of this, though. Tom must have determined his security status before he ever came to visit.

Tom scanned the horizon, then looked back at Hugh. "I am in charge of a group working for the government on a top secret project."

Hugh said nothing, just stared at his brother.

"I found what I was looking for, thanks to you."

"Oh? Really? What was that?"

"Hugh, have you ever heard the term 'triangulation?' "

"Something to do with radio waves?" It was a guess, but knowing Tom, probably a safe one.

"Close. Now look at this."

He knelt down and wiped a spot on the ground clear of leaves and nature's debris. Hugh squatted next to him. Tom picked up a long twig and broke it into three pieces, sticking each one of them into the soil to form a triangle.

"Imagine these are telephone poles with receivers sitting on top of them. Depending on how far apart they are, those receivers are capable of picking up a radio signal from miles away. It could be thousands of miles Hugh, depending on one thing."

"What's that?" Hugh asked, feeling again like the little brother he was to Tom all those years growing up.

"The curve of the earth."

"What does that have to do with it?"

"Radio waves cannot bend," Tom responded. "They only go in a straight, horizontal line. You can't make them conform to the shape of the earth."

"So as the earth curves, the radio waves just go off into space in a straight line."

Tom nodded. "Precisely. Now if you wanted to extend your ability to receive these radio waves, what would you do?"

"Place the receivers higher off the ground?" Hugh replied feebly. He hated being put on the spot by his older brother, even at this age.

"You've got it!"

"So that's why you wanted to find the highest point in Rhode Island."

"Right."

"But why Rhode Island? Why not Cape Cod or coastal Maine?"

"They're in many spots.This was only one of the triangulation points.The others could be as far away as New Jersey and Maine.

"By placing these receivers on top of utility poles and using triangulation, something really interesting happens."

Hugh looked at him wide-eyed, waiting for the payoff. Tom stood up and Hugh followed.

"We can actually pinpoint a radio transmission occurring at that very moment hundreds or even thousands of miles away. In other words, if Nazi naval headquarters radios one of its submarines, we can pinpoint the sub's exact location!"

Hugh was mesmerized. Back then, before television, computers and the atom bomb, this was the stuff of science fiction.

"None of this is really new, Hugh. My outfit once searched for a downed plane in the Arctic wilderness. It was sending a distress signal and we located the aircraft with triangulation among the search planes. The crew was rescued."

With that, Tom glanced at his watch. "Let's go back."

They started walking back to the house. "So this means you can now keep track of everything Hitler does in Europe," Hugh said. "That's incredible."

"Not just Europe or the Atlantic—Africa, too" He stopped walking and looked at Hugh. "We are using triangulation to follow Rommel's troops across Africa."

"No!"

"Yes. Hugh, we can hear what Rommel is telling his tank commanders, then relay that information to the British who are trying to track him down."

"Why?"

"As Rommel advances, we have to keep adjusting our triangulation so we can keep up."

They walked straight to Tom's car.

"Let me show you something."

Tom opened the trunk of his car. It was filled with what was at the time, sophisticated electronic gear.

"What is this for?" Hugh asked.

"It's the same triangulation equipment we have at our receiving station on the hill."

"So why do you need it in the car?"

"Hugh, you are a writer of great mysteries and espionage. You must certainly realize that the Germans have spies planted in our midst."

Hugh nodded, even though he wasn't sure. Everyone suspected that German spies lived in our midst, or at least feared it was so. This was the first time Hugh had come face-to-face with real life espionage.

"There are two other cars with equipment like this. We drive around the area trying to get a fix on illegitimate radio signals."

"Here in Providence?"

Tom looked at Hugh as though he wondered how his brother had earned security clearance.

"Spies are not just in the movies and pulp magazines, you know. Anyway, if we pick up a transmission signal, either going across the Atlantic or coming back, we can then pinpoint the signal within an hour, right down to the street, the house and even the room in the house. Then, gotcha!"

Hugh couldn't remember ever seeing Tom so outwardly pleased with himself.

I asked Cave if he felt sure all of this happened as Tom told it.

"I'll have to admit, at the time it seemed a little far-fetched, but Tom was not the type to make up stories. Yes, he had been bitten at an early age by that very same adventure bug we inherited from our parents, but he was more the serious, practical type, more like our father.

"After that day, I didn't see or speak to him again for another three years. Then, a short time after the war ended, he showed up one day, just like he did three years earlier. This time, when I went out to greet him, he told me to hop in the car.

"We drove to some out-of-the-way spot near the coast. It was off the main road, up in the hills. We weren't even on a road, more like two ruts in the dirt, winding through the woods. They led to a clearing.

"I recognized it immediately, even though I had never been there before. The clearing was really more of an open field. In the middle sat a farm house, abandoned and desperately in need of repair.

"Then I saw them—telephone poles, totally out of place where they stood.

"We pulled up to the farmhouse, got out of the car and walked up the front steps. They creaked under the weight of our feet, each in a little different pitch. The front door was closed but unlocked. Tom just opened it, like he had been there days before, and we walked in.

"On the living room wall hung a huge map of the Atlantic

Ocean, from the eastern U.S., to Europe and down to the Mediterranean. Colored pins were stuck in the faded blue portion of the map. He told me each pin represented a German submarine and the map pinpointed every sub in the German fleet. He knew of only one sub that ever escaped their detection. All this was possible by listening in on the conversations between subs and their home bases in Europe, thanks to triangulation. I walked up to the map, astonished at how many pins were concentrated within an inch of our shores.

"He didn't have much to say after that. We drove back home and talked about my writing, family, general chit-chat."

I asked Cave if he saw more of Tom after the war was over.

"Not at first. I heard from him occasionally, phone calls and even a letter or two. We went fishing together in Maine once, but I'm not sure when. I know he went to Brown University in 1945 and studied Russian while still working for the government. But he never told me much.

"I lost track of him again for a few years. Then, sometime in the mid-1950's, I think, he and his wife Gladys retired at a very young age and moved to Florida, settling on an island near Tampa. After I moved to Florida in 1967 I went over to visit him several times. He had a boat and we would go fishing. His health started to deteriorate after 1980 and he died in 1985.

"Tom may have still worked for the government after moving to Florida. He had a house full of electronic equipment there but he never talked about it. He was always so secretive."

Cave smiled. "He did claim once that he had invented the ship-to-shore telephone. Years earlier, when he worked down at the Cape he had a boat in Chatham and rigged up a device to talk with his wife when he was on the water.

"I really admired him. I only wish I had known him better."

PART TWO: A WRITER IS BORN

Chapter 7: Early Influences

HUGH CAVE'S WRITING CAREER BEGAN IN 1925 AT the tender age of 15, when his first short story, "Retribution," appeared in the *Boston Globe.* His name though, will be forever associated with the pulp magazines popular during the first half of the 20th century.

The pulps actually originated before then. Credit is generally given to Frank Munsey, publisher of *Argosy,* though the date is in some dispute. His April 1894 issue was the first to adopt a traditional 7x10 inch format. The October 1896 issue featured all fiction articles for the first time.

The pulps derived their name from the inexpensive, coarse wood pulp paper used to print them on, which enabled publishers to sell the magazines for a nickel or dime each. Pulp magazines had replaced dime novels as the most popular medium because for the same price, the stories were better written and targeted to an older audience.

In the days before radio and then television became the primary entertainment media in this country, people actually read for entertainment. During the Depression especially, people escaped their bleak world by visiting the neighborhood newsstand or drugstore. For a thin dime, they could select from more than one hundred periodical magazines filled with short stories, novelettes and serials that whisked the reader away from grim reality to a purely fantasy world.

The pulps competed for prospective buyers' attention with flashy cover art and often sensational story titles. Magazines like *Action Stories, Argosy, Dime Detective, Far East Adventure Stories, Modern Romances, Spicy Adventure Stories, Strange Tales, Weird Tales,* and *Western Story,* captivated readers with exciting, romantic, scary and sexy fiction. Many of today's literary genres such as science fiction, horror and romance, first appeared in the pulp days.

The stories were written by a huge stable of writers, some capable of grinding out formula fiction to fill the demand for anything printable and others who went on to be our country's finest authors. Some of the best known (in their time) pulp writers included Max Brand, Edgar Rice Burroughs (Tarzan first appeared as a character in the pulp magazines), H.P. Lovecraft, Clarence E. Mulford (known for Hopalong Cassidy), Frederick Nebel and Manly Wade Wellman. Writers who started in the pulps and then went on to become some of our best known authors were the likes of Robert Bloch (*Psycho*), Ray Bradbury, Raymond Chandler, Erle Stanley Gardner, Dashiell Hammett, L. Ron Hubbard (before the Church of Scientology), MacKinlay Kantor, Louis L'Amour, John D. MacDonald, Richard Matheson (*The Incredible Shrinking Man*) and Tennessee Williams.

Although he is not as well-known, Hugh B. Cave clearly belongs in the second group. He was a prolific writer during the pulp era, churning out stories in every genre from adventure to mystery, romance, western, detective and horror. To sell all he wrote, Cave used more than a dozen pseudonyms (C.H. Barnett, Allen Beck, Judy Case, Justin Case, and Geoffrey Vace, to name a few). He often had more than one story in a magazine. Once he had four stories, each under a different name!

Cave's accomplishments are considered legendary by his peers. The late Robert Bloch described Cave this way at a writer's convention in 1983 where they were both guests of honor. "In one person incarnate we have a virtual living history of pulps. He embodies and personifies that era, and you're not going to get a chance to meet a gentleman of his stature again."[1]

I asked Cave when he started writing.

"After Dad's accident. At some point I began to retreat more into my room where I would draw, or read and write little stories."

Did you cut yourself off from your family?

"No, not at all. Geoff and I were inseparable. Both of us sang in the choir and we liked sports—fishing especially, ice skating, basketball, baseball."

He chuckled to himself.

"Just before I started the seventh grade, I think I was twelve at the time, we moved to 50 Peterboro Street in the Back Bay area of Boston, south of Fenway Park, off Jersey Street. It was a red brick apartment building. Geoff and I would play baseball in a lot next to the building with some other kids from the neighborhood. Some of the Boston Red Sox players actually lived in our building—I don't remember which ones—and when we kids played baseball, a few of them played with us."

I asked again how he began to write.

"Oh, sorry. Let's see, where was I? Yes. I stayed in my room a lot after school and on weekends. Maybe it was to avoid seeing my father. He was like a stranger and made us all very uncomfortable.

"I would write these little stories and then take them to Mother. She was always encouraging and loving about everything I did, even during these tough, tense times. Whatever I did, I showed to her, whether a piece of writing, a sketch, a painting, or some special photograph I had taken. I think I started writing just to please her. God knows she wasn't getting much enjoyment elsewhere in her life.

"I also drew a lot and I could copy any kind of picture. My eighth grade teacher had a thing about etchings of old cathedrals. She had me copy them and then framed my drawings, putting them on the walls of her classroom.

"I remember doing a study of the animals of North America, drawing pictures of every animal I could find in encyclopedias and big dictionaries. Then I wrote a piece about each one. A college professor lived on the first floor of our building on Peterboro Street. He admired my work so much, he took the drawings and bound them into a book, typing up my written descriptions beside every one. It wasn't published, but that became my first book.

"I didn't get serious about my writing until I started high school. Then two things happened. First, Geoff, who was four years older, and also enjoyed writing, had his first story published. After graduating from high school, Geoff actually launched his own writing career, but marriage and its financial responsibilities nipped that career in the bud. I would later use a pseudonym of Geoffrey Vace—that's Cave, of course—in his honor.

"Anyway, as a senior, Geoff was editor of the Mechanic Arts High School paper, *The Artisan.* I remember being jealous of all the attention he received and seeing his byline on stories he wrote for the paper. That's probably what prompted me to start getting serious about my own writing.

"But the second factor that stirred my interest in writing was my ninth grade English teacher, Mrs. Celina Lewis. She nurtured my budding talent and interest. I remember in her class that we used to read aloud from certain books we studied. Then she would ask us to rewrite, in our own words, some scene that interested us. I rewrote the scene from Dickens' *A Tale of Two Cities* in which old Madame Lafarge, I think that was her name, sat knitting while watching people lose their heads to the guillotine. After class that day, Miss Lewis called me up to her desk and told me I had a talent for writing.

"She felt from the start that I had the potential to become a professional writer. In fact, she became so interested in developing my skills that she received special permission to continue as my English tutor throughout my high school years.

"Mrs. Lewis encouraged me to enter the *Boston Globe* writing contest in 1925. I was 15 at the time and in tenth grade. I won honorable mention for my story called "Retribution," about a boy and his horse. A villain steals his horse and is then killed as the boy whistles and the horse throws him. It was significant because they printed "Retribution" in the paper, making it my first published work.

"I remember when I graduated from high school, she signed my yearbook, 'Remember Hugh Walpole's *Fortitude,*' which of course, was the novel about a man's struggle to become a successful writer. It also happened to be my mother's favorite novel, written by the man I was named after!

"Celina Lewis was not the only one who influenced my decision to write, however. There was one other significant adult in my life at the time, a man who would become more of a father to me than my real father had ever been. His name was Albert Snow.

"Albert Snow served as the organist and choirmaster at my church. He was also organist for the Boston Symphony Orchestra at some point in time as well. Mr. Snow encouraged my love of music. After all, it was he who directed Geoff and me in the choir at Emmanual Church all those years, from the time I was seven or eight until I graduated from high school.

"He was tall and good-looking, a quiet, gentle man, who never raised his voice and had a great sense of humor. At rehearsals he would hear sour notes and stop us, then say let's do that again—except you two don't sing this time. He was never the Prussian general type; every one of us boys loved him. I tried to emulate him then and long afterwards. Mr. Snow is responsible for the kind of man I became and am to this day.

"He seemed to take a personal interest in Geoff and me, frequently visiting our home. It was much later that I realized he had also taken an interest in our mother.

"Every summer, Geoff and I attended a summer camp down on Cape Cod. Camp Ascension was owned by the Episcopal Church and I believe Mr. Snow was camp director. He actually drove us to camp each year in a covered truck. The camp lasted for two weeks, which we spent in old army tents at first, then later they built cabins. We fished, hiked and swam. We had a lake there called Hedge Pond, about a half mile across. At the end of the two weeks, you had to prove you knew how to swim by swimming across the lake with an escort of rowboats.

"They had a circular fire pit in the center of the camp, which at one time had been the site of a sawmill. There was still a huge pile of sawdust behind our tents. Every night we had a campfire. The pit was about as big as my bedroom. All the kids, about 40 of us, sat around the fire on wooden benches while Mr. Snow read stories. As I remember it now, he read ghost stories and mysteries—Edgar Allen Poe, Arthur Conan Doyle, Ambrose Bierce, that sort of thing. I sat right next to Mr. Snow. When he read, you could hear a pin drop, except for the crackle of the fire. I loved it. He was like a surrogate father to me."

Cave laughed. "I hold him personally responsible for my lifelong interest in weird menace stories. Many of them probably started as ideas and images kindled as we sat around that campfire."

Albert Snow's name would come up frequently in our meetings together. He was quite fond of the man. I asked about Snow's interest in Cave's mother.

"He wasn't interested in her at first. He came around occasionally when I was younger, then more frequently after Dad's accident. He didn't seem to show a personal interest in my mother, at least none that I recognized, until well after my father left us.

"I don't think they ever dated or spent any time together alone, but at some point, he must have indicated to Mother his fondness for her. I found out later that he had actually asked her to marry him. Had I known this was a possibility at the time, I certainly would have encouraged it. However, he was very discreet about it; that's how you were in those days.

"Anyway, my mother was nine years older than Mr. Snow. I don't know if that was the reason she turned him down, but she did. He eventually went on to marry a Boston socialite."

Cave's voice creaked with disappointment, even today. "A few years after that he died of cancer."

He paused, reflecting. "Mr. Snow was a wonderful man—and he would have made a great father.

"Mother never remarried. I don't think she ever had a gentleman friend after Dad left. She just devoted her life to us—and probably in remembrance of her love for Dad. She must have kept alive her memories of when she was a 20-year old student nurse, the romantic years with him in South Africa, coming to America and raising a family together—right up to the accident. That's when her life as his mate ended. I don't think she could have found someone else and invested another lifetime in a relationship. It was easier for her to relive the good memories of Dad.

"Whatever the reason, she left no room in her life for Albert Snow, and I lost my only opportunity for a father who might have loved me as my mother did.

"Mother eventually retired to live alone in a modest apartment near my brother Geoff and his wife Alice in East Douglas, Massachusetts. Toward the end of her life she suffered from amoebic dysentery—a reminder, she said, of her childhood in India. At that point Geoff and Alice insisted she move in with them. She died of a stroke soon afterward—a good, brave, honest woman whom I dearly loved, and who loved me dearly in return."

Cave's eyes filled with tears. I felt he spoke directly to his mother, wherever she may be. I also felt he spoke to her often over the years.

Chapter 8: Coming of Age

Aside from the wrenching circumstances that began at age nine with his father's accident, Cave lived a typically normal childhood. About that age he joined the Emmanual Church choir—singing soprano—an activity that gave him much joy and comfort until he graduated from high school.

He and his brother Geoff were close during those years and remained so until Geoff died in 1988. Tom had already left home in 1919 and was a shadowy figure in Cave's life until his 1985 death.

In 1921, when Cave was 11, the family moved to Peterboro Street in Back Bay. There he attended Prince School, riding his bike two miles to get there or taking a streetcar. Geoff went to Mechanic Arts High School. They lived in an apartment across from the Charles River, by a wooded area. They were near Boston Symphony Hall, where he and Geoff would go and listen to concerts as guests of Albert Snow, sitting in the balcony.

By his own description, Cave was a quiet, obedient boy. He had friends and playmates, but seemed happiest when within the womb of his home. There he led a secret life of adventure, an escapist with a fascination for the written word that transported him away from his normal, though sometimes painful life, into a world of exotic lands, heroes and intrigue.

As he grew older, Hugh enjoyed sports, including the team variety, but didn't possess the kind of competitive spirit necessary to excel in them. Cave was a shy sort around people and his most detailed memories revolved around the family living room. He loved to sing and listen to music, but showed no particular aptitude for playing a musical instrument. He drew a lot, he read, and his talent for writing began to emerge. It was during those middle childhood years that his love of adventure blossomed, the ultimate escape from reality.

If you visit Hugh Cave's home today, you will find it to be a typically Florida, ranch-style, concrete block construction, with wood and brick trim on a one third-acre lot. The lawn and flowerbeds are neatly manicured. Inside, the tiled entryway leads to a spacious living room with sliding glass doors that open up to a cheery back Florida room, essentially a closed in patio. The galley-style kitchen connects the living room on one end and a breakfast nook on the other end, overlooking the front yard.

It should come as no surprise to Cave fans that he ended up making his home in Sebastian. It is located in a part of Florida called the Treasure Coast, so named because this is where the first sunken Spanish treasure galleons were discovered about 40 years ago. He couldn't have created a better setting for a writer of adventure yarns.

Whenever I arrived for our weekly get-together, Cave was prepared with books, articles, photos and other documents to illustrate subjects that we had been covering or would cover that particular day. The materials were neatly piled on the kitchen table next to a yellow legal pad and pencil. His Mr. Coffee carafe was filled with freshly brewed decaf for my visit, on the kitchen counter with several coffee cups, spoons, sugar and skim milk, sometimes a tray of cookies. Occasionally, I brought muffins or pastries.

Peg began to join us at the fourth interview, coming to sit at the table from time to time when she wasn't out shopping or busy elsewhere in the house. Peg probably wanted to sit with us every time I came over, but didn't, knowing this was Hugh's time. It was an expression of her love and respect for him.

"I think my most vivid childhood recollections start at the time we moved to Brookline in 1923. I was 13 at the time and just starting the ninth grade at Brookline High School. I was often the youngest in my class since skipping fourth grade. My situation at home overshadowed any problems I may or may not have had in school. It was about the time of my father's accident and painful—for the family—recovery.

"Geoff had already graduated from high school and he was working. Dad still lived with us, but he seemed more like a boarder than a father. He had resumed his accounting practice in the city and we didn't see much of him.

"We lived in a two-story, white frame house, rental of course. It had almost no backyard, but the house was only five minutes walk from my high school. In front of the school was a huge park with a bandstand, gym and a building that housed the school swimming pool. It was a pretty place.

"So we had plenty of room to play, especially sports. In the evenings, I played handball at the high school with whoever else showed up. I used to love gymnastics, which I was good at because I was skinny. I also climbed a rope faster than anyone."

Cave laughed aloud. "We had a long corridor in our house and I would put down a mattress at one end, then run, dive and somersault on that mattress. Mother allowed it—encouraged me, actually. Of course by that time, Dad didn't say anything about it one way or another."

Although Cave was shy around others, he seemed to have a real interest in sports.

"Yes, in some respects. I was good at gymnastics, swimming, and I loved hockey—the playground in front of our high school was flooded for skating every winter and I played a lot of pick-up hockey, but wasn't good enough for the high school team. I was too light for football and not too keen about baseball, then or now. Tall and skinny is okay for basketball, but our school didn't have a team. I did, however, play on the church basketball team. There was an adult church league. One team, the Ascension Alerts, became semi-pro. I tried to make it with that team, but didn't get far. By the time I finished high school, my basketball days were over.

"I was very good at table tennis in high school, though it wasn't considered much of a sport back then. There was a league at the time, with six or seven teams. My team usually won. I even wrote some articles about table tennis later, one for *Elks Magazine* as I recall.

"I started playing a banjo-uke around the time we moved to Brookline. I had tried piano but couldn't figure it out. Eventually, I gave up the banjo too, but not before I painted the face of a pretty girl on it, copied off the cover of a *Good Housekeeping* magazine. I had sketches and paintings all over my bedroom walls.

"I remember illustrating my history notebook with a picture of Columbus standing on a rum barrel on the deck of his Santa Maria, a spyglass to one eye as he discovered America. Later in life, I took some art courses and did quite a few oil paintings, especially in Haiti. I sold a few of them too, but it was never much more than a hobby.

"The same with photography. My mother bought me a cheap Brownie box camera and I became very interested, even to the point of developing and printing my own pictures. Around that time I found an article in *Popular Mechanics* on how to build an enlarger using a wood box and a window. I built one and it worked. I also painted pictures from my photos. From then on and up until just recently, I was hooked on photography. My two most popular travel books, *Haiti: High Road to Adventure,* and *Four*

Paths to Paradise: A Book About Jamaica, both contained many of my photos. The photos helped me sell those books, which both became best sellers. I ended up with over 1,000 8x10's and I sent them in batches to newspapers. You could make five to ten dollars a picture when they were used. I sold to publications like the *New York Journal of Commerce.* By the time I went to Haiti, I owned a Speed Graphic professional camera. Photography never became more than a hobby either. Writing took up the majority of my time.

"Of course, I loved to read as a teenager. In Brookline we lived within walking distance of the public library. Geoff and I spent many an evening there. By the time I graduated from high school, I think I had read just about every fiction book they had!"

I asked him if there were any defining moments in all those events or activities.

He pondered my question, immediately putting aside his treasure trove of memories. "You mean that helped set my life's course?"

I answered affirmatively, because other than the troubles resulting from his father's accident and eventual departure, his life seemed typically Middle America to this point.

"Milt, who can say what makes people do the things they do? Some of the world's greatest people had what you would consider a typical childhood, while others came from the most deplorable conditions. The same is true of bad people."

I wasn't satisfied. I pointed out that many writers never accomplished a fraction of what he has in his lifetime. And there are millions more who say they want to be writers but never do it. Was there some trigger that sent him off on his life's course?

"I suppose my father's accident was a defining moment. But let's go back to that list of ingredients you asked me about to become a writer. Here's one—dreaming."

Dreaming? I asked.

"Yes, dreaming. Imagining yourself somewhere or doing something exciting."

Oh, I answered, you mean daydreaming.

He shook his head. "No. Milt, when you were 13 or 14 years old, didn't you have dreams and fantasies?"

Sure, I said. I wanted to be Buster Crabbe as Flash Gordon. I wanted a submarine like Captain Nemo in *Twenty Thousand Leagues Under the Sea.* I wanted to be a baseball star."

"So what did you do about it?"

I told him that I lived out these fantasies when I played with friends.

He asked again, "No, what did you *do* about it?"

He stopped me cold. My safe little life back then didn't allow for me to do something about my fantasies. Okay, Hugh, I told him, you've made your point. Now why don't you tell me what you did about it and maybe we can find a defining moment somewhere.

"I think I may have an example for you."

Good. I was relieved that the pressure was off me and back on him. After all, he could learn nothing from my life's story.

"First, you have to remember that I grew up somewhat restrained by the Victorian upbringing of my mother. But I had this fascination for the written word that transported me from my Victorian, sometimes unpleasant life, into a world of exotic lands, heroes and intrigue. I wasn't interested in becoming a policeman, fireman, lawyer or doctor. I wanted to be an explorer, go off to strange, far-away places. I read those kinds of stories—H. Rider Haggard, *Tarzan of the Apes,* and wanted to see the world of my fantasies. Even though I didn't follow through until well into my adulthood, I never lost the desire for adventure. I think it enabled me to write so many adventure tales, because I imagined myself right in the middle of them. However, I did have one adventure as a teenager that gave me a taste of the world I desired.

"The summer between my sophomore and junior years in high school, before my 15th birthday in 1925, a friend of mine who sang with me in the Emmanuel Church choir suggested we do something daring. His name was Shirley Goodwin—that's right, he was a boy. He said his parents wanted a girl and planned to name her that, if you can believe it.

"He was a year older than me, but we were in the same grade. Shirley was my best friend. Ernie Stokes and Everett Knudsen were other friends, also in the choir, but not friends like Shirley. He suggested we go on a 'grand adventure' in the Adirondack Mountains. It started as sort of a joke, then we kept talking about it, working ourselves up until something had to be done. We decided to run the idea past our parents one afternoon, then meet the next morning before school to compare results. Well, back in those days you could do something like this without fear of meeting up with some pervert or serial killer along the way.

"Much to our surprise, we were given conditional approval by our parents. In my case, it was Mother; I don't think Dad knew anything about it and probably wouldn't care one way or the other if he did.

"So that summer, armed with a letter of introduction from Choirmaster Albert W. Snow saying we were good kids, etc., in case we were picked up as runaways, Shirley and I left on our big adventure. We set out to hitchhike from Brookline, Massachusetts to Niagara Falls and then to the Adirondacks, armed with blanket rolls, a change of clothing, and some money to feed ourselves.

"The trip ended up taking about a month, but when we started, we didn't know if it would be a day, a week or all summer. I can't imagine kids our age doing this kind of thing these days. There's just too much bad that could happen.

"Back then there weren't so many cars on the roads, so we did more hiking than hitching. We slept outdoors mostly, usually along the road, sometimes in barns with the owner's permission. At one point a high school teacher picked us up and we stayed at his house a few days. I remember he lived on a farm in Painted Post, New York. Often people would pick us up and we might stay with them two or three days. They might just be on vacation themselves and take us along with them. We wrote home every day to let our folks know how it was going.

"Once we spent the night in a quarry. It was a bit scary to us, especially when this wild-looking man suddenly came out of nowhere and wandered into our campsite. He was a bum, big and tall, unshaven with a bushy beard. I hate to say it, but he reminded me of my father after the accident when he stayed in his room all the time. But he didn't threaten or hurt us, just sat by the fire and talked for a while, then went on his merry way. I must admit we both kept one eye open all night, but never saw him again.

"When we crossed into Canada there were no customs houses or gates to indicate we were in another country, just a small sign that read, 'You are now in Canada.'

"At Niagara Falls we did all the usual things—rode the 'Maid of the Mist' boat that went right up to the foot of the falls, went into the 'Cave of the Winds,' and so on. In the Adirondacks we climbed, on successive days, two of the highest peaks, Marcy and Whiteface. We were just two kids with knapsacks, cameras, change in our pockets and an exhilarating spirit of adventure.

"By the time the trip was over, we were glad to be home again. My need for adventure had been satisfied for a while. Shirley and I remained friends for many years, until I moved to Rhode Island in 1931. I became a writer and he became an Episcopalian minister.

"But an important bridge had been crossed that summer, Milt," Cave said as he leaned toward me and tapped his forehead, "from the land of fantasy that had only resided up here, to the possibilities that lie out there." He made a sweeping motion toward the kitchen window.

Chapter 9: The Course is Set

The summer of 1926 began just as it did the four prior years, with two weeks at Camp Ascension. Cave was now, at age 15, one of the oldest boys in camp, and he probably had some sense this year would be his last. Cave had begun the transition from childhood to adulthood.

Upon returning from camp, Cave learned that his English teacher, Mrs. Celina Lewis, aware of his family's tight financial situation, had found him a job for the summer. He would be working at an old family-style hotel on Martha's Vineyard, called Wesley House.

"I was the only high school kid there; the rest were college students. They initially had me working as a bellhop, but then they put me in charge of the print shop. We printed menus every day for the guests on an old-fashioned, hand press. I worked part of the day as a bellhop, then I would write out menus and print them. I took the liberty of writing short poems at the top of each day's menu."

The summer went quickly and Cave enjoyed his independence, the opportunity to express his creativity and the satisfaction of having cash in his pocket.

When Cave began his senior year at Brookline High School, the situation at home had settled into a comfortable normalcy. The family still struggled financially, but no one complained. Cave continued working before and after school at Delano's, still riding his bike there in the morning, coming home for breakfast, then to school, making deliveries afterward. He saw less and less of Geoff, who worked full time and spent almost every day with his girlfriend, Alice Bascomb.

"They named me captain of my Emmanuel Church basketball team when the season started in October. We played at the Boston YMCA. Basketball was a different game back then, two-handed set shots, lots of passing. A high score might be 35–31.

During this time, firehouse basketball came on the scene. Rhode Island coach Frank Keaney came up with the fast break; his teams were the first to score 100 points in a game. 'Point-a-minute' they called it."

Cave's sports career soon ended because he devoted more and more of his time to writing. Prompted by his success writing poems on the Wesley House menus, Cave regularly submitted poetry to various publications. He also received a Lincoln Medal (still in his possession) for a contest he won with an essay on Abraham Lincoln, submitted under the pen name, "John Bull." He would have many more pen names in the future. This was his first writing award, not counting the honorable mention for "Retribution." He also won a gold award during the school year for excellence in English. "I kept the medal for many years, then gave it to Peg, who took some of the gold and had it made into a ring for her grandson."

Whatever influenced his desire to write—Wesley House, his reading, his English teacher, the Adirondacks adventure, campfire ghost stories at Camp Ascension, seeing his brother Geoff's success writing in the school paper—one event probably galvanized his career decision to become a writer.

"Late in 1925, Celina Lewis showed me a Sunday School newspaper, I can't remember the name of it, published by the D.C. Cook Company. The paper carried short stories in it, and not only that, they paid the writers for these stories. She felt the quality of my writing at the time was good enough to be published and encouraged me to submit something.

"I was so excited, I went out and bought an old secondhand typewriter. I then wrote a short story and mailed it to the company. You can imagine how thrilled I was to receive a reply. The letter said 'Your story is far too long for our publication, Mr. Cave; however, we will run it as a serial, and kindly, in your next story, would you double-space it?"

Getting his story published was a thrill; getting paid for it transformed his hobby and passion for writing into a potential profession. The course had now been set.

In January 1927, the family moved again, to the Linden section of Malden, north of Boston and near Geoff's fiancée, Alice. Geoff had found this home for them and they rented the second floor. The move meant Geoff would see more of Alice and have his mother close by. The new arrangement didn't favor Cave though; instead of five minutes, the commute to school now took him one and a half to two hours. "I took a streetcar to Boston, then the elevated train, then another streetcar, to get to Brookline. In the evening, I would do all my homework on the streetcar."

To this point, Cave had shown little interest in the opposite sex. He says he didn't have girlfriends because he always had to work after school and never had time to get involved. He also admits being very shy around girls, never once attending a high school dance. It was not until his senior year, with graduation in the not-to-distant future, that Cave had his first date.

"She was a red-haired beauty named Deborah Roud, and one day I worked up the courage to ask her out. Paul Whiteman was in Boston for a silent war movie called 'The Big Parade.' It was playing downtown at the Tremont Theater with Whiteman in the orchestra pit. You had to dress up for events like this, so I borrowed Geoff's tuxedo, which was too big on my skinny frame.

"I took the streetcar to her house—she lived near Beacon Street —and we went downtown to the movie. We had a good time and I liked her, but our budding friendship abruptly ended when I took her back home.

"I didn't know it at the time, but she was Jewish. So when we got back to her house after the movie, her mother and father began asking questions. When they found out I wasn't Jewish, they wouldn't let her go out with me anymore. My very first date then ended up being my last date in high school."

While his love life remained dormant, his writing life blossomed. Cave became short story editor for the Brookline High School newspaper, *The Sagamore*. His poem, "Reason For Pride in Brookline High," won him the Excellence in English award and a college scholarship. It began as follows:

> The morning doors of Brookline High admit me for the day.
> (I say "admit me," yet 'tis more; 'tis "welcome" I should say.
> For as I pace along the aisle and leave my books the while,
> The master greets me with "Good Morning!" and a cheery smile.
> 'Tis but a minor thing, I know; it means not over-much,
> And yet it lends the coming day a golden starting touch.
> The start! It makes for better work, it drives away the gloom,
> Breaks down the barrier and makes that room a sunny room.)[2]

He also submitted a second entry in the *Boston Globe* writing contest entitled "Great and Small," and again won an honorable mention. He had an article published in the *Boston Post,* and his poetry now appeared regularly in newspapers as well.

In June, Cave graduated from high school, one month short of his 17th birthday. With a college scholarship in hand, Cave decided to return to Wesley House on Martha's Vineyard for the summer.

"They had sent me a letter offering my old job back as bellhop and printing press operator if I wanted it. Geoff told me not to go, to get a real job because this was only a summer thing. But tips were good and it was better than most jobs I could find right out of high school at 16 years old."

Cave was still the youngest employee, but as a college-bound high school graduate, the other employees now viewed him as more than a kid. He would soon find himself in very adult-like situations.

"Ten students were employed at Wesley House, five male and five female. We worked together all day every day, but after work, the boys and girls were forbidden to mingle. The five girls stayed on the top floor of the main building and the five boys stayed in one of the cottages. Of course, being forbidden to mingle, we went ahead and mingled anyway, eventually pairing up. In the evenings, all ten of us would sneak out and walk down to the beach. I was the youngster of the group and had no experience at all with the opposite sex to that point, so I wasn't looking to pair up with anyone. One girl had not paired up with anyone either, so we found ourselves thrown together as a result."

That girl was a waitress named Margaret Long. Margaret was nearly three years older than Cave, a student at Rhode Island College of Education majoring in Physical Education. A tall, thin girl with a boyish figure, she hadn't shown an interest in Cave or any other boy for that matter. They were left alone on the beach, however, and Cave, clueless about matters of the heart, thought of her as his first girlfriend.

"I guess I was attracted to Margaret because of her maturity—she was more than two years older than me, possibly a mother figure—and the fact she paid attention to me. I didn't recognize it at the time, but Margaret was standoffish, only interested in idle conversation, nothing more. That only increased my interest in her."

By summer's end, having been thrown together in this captive environment, and Cave's penchant for fantasy, he thought he was in love. They parted company, she for Rhode Island and he for Boston, with vague commitments to stay in touch.

* * *

Cave quickly refocused on the next phase of his life. Geoff had become a bookkeeper like their father. Mother was still doing private nursing in people's homes. Cave had won a scholarship and started taking evening classes at Boston University, but knew he also had to find work in order for him to afford school and do his part to help with the family finances.

"I went to an employment agency looking for a job and they sent me to Otis Elevator Company. They hired me as a 'Learner Serviceman,' repairing elevators. I went with a crew of three big, burly men to office buildings in the downtown Boston business district. I was the kid who handed them their tools while they repaired broken down elevators. I was no damn good at it and hated the job. After three weeks, I quit.

"So I went back to the agency and they sent me to B. L. Makepeace Company on Washington Street, where I was hired as a clerk. They sold instruments, materials and supplies for architects, surveyors and draftsmen. I spent a lot of time in the blueprint room, but didn't sell over the counter because I didn't know a transom from a level. I worked there for six months, going to college and continuing to write poetry in my spare time, getting it published in various newspapers and small magazines."

His poems appeared in the *Boston Post, Presbyterian Advance* and even the *Los Angeles Times*. Cave was a lovesick young man, pining for Margaret though he never knew if she cared at all about him. "I didn't realize at the time that this wasn't working."

His feelings became a matter of public record, aired regularly in his poetry:

DOUBT
Hugh B. Cave

My heart beats madly!
If I knew
She loved me,
Maybe
It would drop . . .
I'll ask her!
No—I do not dare—
She might say "No!"
And then
'Twould stop!

Boston Post
Date unknown[3]

FORGET?
Hugh B. Cave

Forget?
What would you have me do,
Forget those days
With you?
Forget your promise too,
The vows I made
To you?
Because
Our dreams did not come true,
You wish me to
Forget?

Los Angeles Times
Date unknown[2]

Cave stayed at Makepeace for six months, until he was elated to find a job in the spring of 1928 at The Four Seas Publishing Company in Back Bay across from the Boston Repertory Theater. Four Seas was a vanity publisher for writers who don't have enough talent for a traditional publisher, but had enough money to print the book themselves. Four Seas also published a magazine, *Author and Journalist,* and edited other publications.

"The job paid $15 per week. I started out designing book jackets, then proofing galleys, writing blurbs for book flaps and editing copy for a parent-teacher magazine and a granite industry trade journal, something called *Chips and Spalls.* Eventually, my boss allowed me to rewrite manuscripts so they were more publishable. I saw my first electric typewriter at Four Seas—a secretary had it, not me. I did write an article for one of their magazines, 'Confessions of a Vanity Publisher's Assistant,' but I wrote it under a pen name because I didn't want to lose my job."

PART THREE: A CAREER IS LAUNCHED

Chapter 10: Death on the Highway

WHILE WORKING AT FOUR SEAS, CAVE DECIDED it was time to move out on his own. Geoff would soon be married to Alice and his mother lived away for days at a time as a private duty nurse, so the family decided to let their upstairs Malden flat go.

"I found an apartment at 55 Queensberry Street in Back Bay for $50 a month. It was a studio with an alcove that I curtained off from the kitchenette as a sleeping area. My mother stayed with me between her live-in nursing jobs."

Cave had begun visiting Margaret in Pawtucket, even before going out on his own. "I took the train down on Friday after work—it was a one hour trip—then walked five miles to her house and would stay for the weekend. We'd get a group together and go out dancing on Saturday. Then I would walk back to the station early Monday morning, sometimes in the bitter cold, and take a train, getting off at the Back Bay Station. I went straight to work by 9 a.m."

I asked Cave if Margaret lived alone in Pawtucket.

"No, she lived with her mother and a maiden aunt."

And you were allowed to stay at their house? Wasn't that a little unusual back then?

"Yes; people didn't just sleep together; everything was prim and proper. I think she viewed our relationship as merely a friendship, nothing romantic. I was the one who thought otherwise, naïve as I was about such matters."

Did she visit you in Boston?

"I don't recall her ever coming to see me until I had my apartment on Queensbury Street. Then she would come up with girlfriends to visit, spend a few hours and leave. She never came alone."

He considered his relationship with Margaret to be long term, regardless of how she perceived it. His relationship with any other women he may meet was strictly platonic. Ironically, it seemed obvious that Margaret's interest in Cave was just as platonic—obvious to anyone but a young, love-struck Hugh Cave.

*Hugh was delighted to hear from Gary Swanson (*These are not actual names; Hugh could only remember the incident*), a student at Holy Cross from Connecticut. They had worked together for two summers at Wesley House on Martha's Vineyard, both as bellhops. Except for Margaret, Hugh had not heard from any of his co-workers after they headed back home in the fall almost a year ago.*

"How did you find me?" Hugh asked.

"I called Wesley House," Gary answered gleefully, "and they gave me your home phone. I then spoke with your mother and she told me how to get in touch with you at work."

"Well, it's good to hear from you."

There was an awkward pause, the one that comes when two people who once shared a tiny part of each other's lives and suddenly find themselves reunited with nothing else in common.

"You're probably wondering why I called, Hugh. Do you remember Sally Westerman?"

"Sure, wasn't she in housekeeping?"

"Uh-huh."

"And you two seemed to have something going when we used to go down to the beach."

"Right again. Last fall Sally dropped out of Boston University and disappeared from sight. Then she called me the other day and said wouldn't be great if we got together again with the Wesley House crew for a night on the town. So that's why I'm calling."

Hugh remembered feeling like an outsider at Wesley House, not as much the second summer, but still more of an afterthought when everyone got together evenings after work. "That sounds great; who else have you contacted?"

"Well, unfortunately there aren't many of us left in town and so far it's just us. Say, what about that girl you spent time with, you know, the waitress? I can't seem to recall her name."

"Margaret Long," answered Hugh in a monotone.

"Yeah, that's it, Margaret. Do you know how to get in touch with her?"

Hugh remembered Margaret didn't like Gary Swanson; he also knew she would probably turn down an opportunity to visit Boston as she had every other time he asked her. "Yes, I've spoken with her once or twice," he lied. "She's getting married this summer."

He hoped Gary would drop the issue.

"Really? No offense Hugh, but I figured her out as a girl who didn't like guys. So who are you dating these days?"

"Well, no one really. I have this new job and it's taken all my waking hours just to stay on top of it."

"Great! I'm glad for your job and all, but you are in luck. Sally came to town with her sister, Nancy so we can double date. How about it?"

Hugh had little interest in spending an evening with Gary Swanson and no interest in a blind date, but the idea of getting out for an Saturday evening of fun was long overdue.

"Sure, I'd be glad to."

Gary picked Hugh up at his apartment. Sally Westerman and her sister were also in the car. Hugh felt awkward seeing Sally and Gary, both good-looking and inaccessible at Wesley House, now gushy and acting like best friends. Sally and her sister both had auburn hair but styled differently. Other than that, they bore little resemblance to one another. Sally was gregarious, slim, well-proportioned with an infectious smile and flawless complexion. Nancy was reserved, a little overweight and had a face that didn't reflect much joy. In a way, she reminded Hugh of Margaret, so he soon felt comfortable with her.

They decided to get some dinner and then go dancing at Revere Beach. The evening turned out to be fun for Hugh. He and Nancy didn't dance much, but they chatted while Gary and Sally danced, then listened while Gary and Sally talked at the table, chattering endlessly about their fun experiences at Wesley House.

Hugh jumped in on situations he recalled, but felt uncomfort-

able because most of the interesting experiences Gary and Sally talked about were news to him. Nancy was attentive, laughing when they laughed, but had nothing to add since she was even less a participant than Hugh. He enjoyed himself though and they stayed until one o'clock in the morning.

They didn't talk much as Gary sped home along the two-lane highway in his 1925 Ford. Sally rested her head on his shoulder and he with his arm around her. Nancy just stared ahead, occasionally asking Hugh if he was tired.

Suddenly a loud popping noise caught their attention. Gary gripped the steering wheel with both hands. "Sorry folks, we have a flat."

Gary pulled off as soon as he saw a clearing. The road had been built through an area of thick underbrush that crept right up to the narrow sand shoulders.

They all climbed out and inspected the flat rear tire. Gary brought out the spare and Hugh helped him while the girls stood by and talked quietly with each other.

The tire fixed, they all piled back in the car. Hugh had opened the back door for Nancy, then slid in next to her. From out of nowhere a blinding light filled the inside of the car. Hugh glanced out the rear window in time to see two headlights bearing down on him. Then came the sound of screeching tires.

Hugh woke up lying in a strange bed. He looked around the dimly lit room and immediately knew he was in a hospital. Moving his head made him acutely aware of a buzzing pain. He also found it difficult to focus his eyes. One by one, he moved his arms and legs to be sure they were attached, then tried to sit up. The dizziness made him drop back and close his eyes. He now felt nauseous as well and placed a hand on his forehead, which was wrapped in bandages.

He heard footsteps come into the room and opened his eyes to see Mother and Geoff. Mother's eyes were red from crying as Geoff spoke. "Thank God you're awake."

"What happened?" asked Hugh, fighting a wave of nausea as he spoke.

"You were in a serious accident," came another, strange voice from the doorway.

In walked a man wearing hospital whites accompanied by a uniformed policeman.

Geoff then spoke. "You were apparently parked along the side of the road when a car came along and rammed right into you."

"It was a big Hupmobile," added the officer, "Going way too fast. Your friend's car was totaled."

Hugh sat up quickly. "What about the others?"

The pain overwhelmed him and he fell back, closing his eyes again.

The man in white came up and placed a stethoscope to Hugh's chest. "I wouldn't try that again if I were you. You had a concussion and a pretty nasty bump on the head. Now take a deep breath."

"Your friends will be okay," said the officer. "The two in the front seat got banged up on the windshield. They were knocked out cold and pretty bloody when we arrived on the scene. The woman in the back seat with you is in about the same shape as you are, but like I say, they will all be alright—which is more than I can say for the guys in the other car."

"What do you mean," asked Hugh, wincing at the pain.

"Three of the passengers were thrown from the car; broken bones, cuts and bruises, but they'll live. The driver wasn't so lucky; he was killed on impact."

"No," said Hugh somberly.

"He was going way too fast for that road. The shoulders are so narrow you can't entirely pull off if your car is disabled. Enough of your Ford was on the road that he just plowed right into it."

Cave sat quietly for a few moments. "You know, Milt, that was the second time I came close to death, the first time on the boat coming over from England."

I asked whatever happened to Gary, Sally and Nancy.

"After saying our good-byes at the hospital, I never saw nor heard from them again. However, I still have a scar here on my forehead to remind me of that night."

He chuckled. "Something good did come of that experience, believe it or not. I hadn't told you anything about my boss at Four Seas, Edmund R. Brown. He ran a tight ship, which he had to as a small publisher of books and magazines.

"I don't recall how long I stayed in the hospital, but one day Mr. Brown came in to see me. He asked how I was, then handed me a folder with a manuscript, rubber-banded together. It was a book of poems with the title, *Pan and Peacocks,* by W. Adolph Roberts. As he handed it to me he said, 'Since you aren't doing anything else right now, could you please proofread this?'

"I did it, of course, and actually designed the jacket flap, too—I used a wallpaper pattern as I recall. Anyway, I worked on this book in the hospital and after returning to my job, I corresponded frequently with Mr. Roberts. I didn't find out until I was well into this project that Mr. Roberts was also the editor of a pulp magazine called *Brief Stories.*"

Cave was well familiar with pulp magazines, being such an avid reader. "By now I was subscribing to *Author & Journalist* and *Writer's Digest* because I wanted to get into pulps. As soon as I found out that Roberts was editor, I went to a drugstore and bought a copy of *Brief Stories.*

"Adventure stories, especially South Seas adventures, were my favorites from childhood; in fact, they still are to this day. I used to read every book or story I could find about those exotic, faraway places. My interest had been fueled by stories from relatives about Africa, Borneo, Australia and the South Seas. That was the type of story used in Roberts' magazine, so I decided to write one and submit it. The story was 'Island Ordeal.' Imagine my excitement when he accepted it for publication!

"Then I wrote a second story, 'The Price of Vengeance,' submitted it to a different pulp, *Action Stories,* and it was also accepted for publication. I wrote another one for W. Adolph Roberts, 'Pool of Death,' and he accepted that one, too."

By the time Hugh Cave and W. Adolph Roberts finally met, Roberts was surprised to see that Cave was only a teenager. He had submitted both stories with his job title of associate editor. Cave was also surprised. Roberts came from Jamaica, but had very light skin. According to Cave, he could have passed for white. Although these were the only two Hugh Cave stories he ever purchased, the two of them crossed paths again many years later.

Cave stayed at Four Seas until July 1929. By the time he left, he had been promoted to Literary Editor of the General Magazines Division. He also developed a lengthy resume of publishing credits which by then demonstrated his budding versatility as a writer. Cave's *Brief Stories* submissions would be published in July and August 1929. "The Price of Vengeance" appeared in the August 1929 issue of *Action Stories,* and in October 1929, they published a fourth story, "Jungle Loot." In addition, he had two short stories published that year in *Mystic* magazine. As of the date this book was written, there are no copies of these stories in existence.

He also published an article about writing in *Author and*

Journalist entitled, "Onomatology and Onomatopoeia." His previously mentioned poems appeared in numerous publications, including *Bozart Poetry Magazine*. While at Four Seas, he designed cover art for *The Broad Highway*, a book of poems by Emma Doan. Syndicated sports columnist Grantland Rice frequently accepted poems by Hugh Cave. Cave also created a series of sayings that he illustrated under the heading, "Ah Foo," which were published in *Boston Young Men's News*, a publication of the YMCA.

> All of us can rise and "I may"—
> But he who says "I will!" will win the day
>
> Ah Foo
> Date unknown[4]

By the end of June 1929, finding publishers willing to print just about anything he wrote, Hugh B. Cave made the decision that would chart his life's course from that point onward. "I decided I had enough talent to make it as a writer, so at the ripe old age of 18, I quit my job to write full time. I never looked back."

Chapter 11: Write to Live

The career path he chose would bring him a good, solid living and lifelong fame. But at the age of 18, just spreading his young wings, he was as yet unaware how precarious a career his chosen field might become. Robert Kenneth Jones, in his book, *The Shudder Pulps* (1975, FAX Collector's Editions, Inc., West Linn, Oregon) describes the pulp publishing business:

> These days, Madison Avenue would chuckle at the modest circulation figures and unprepossessing financial statements of the pulps. Yet thirty-five years or so ago, sales in the neighborhood of two hundred to three hundred thousand copies of an issue meant a fair profit to a publisher. He thought in terms of thousands—and sometimes, hundreds—not millions.
>
> In this heady environment, survival depended on newsstand sales . . . where the gaudy covers slugged it out with each other for the customer's dime. It was a fight to the (coated) finish. Publishers scanned newsstand sales returns as ardently as television producers today agonize over the latest viewer ratings.[4]

By the fall of 1928, Geoff Cave had married Alice Balcolm and Hugh Cave now lived in his own studio apartment on Queensberry Street. The Cave household that defined his life to this point, no longer existed.

He visited Margaret regularly in Pawtucket on weekends, arriving back in Boston on Monday mornings in time for work at Four Seas. If Cave at any time had stepped outside of his lovelorn haze to see what was really going on between them, he would have stopped seeing Margaret. However, the mesmerizing effects of first love to someone who, at age 18, had no practical experience dealing with the opposite sex, prevented him from applying any common sense to the situation.

"I thought we were in love, although there was nothing romantic about our relationship. Even after we married, there was little romance. To this day, I don't know how she really felt about me. All I know is that in my mind we were a couple and I accepted everything about our relationship, good and bad."

One of Cave's numerous poems published during his first years as a writer entitled "Description," appeared in the *Bozart Poetry Magazine*'s January-February 1929 issue and provided another window into his relationship with Margaret:

There is no passion,
No abandon, in her soul.
Her smile is a mechanical thing,
Turned to a premeditated angle,
Intended to please,
And pleases—but never delights.
She loves without loving,
Dances without hearing the rhythmic stamp
Of the orchestra,
And says calmly:
"How perfect the moon is tonight,"
Instead of whispering, "Look!—
Look at the moon!"
She is always conscious, always deliberate.
She kisses without closing her eyes.

—Hugh B. Cave

Margaret's mother, Agnes, came to the U.S. from Scotland. According to Cave, "She was a nice old lady with a Scottish brogue you could cut with a knife."

Agnes had worked as a master weaver in a fabric mill back home and came here to work in the Pawtucket mill. Margaret's father, Edward Hunter Long, was born in England, but emigrated as a teen and served in the U.S. Army during the Spanish-American War. They lived with Edward's spinster Aunt Maggie in a company-owned house about 100 yards from the mill outside Pawtucket. All three of them worked at the mill. "The whole street was cookie-cutter frame houses, non-descript, devoid of personality or character. They were fairly small, two-story. I remember the bedrooms to be icy cold in the wintertime when I would stay there.

"Margaret's father left home when she was ten years old, leaving her to be raised by her mother and maiden aunt, Margaret Picken Long. Interestingly, Aunt Maggie, as she was known, had also raised Margaret's father when he was a boy.

"Both Agnes and Aunt Maggie hated men. Margaret's mother felt men were not to be trusted and sex was a bad thing, something men insisted on and women had to do, but it wasn't nice. That wasn't an uncommon point of view then, especially from women of a European background. I'm not surprised Margaret's father left a home where such an attitude prevailed. Probably I should have learned from that.

"Not surprisingly, Margaret didn't care for men, either. Even after we married, she would have nothing to do with my men friends. To be fair, we had good times, though. When I visited her in Pawtucket, we went for long walks in the woods across from her house and talked a great deal. I know we were friends if nothing else."

By the end of 1929, Cave had published eight short stories. In addition to the previously-mentioned stories, his "Wolf Breed" was published in the November 1929 issue of *Action Stories*, and "The Shadow of Tsiang" in the October 25, 1929 issue of *Short Stories*.

Although the latter story became Cave's first to use what would evolve as the popular Tsiang House name, it was set in Africa and the main character, Major Corony was a diamond trader as well as the man in charge of the jungle post. The next Tsiang House story, "The Sins of the Fool," would be set in Borneo.

"My father used to talk about Borneo a lot, and I believe he had a brother who went there, to British North Borneo. That's probably where my fascination with that part of the world began. As far back as I can remember, I always wanted to be an explorer, go to strange, far-off places. Those were the kinds of stories I read. I never wanted to be a policeman, fireman, lawyer or doctor.

Writing gave me the opportunity to live my fantasy life while all my other childhood friends went on to more mundane pursuits."

"The Sins of the Fool" appeared a few months later, in the February 10, 1930 issue of *Short Stories*. It would capture the imagination of readers and result in one of Cave's most famous pulp series.

The story opens when a body is discovered by Captain Bruce Deragon, who would also become a series regular.

> This was Tsiang House, home of the British Governmental supervisor of the local native tribes. Tsiang House, with its darkened rooms and whispering walls! With its silent, creeping river of mystery, the Molo, drifting past under the veranda. With its Harrington, Lord Harrington, hanging dead over the table—murdered.[3]

Then Deragon and the aforementioned Major Jack Corony, no longer a diamond trader, proceed to solve the murder. They suspect a plot by one or more of the locals bent on eliminating their colonial masters. They are correct, of course, and in a climatic scene, they surprise an attacking mob of bloodthirsty natives with a hail of machine gun fire.

> There was no retreat, no possible chance of escape. Moreover, the savages of the interior do not recognize the meaning of fear. They came forward mechanically, hurling themselves into the passage in a futile endeavor to reach the murderous gun that was mowing them down. Snarling faces filled the darkness, only to drop back with sobs of sudden surprise as the line of destruction seared into them.[3]

Keep in mind these stories were written at a time when colonialism was considered proper economic and social policy.

Eventually, writing about those places would earn Cave the opportunity to visit them. But first, he wrote just to make a living, and in the process of making a living, he became a better writer. Those bleak Depression years would provide the ultimate test of his commitment to the writing life.

Cave quit writing poetry late in 1930 after his feet were planted solidly in the pulps. One of his last poems, entitled, "Men," appeared in *Sunset Magazine,* later put to music by Carlyle Davis. Oliver Ditson Company published the resulting song, and Carlyle Davis performed it at Carnegie Hall in 1931. "I received tickets to the concert but couldn't attend, so I gave them to a friend in New York. He went and said Davis did a great job on it."

They go at morning,
Come at night.
Eternally they fight
And fight . . .
And . . . fight . . .

They slave—
Release them from the rut,
Lift them above,
Unbonded, free,
And they will come again
For love
And be—
Just men.

Sunset Magazine, circa 1930

For the year 1930, he published 19 of his pulp stories, ten of which appeared in *Short Stories.* This was at a time when the country's economy was freefalling.

I asked Cave how the Stock Market Crash and years immediately following it affected him.

"A number of magazines went out of business. The Clayton Company's *Strange Tales* was a victim. I began to think I was a jinx about then. Every time I sold to a new pulp magazine, the damn thing would go out of business. They were folding like flies during the Depression. Yet I still made $5,000 a year when college graduates were lucky to find jobs paying $18 a week. I didn't know anyone making that kind of money."

Of the 19 stories Cave published that year, most were adventure tales, usually set in the South Seas. However, he also published a western and several detective stories.

The time frame between writing a story and seeing it in print would range from a few months to years. One of those stories, a Tsiang House tale called "The Midnight Horde," was originally written in 1930.

" 'The Midnight Horde' came out in Fiction Publishers' magazine, *Far East Adventure Stories,* as a serial, beginning with their September 1931 issue. Unfortunately, the magazine ceased publication after just three installments. Several years later, I sent it to Gwen Cowley, fiction editor at the *Toronto Star Weekly.* She had been buying my new stories and reprinting others—eventually more than 50 of my stories appeared in that publication. She bought 'The Midnight Horde' to be published as a complete novel, but it didn't come out until February 7, 1938, seven years after partially appearing in *Far East Adventure Stories*.

"The Midnight Horde" concerns an illegal gun runner, Andre Gervaine, who is supplying Borneo Dyak natives with rifles to rebel against the British Foreign Service. Captain John Halliday, also known as Johal, is seeking information about Gervaine and is led to him by a beautiful woman, Regine, who turns out to be a Gervaine associate. About to be killed, Johal escapes. Gervaine plans to ship four native boats loaded with guns up river, past the remote British outpost of Fort Tai-Tzu. Major Jack Corony and Captain Bruce Deragon of Tsiang House fame have been sent to take charge of the fort. They foil all of Gervaine's attempts to move the guns past the fort, as well as a fierce native attack. Johal eventually confronts Gervaine and kills him, then finds out the beautiful Regine is actually a spy and daughter of the British Foreign Service chief.

"After *Far East Adventure Stories* folded, they returned the unpublished fourth installment, which I then sent to Gwen Cowley some years later. But when the *Toronto Star Weekly* printed the story, it turned out to be only a condensation. They never returned the original manuscript, so that complete fourth installment is gone forever."

The story of how Cave came to write "The Midnight Horde" provides some insight into his uncompromising work ethic, which enabled him to sell 300,000 words of copy per year in the 1930's.

"I loved to go fishing, and one of my favorite fishing spots was Frost Pond at a Maine lumber camp. I went there in the summer of 1930 with Margaret's brother, Ed Long. It was up in the Ripogenus Dam country on land owned by the Great Northern Paper Company. There were many great trout spots up there and Frost Pond was one of them. We had to get special permission to cross the dam and a gatekeeper guarded the entrance. I tooted my horn and he would open it. After two or three trips, he knew me and just let us in. Then we followed a logging company road to the lake."

He laughed. "One night, I think it was this trip, a big Jack Dempsey fight was being broadcast on the radio. The lumber company had a warehouse in the area and some guys were staying in the building overnight for some reason. I went there hoping to hear the fight. The lumber company had installed a telephone wire along the forest road to the warehouse. I drove my Model A Ford to the building and we ran the telephone line down to my car radio. That became our antenna so we could listen to the whole fight. Had a great time that night.

"Few things interfered with one of my fishing trips, but I usually brought along my portable typewriter or a notepad in case the muse struck me. Well, that first night at Frost Pond, Ed Long and I sat at the campfire talking and then went to bed in our pup tent. Lying there, I suddenly had this idea for a story. By morning, I was sitting under a tree, furiously pounding the keys of my portable typewriter. Ed woke up and got ready to go fishing. I told him to go ahead and I would join him later. I spent the whole day on this story and never did go fishing on that trip."

In 1931, Cave had 37 stories published in addition to "The Midnight Horde." His willingness and ability to spend double-digit hours at the typewriter churning out respectable copy earned him a respectable income. The average pay for those 38 stories was only about $100, but this was at a time when college graduates only made $1,000 per year. Not only did he write for many different publications, but continued to write in a variety of genres, including adventure, horror, western and detective. That year, the *Boston Globe* started reprinting his stories in its Sunday magazine for $15 each. It was his first foray into slick paper publications, a course he would pursue with increasing vigor in the coming years.

Chapter 12: "Dear Mr. Cave"

The booming pulp market enabled Hugh Cave to learn his writing craft 'on the job.' Demand for writers had never been greater, nor would it ever be as strong again. Because he had talent, and more importantly, because he was willing to put in the hours, Cave fine-tuned his writing skills while earning a living at it.

Many well-known writers began in the pulps, but many "wanna be" writers also began—and ended—their careers writing for pulp magazines. One of those would-be writers was Geoffrey Cave.

"When I started selling to the pulps, my brother Geoff did too. He always wanted to be a writer and certainly had the talent for it. However, he was also married and eventually had three children. It was difficult enough trying to earn a living at a penny a word working up to 18 hours a day. It was impossible with a family to care for. So after a promising start, he was forced to stick with his more traditional job. He never wrote again."

Cave kept his brother's name alive, though. Whenever he sold two stories to the same magazine, he wrote one under the name Geoffrey Vace. It would be the first in a long list of pen names, but the most significant since it was in honor of his brother. "I'm not exactly sure which was my first Geoffrey Vace story." (Cave's bibliography shows it to be "Up River From Sandakan," which appeared in *Oriental Stories,* December 1931.)

Cave's South Seas adventure stories left readers wanting more, which he gladly provided them. "I sent one story to Clayton Magazines, which published *Wild World Adventures, Strange Tales* and many others. They had a consulting editor, an older man, whose name was Dr. Douglas Dold. Dr. Dold was curator of snakes at a zoo in New York and had actually spent two years exploring Borneo.

"So one day I receive this very long letter from Dr. Douglas Dold. He wrote and said he liked my stories and my style, but I was making a few mistakes about Borneo and he offered to help me out.

"I wrote back and took him up on it. Then every month I would receive a letter, partly letter, partly pages of notes about Borneo —for instance, different birds, what they looked and sounded like, snakes, all the background I needed to make my stories more authentic."

Once the relationship blossomed, Cave began selling stories to *Strange Tales,* through Dr. Dold to Harry Bates, editor of *Strange Tales* at the time. Cave's most famous weird menace tale, "Murgunstrumm," was one of them.

Dr. Dold also came up with story ideas, which he passed on to Cave. One of those ideas became another Hugh Cave classic, "Stragella."

"He had suggested a story involving the Indian Ocean, sea snakes and a derelict ship with vampires on it. I offered to include his name on the story when it was written, but he wouldn't let me."

Dr. Dold and Cave never met in person, only through letters. It was in one of those letters that Cave learned something remarkable about the man. Dr. Douglas Dold was blind.

"Dold became blind as an adult from injuries he suffered during World War I. He learned how to type by touch alone. He had someone read my stories to him aloud, then he would comment on them in his letters. I received pages and pages of notes from him that he had taken over his two years in Borneo. From those letters I knew the sound of every insect, where rivers went, what the natives looked like, their ceremonies, and much more, all of it first hand from someone who had been there. Dr. Dold became a mentor. Several of those stories also won honorable mention in the O'Henry contest and I have him to thank for it; his details made my stories real."

The correspondence with Dr. Dold continued until he died around 1934, "from too many snakebites," according to Cave. Dold became like a father advisor too, for instance, recommending that Cave put ten percent of every check he received in the bank and leaving it there. Incidentally, Dr. Dold was the brother of science fiction illustrator, Elliott Dold.

The South Seas became ground zero for many of Cave's pulp stories. They were based on his accumulated knowledge about the region from reading, hearing accounts from family members, and eventually his relationship with Dr. Dold. "In writing for the pulps, I would draw on what I had read for background, then from people and events in my life for characters and story. I didn't just invent a character; something of my real life memories and associations always went into the development of that character. I always boned up on backgrounds. I read everything I could get my hands on about, for instance, New Guinea. Later, during World War II when I actually had the opportunity to visit New Guinea and Borneo as a correspondent, I knew more about it than the guys who were there. I could tell them what was back there over those mountains."

One of his Tsiang House Borneo stories precipitated a fan letter that also resulted in a long-term correspondence-based relationship.

The story, "Green Eyes of Confucius," concerned "a very clever crook, posing as a genteel church missionary," who stole precious gems from native religious statues. Carl Jacobi, a young, aspiring pulp writer like Cave, read it and loved it.

So he wrote Cave a letter dated August 14, 1930, congratulating him on "The Green Eyes of Confucius," first published in the August 1930 issue of *Short Stories* magazine. Cave wrote back and that began an exchange of letters for the next 62 years until Jacobi, by then in a nursing home with Parkinson's Disease, could no longer write. From that point until Jacobi's death in 1997, Cave only heard from him through his caregivers.

Most of Jacobi's letters to Cave were lost in the fire of 1967 that destroyed all his pulp magazines. However, Jacobi saved most of Cave's letters to him. A selection of letters from their years of correspondence was published in the 1994 book, *Magazines I Remember* (Tattered Pages Press). Those letters provide insights into the times and both men's writing careers. They will be referenced frequently throughout this book.

Probably the most extraordinary aspect of their 67-year relationship is that the two men never met in person. "I did call Carl once—I think it was 1979 or '80, when I lived in Lake Placid, Florida—and I remember being surprised at his high-pitched voice. It wasn't much of a conversation and I never tried to speak with him again after that. My last correspondence was actually with the people taking care of him, because Carl could no longer put pen to paper."

Cave carried on a more limited correspondence with two other pulp writers, Bob DuSoe and Bedford Jones. "I don't remember why we exchanged letters, probably just one pulpster writing to another about some story or other."

Chapter 13: Moving to Margaret

Up to now, Cave had characterized Margaret's attitude toward him as "apathetic." There had been nothing romantic in the relationship or even, it seemed, the promise of romance. He insisted that they were good friends, however.

As he began to achieve some financial success with his writing though, she began to show more interest in him and the relationship was not as one-sided as it had been to this point.

I asked Cave if he realized her growing interest seemed to coincide with his growing financial success.

"I may have, but I was already in love with her, so when she became more interested in me, that only intensified my feelings."

Those feelings motivated his decision to move from Boston to Pawtucket in 1930. "Margaret encouraged me to move down saying why live in Boston and go through all this trouble of commuting back and forth all the time. I was earning good money and it didn't really matter where I lived as a writer. Frankly, I was tired of the endless train rides and didn't need much encouragement. I really didn't like Pawtucket—it was a mill town and no Back Bay—but she was there and I wanted to be with her."

Cave found a place to live in Pawtucket's only apartment building. It was located at 86 Montgomery Street, in the heart of town near the railroad station. His apartment had a bedroom, living room, kitchenette and it was furnished. Cave brought his own phonograph and books for a personal touch. "I probably took that place because I had walked by it on my way to Margaret's house each visit."

While his relationship with Margaret was frustrating at times, Cave had no such problem with his career. He spent hours each day grinding out copy and getting it published. He loved his work and it loved him in return, giving him pleasure and rewarding him financially for his efforts. However, the hectic pace led to a lapse in judgement which almost scuttled his career just as it gathered momentum.

Cave did not publish everything he wrote, which might be expected since he churned out copy at such a feverish pace. Time was money though, and he could not afford to invest time in a story, only to toss it out if an editor rejected it. "My custom in those days was to put a rejected story aside for revision at a later date because I was always working on something new.

"As I recall, I had maybe half a dozen stories put aside this way, and suddenly I needed a Tsiang House tale for *Short Stories* magazine. These stories had been running for some time and they were very popular with readers. I knew because whenever one was coming up, the magazine ran a half page ad announcing 'Another Tsiang House story by Hugh B. Cave in our next issue.'

"Well, I needed one, so I looked through the half dozen rejects I had on hand and found one that could be rewritten in the Tsiang House setting. I rewrote the story and mailed it off to the editor of *Short Stories,* Roy de S. Horn. In a moment of carelessness, I put the original manuscript back in the reject pile."

He doesn't recall which two stories were in question, but they were probably "The Thin Flame of Courage" (*Top Notch*) and "The Silent Joker" (*Short Stories*).

"Roy Horn bought the Tsiang House tale. A little later, I went through the reject pile, as was a habit of mine, and mailed those stories out again. The original of the one I had revised for *Short Stories* went out to another pulp magazine, *Top Notch,* and Heaven help me, they bought it!"

Cave didn't realize what he had done until the two stories appeared on the stands at the same time, in issues dated November 1931. "All kinds of letters began arriving at the editorial offices of both magazines. 'Hey, I just read this story in *Short Stories!*' 'Hey, I just read this story in *Top Notch!*' 'What are you guys doing!'

"I had letters from both editors asking me what was I trying to pull. I confessed to having been stupid, and pointed out to both editors that no sane young writer would jeopardize his career by doing such a thing deliberately. They suggested—no, demanded—that I come to New York and talk things over."

Cave handled the situation as diplomatically as a 21-year old aspiring writer could. "I believe I went first to the editor of *Top Notch,* who was both sympathetic and understanding. He phoned Roy Horn of *Short Stories* and suggested the three of us have lunch. We went, if I remember right, to the Army & Navy Club. Mr. Horn had a military background. It was a pleasant lunch. Both men seemed to understand how such a thing might happen to a very young man who was working his tail off to make it as a writer. The solution they came up with was that I agree to write separate, individual letters to each of the complaining readers, explaining to them what had happened.

"It took me days to write the letters. But you know something? Many of those readers became fans of mine and continued to write to me—or to editors about me—long after the incident of the two stories had been forgotten."

The incident taught Cave a valuable lesson, but it also resulted in his decision to take another step in furthering his professional career—he hired an agent.

The agent was Lurton Blassingame, who operated a one-man agency out of New York. He had a number of successful clients, including at one point, noted science fiction writer, Robert Heinlein. Blassingame was about ten years older than Cave. "I had been working without an agent, selling stories to, among others, several magazines put out by Popular Publications. The big editor at Popular then was Rogers Terrill. He wrote to me that I really ought to have an agent and one of the best was Lurton Blassingame who, just coincidentally, submitted stories in blue folders as I always did. In fact, said Rogers, every time a story of mine came in he thought it was one sent by 'Count,' which is the name everyone called Lurton.

I think I gave Rogers permission so he could talk to Lurton about me. Lurton then got in touch with me and became my agent."

By the end of 1931, Cave published 300,000 words of fiction, an amazing feat by any standard, but a necessity for writers at the time struggling to earn a living in the pulps. He already saw, however, that the long term future of pulp magazines might be limited and many of his contemporaries were making the move out of pulps into much better paying slick paper magazines and books. Slick paper magazines paid more money for a story and they were higher class publications. Cave felt he needed to move his career up to the next level and the slicks would give him more visibility.

Unfortunately, he met with limited success. The first slick sale (other than reprints, to be discussed below) was to Tower Magazines' *The Illustrated Love Magazine,* which paid 3½¢ a word, slightly better than the pulp range of 1¢ to 3¢. His second U.S. slick sale wouldn't occur for another year, in the October 1933 issue of *Household* magazine ("Scarecrow in Scarlet," featured on the issue's cover). However, he did not sell his work to the slicks with any consistency until well into the 1940's. His first major U.S. slick sale, "I Saw the Helena Go Down," appeared in the January 22, 1944 issue of *Saturday Evening Post,* and it was actually an excerpt from his non-fiction war book, *The Fightin'est Ship.*

Cave did much better selling reprint rights to Sunday supplements, religious and Canadian magazines, which were more or less the middle ground between pulps and slicks. His first foray out of pulps was to the *Boston Globe Sunday Magazine.* He convinced them to purchase reprint rights to his stories, his first being "The Green Eyes of Confucius" in the *Sunday Magazine*'s April 9, 1931 issue. Interestingly, the *Boston Globe* had published his very first stories, written as a high school teenager, just five and six years earlier.

Cave also saw the Canadian market as an opportunity for selling secondary rights to his original stories as well as first rights to stories he could not sell to U.S. publications. It was an original story, "Improper Lady," that first appeared in *Canadian Magazine* on April 5, 1932. "Ordeal by Battle," another original, appeared in the magazine in its November 1932 issue. He would sell them a total of 11 stories over the next two years. Other Canadian publications he wrote for included *Chatelaine, Family Herald & Weekly*

Star, and later in the 1940's, *Toronto Star Weekly.* He also found success with religious magazines, including *Christian Herald, Extension, Sacred Heart Messenger* and *The Sign.*

The pulps were his domain, however. In 1931 and 1932, Cave sold 49 stories to the pulps and the market for his work just kept growing. Between 1933 and 1934 he sold 82 stories to 27 different publications. His cross-genre talents were in clear evidence: he published six stories in *Weird Tales,* six in the *Boston Globe Sunday Magazine,* nine tales in *Western Story,* nine in *Canadian Magazine,* and 12 in *Dime Mystery* magazine. In 1934, he sold the first of ten stories to one of the pioneer hard-boiled detective magazines, *Black Mask.* Over the next five years, he would flourish in the detective fiction market.

I asked Cave how he changed genres so easily and wrote for so many pulp magazines.

"I started by just sending stories out myself. I bought a magazine, read just enough to find out what they were publishing, then sent in a story. Or if I wrote a western story, for instance, sent it to *Western Stories* magazine and they turned it down, I looked through the list of other western magazines and mailed it to them. I used *Writer's Digest* and *Writer's Market* quite a bit. I spent about six hours a week sending out stories and researching markets. If a story came back, I wouldn't necessarily mail it right out again, but put it in my reject pile. When I had the time, I worked that reject pile, usually every week or two, and decided what might sell where and resubmitted it.

"We had no such thing as query letters back in the pulp days. You simply mailed out stories. Half the time I didn't even send a cover letter; just mailed the story. The editors knew who the writers were. They might write me and request that I submit a story, so I would write one—often in a day or two—and send it right out. Today, some magazines, especially small press publications, want to know who you are before having you send them something. Back then, the editors all knew Hugh Cave and the other regular writers. The market was much larger and there were fewer writers; today it is just the opposite.

"Milt, where else in the world could a beginner get paid while he is learning and have fun in the process? Pulp writers weren't master writers yet, at least the younger ones. You learn to write by writing. It's a shame those days are gone. I read an article by a top editor at Tor Books in a writer's magazine recently and she said the average shelf life of a paperback today is six days. Imagine that, six days! How can anyone make money when it's on the shelf only six days? Pulps used to be out for a month."

By 1932, Cave was anxious to advance his career. He decided the best place to do it, the most direct route to success, was in the heart and soul of the publishing business—New York City.

Filled with visions of fame and fortune, he announced his decision to Margaret. She voiced her disapproval, possibly because she would miss him, or possibly concerned that away from her influence, he might find someone who truly cared for him. Her concerns did not deter him though, so he gave up his Pawtucket apartment, packed everything he owned into his secondhand Chrysler coupe, and took off for the Big Apple.

"My memory is a bit hazy about all this now, but I know I rented a room somewhere near Columbia University, thinking that it must be in a respectable part of the big—and to me—terrifying, city. I figured I would try to live there for a while and if I liked it, then seek out an apartment."

Over the next week, Cave visited a few editors that he knew and quickly discovered something he could have found out over the telephone. "Editors didn't give a damn whether I lived nearby or on the moon. Most of them, for that matter, didn't live in New York but commuted from Long Island, New Jersey or Connecticut. One editor, Ken White, told me straight out that he preferred NOT to meet his writers face to face. 'You build up a mental picture of some big, brawny writer based on the characters in the stories,' he said. 'Then the author would come in and look like he wasn't big enough to lick a postage stamp.' "

Ken White eventually became one of Cave's fishing buddies, but they first met on this trip to New York.

He made friends with several other pulp writers during his New York stay. "We would meet at Arthur J. Burks' apartment, three or four of us. Manly Wade Wellman was one of them. We drank Art's booze and filled the room with talk while Art was off in a corner on his manual typewriter banging away to meet some deadline. He was a prolific writer. One time we were all talking about how writing would be so easy if you could get ideas for plots. Art overheard us and stopped working. 'Hey,' he said, 'there's plots all around here; what are you guys worried about? Pick any object in this room and you can make a plot about it.'

"So someone says, 'Okay, Art, let's have a plot about that glass doorknob over there.' Art said, 'Go ahead and talk; give me a few minutes and I'll think one up.'

"He sat for about five minutes, talking to himself at the typewriter like I do when I write, and then he said, 'Okay, I've got one for you.' He came up with a fully schemed mystery plot about a diamond hidden in a glass doorknob. You couldn't see it because the diamond looked like glass. I think he ended up writing it some time later as a story."

In spite of his newfound friendships and proximity to the epicenter of pulp magazine publishing, Cave quickly became disenchanted with life in New York. After just two weeks, determining that editors and publishers didn't care where their writers lived, plus encouragement from Margaret who was against this move from the start, Cave decided his future didn't lie in the Big Apple. "I guess I always felt uncomfortable in big cities; all through my life I opted for smaller, out-of-the-way places."

His decision to leave came in the middle of one sleepless night. "With my rent paid in advance and no need for me to say goodbye to anyone, I repacked my old coupe before daybreak, anxious to return to Pawtucket. It was then I discovered the car wouldn't start. Well, a balky starter was part of this car's personality, so I knew what to do. In the pre-dawn darkness, I took out the crank and got her going—but sprained my wrist in the process. I had to drive back to Pawtucket with one hand. Within 50 miles of home, I had a flat tire. Since I had already changed one tire on this trip, I no longer had a spare, so I drove the remaining 50 miles on a flat. So much for life in the Big Apple."

Cave needed to find a place to stay upon his return. A friend of Margaret's owned a small cottage and offered to rent Cave the cramped second floor. He accepted without hesitation.

Comfortable that he had made the right decision, Cave went back to work immediately. The security of his preferred small town way of life however, did not insulate him from facing yet another life or death situation.

That winter his mother, Edith, came down for a visit. One night during her stay, a gas leak developed in Cave's quarters. "The stove backed up, spitting out deadly fumes that made both my mother and me very ill. We were almost overcome. I struggled to get her out of the building, nearly succumbing myself to the gas."

They made it out unharmed, and Cave found another apartment next door to his first one in downtown Pawtucket. He would live here until early 1935, when he and Margaret finally moved in together.

PART FOUR: CAVE OF A THOUSAND TALES

Chapter 14: Murgunstrumm and Others

> Hugh Cave (now there's a name for a mystery writer) has been described as a master of the livid phrase. He larded his narratives with such expressions as "agony-mist," "corpse-creature," "retching face," and "shrieking heap." His tales built up slowly and suspensefully to a final harrowing scene. He proved adept at this, although he modestly explains that he "just plugged away, trying to learn how to write by writing."[4]

FEW PEOPLE TODAY UNDER THE AGE OF 75 CAN recall living through the darkest Great Depression years from 1930 to 1935. Life was difficult for most people, especially those who had lived through the upbeat Roaring 20's. Fiction writers and movie producers during this time were challenged to come up with stories so horrible, they made life in the Depression seem idyllic by comparison. The movie horror genre peaked with films like *Frankenstein* and *Dracula* in the early 1930's, but continued in the pulps.

The leading horror pulp was *Weird Tales*. First published back in 1923 (and one of the last of the pulps to cease publication in September 1954), *Weird Tales* focused on the weird, bizarre and terrifying side of life. Many well-known authors started their careers writing for *Weird Tales,* including Robert Bloch, Ray

Bradbury, H.P. Lovecraft and Tennessee Williams. The magazine has been revived several times since 1954 and today is again publishing top new horror fiction.

Hugh Cave wrote 11 stories for the original *Weird Tales,* his first in the May 1932 issue. Entitled, "The Brotherhood of Blood," it made the magazine's cover, quite an honor to the aspiring, 21-year old writer—especially since it was the first story he ever submitted to them!

A new form of horror fiction made its debut in the October 1933 issue of *Dime Mystery* magazine. "Weird menace" or "shudder pulps," as it came to be known, featured horror at its most twisted—

> Usually, some horrible, devilish, and to some degree, supernatural being was threatening the well being of all, but in most cases caused a great deal of torture and sadistic attacks on women. The pulp covers usually captured the essence of the torture and showed girls in various stages of torture and nudity. Our hero, usually after his girlfriend has been taken hostage, must now confront the evil villain. After saving the day, our hero then explains how the devilish villain is only human and was using the latest in high-tech science to scare the victims so that he may gain in worldly possessions.[4]

Dime Mystery is considered the first "weird menace" pulp magazine. It premiered as *Dime Mystery Book Magazine* in December 1932, then shortened its name and changed focus to the weird side with its October 1933 issue. That issue featured a Hugh Cave story, "The Graveless Dead." He had already become known as a horror writer and wrote 19 stories for the magazine over the next three years, including one of his better-known tales, a novelette called "The Corpse Maker."

Though he had by now written in almost every pulp genre, Hugh Cave is probably best remembered for his weird menace stories. He began writing them before the term was coined. His first weird menace tale, "The Corpse on the Grating," appeared in *Astounding Stories,* February 1930.

One of Cave's signature tales, "Stragella," appeared in the June 1932 issue of *Strange Tales.* "Stragella" was the story suggested by Dr. Douglas Dold, that opens . . .

> Night, black as pitch and filled with the wailing of a dead wind, sank like a shapeless specter into the oily waters of the Indian Ocean, leaving a great gray expanse of sullen sea, empty except for a solitary speck that rose and dropped in the long swell.

> The forlorn thing was a ship's boat. For seven days and seven nights it had drifted through the waste, bearing its ghastly burden.[5]

Cave himself describes the story. "It is about two shipwrecked sailors on the Indian Ocean. Trying to reach shore in a leaky open boat, they seek refuge on an apparently deserted ship. But the ship is not deserted. It is occupied by vampires, led by a woman named Stragella, who live aboard the hulk while preying upon the inhabitants of a nearby penal colony."

He reveals a succession of frightening images in this tale, enough to fill half a dozen stories for most writers: two survivors near death at sea in a small boat, waters teeming with sea snakes, a derelict ship littered with human and animal bones, a beautifully grotesque flowering vine, giant bats, a gorgeous vampire . . .

Hugh Cave's most famous weird menace tale, published in *Strange Tales*, January 1933, had its origins in a real life experience. "I was trout fishing one Sunday morning, alone, in rural Rhode Island. I parked my car on a country road and followed a new stream—new to me, at least—fly fishing, without much luck. I came to the ruins of an old farmhouse in a clearing—just the cellar, mostly, divided up by old, broken down walls, into small rooms. I thought I'd take a rest and explore it. While I was doing so, a man appeared with a shotgun. 'What you think you're doin' here?' he said, waving that gun at me. 'Oh,' I answered with a grin, 'just looking for some story ideas. You see I—he then said with a snarl, 'You get the hell outta here right now, fast! Or I'll use this thing on you!'

"Well, he was the ugliest human being I had ever come face to face with. ANY writer would have used that incident in a story, especially a writer of horror tales. So I went home and began 'Murgunstrumm.' I made that farmer the title character to get even with the old coot if for no other reason."

And get even he did . . .

> An ugly face it was, in the full horrible significance of the word. A sunken savage gargoyle, frog-like in shape, with narrow close-set eyes blinking continually beneath beetled brows that crawled together, like thick hairy fingers, in the center. The broad nose, twisted hookwise, seemed stuck on, like a squatting toad with bunched legs. And the mouth was wide, thick, sensuous, half leering as if it could assume no other expressions.[6]

The story centers on a back road country inn, The Grey Toad

Inn, where a group of modern party-set vampires bring their victims. The victims are usually attractive young women who are drained of their blood. Their bodies are then used to feed unsuspecting guests. Murgunstrumm, the title character, is proprietor of the inn who does the vampires' bidding.

Paul Hill is the story's protagonist, who is considered insane after an earlier run in with the vampires. He escapes an insane asylum to return to the inn and look for his girlfriend, who was with him the first time.

"Harry Bates bought the story for *Strange Tales* and gave it a solo cover. Karl Edward Wagner used it as the title story in a collection of my horror tales and the World Fantasy people gave it their award for Best Collection."

"Murgunstrumm" went on to be a trademark Hugh Cave tale, published eight different times over the next 63 years (and almost turned into a movie!). Ironically, this, his most famous story, happened to appear in the last edition of *Strange Tales* before it folded after just seven issues. Cave had been attracted to the magazine because it paid writers higher rates than competitive magazines. He never received a single red cent for his most enduring pulp tale.

As previously mentioned, *Far East* magazine folded before publishing all installments of his first serialized novel, "The Midnight Horde." The Great Depression not only put many of Cave's pulp magazines out of business, it often left the surviving magazines without enough money to pay their writers. In his letter to Carl Jacobi, dated December 10, 1932, he writes:

> This fiction factory is in the doldrums and, between you and me and the storm clouds, is getting desperate. A checkup on the year's work reveals 54 stories written so far, including a dozen long novelettes and a dozen slick-paper attempts. The slick stories were a downright gamble, so I can't legitimately call those stories a part of the routine year's work. That leaves just about 40 yarns written this year which should have sold—allowing, of course, for a few duds which creep into the best of families. Well, so what?
>
> The files show a record of 32 stories sold. Of those, I've been paid for 19. Only in a few cases have I received more than a cent a word, and in two instances I received less than that. I'm getting low in reserve funds and yet have more than $1,500 owing to me. Did you ever see such conditions before in the fiction business?[1]

While most of his waking hours were spent at the typewriter, Cave found time to help establish the American Fiction Guild's Rhode

Island chapter. This resulted from his brief fling in New York City. The pulp writers he met during his two week stay all belonged to the American Fiction Guild's New York chapter, which was quite active. They wanted to start up a group in Rhode Island under their direction and asked Cave to do it, naming him president. One of his first responsibilities was to contact other pulp writers in the state. So he wrote letters to every writer he could find that lived in Rhode Island. One of those writers was none other than H.P. Lovecraft.

Cave recalls his brief relationship with the legendary writer. "Howard Phillips Lovecraft lived in Providence. At the time, I was writing for a number of pulp magazines making a lot of money. He was writing for one, *Weird Tales,* and a few fan magazines, making barely enough to eat. He died at 47. Lovecraft's style was archaic, but he created great mythos and had a tremendous ability to carry the reader along to a dashing climax.

"I had several letters from H.P. Lovecraft and they were all written in longhand. As I recall our brief exchange, we admired each other's work and swapped a few comments on editors. It never turned into a real correspondence, however, and although we were residents of the same city, we never got together.

"Somewhere along the line, we got talking about rates and he said something to the order of not caring about rates, that he just wrote because he was an artist, or his art was more important than what he got for it. In one of my replies, I made the crack—I think it was by Boswell in his book about the life of Samuel Johnson—that 'only a blockhead wrote except for money.' I was a juvenile jerk at the time, much younger than Lovecraft, feisty, making about $5,000 a year while he wasn't making enough to eat on.

"He didn't like that. He repeated the comment in a letter to someone else and called me a 'Philistine.' I believe the incident was mentioned in L. Sprague deCamp's biography of Lovecraft. The letters stopped after that and I never heard from him again."

Cave wrote 11 stories for *Weird Tales,* 13 in *Terror Tales,* 19 in *Dime Mystery*, and four for *Strange Tales*. That was a modest amount in four of the leading weird menace pulps, especially considering the prodigious amount of work—more than 800 stories—he published in all the pulp magazines. Yet, his reputation as a writer of weird menace tales would prevail over the years. That was because stories like "Murgunstrumm," "Stragella," and "The Corpse Maker" had remarkable staying power. ("For sheer menace and a sense of implacable doom, "The Corpse Maker" in the

November 1933 issue of *Dime Mystery,* rates among Cave's best."[4]

> The face beneath was a living hell which would haunt Carlee Ryne's memory until eternity. Its eyes were gouged pits; its distorted mouth extended in a permanent grin along the entire length of one decayed cheek. Black stumps of teeth filled the jaw. "Corpse-face" was in truth the right name for that gargoyle countenance. It belonged on a dead man, on a man long dead. It was the face of Erno Zaran![8]

One of Cave's early weird menace tales, "Dead Man's Belt," (*Weird Tales,* May 1933) started out under another name as a story for the slick publications, but Cave found no takers. "It still opened new markets for me, because many slicks wrote back and invited me to send them other stories."

As he so often did when churning out 300,000 words of copy a year, Cave came up with another way to sell the story—turn it into a tale of horror. The story concerns two black men and a black woman who lived in a dump. One man kills the other to have the woman to himself. He uses the victim's own belt to strangle him. Then the belt comes back to kill the murderer.

The story became one of Cave's most popular. It was reprinted in the 1977 *Murgunstrumm and Others* collection. "A French editor told me it was his favorite Cave story, but he couldn't use it because the black dialect didn't translate into French."

This was one of only two short stories Cave ever wrote where the main characters were black, the other being "The Prophecy" (*Black Book Detective,* October 1934). That reflected his experience with African-American people to this point in his life, which had been limited. "I didn't have any blacks in my high school and I don't recall encountering racially motivated friction at any time, before or since. When Margaret and I first visited Florida back in 1935, we rented a house in Delray Beach for the winter. It was located near the black section of town and I used to buy fish in the black marketplaces. Once I wanted to gig frogs in the Everglades, so the 12-year-old son of a black woman who did our laundry took me with him in his boat."

From 1949 to 1980, Cave would spend much of his time in Haiti and Jamaica, two black countries where he found himself accepted by the locals as practically one of them. His humble, accepting manner helped him gain access to people and experiences many writers are never privileged to encounter. Paradoxically, that same manner probably worked against him in the competitive popular fiction market. If he had possessed more of an affinity for self-promotion, he might be a household name by now.

One of his experiences with minorities, in 1934, gave him some initial insights into black subculture and paved the way for his later Caribbean adventures. "There was a black religious group I had heard about in Pawtucket. They were reportedly of a 'strange and unusual nature.' I don't remember how I heard about them. They met at night in an old building in the poorest section of town. I decided I had to go there and talked a group of friends into going with me. The group included Margaret, her brother Ed, her friend Rosemary Dunn, and another couple we knew, Dick and Emily Phelan. We drove over there and were warned to lock our car if we left it.

"This religious group met on the second floor, so we went up and slipped in during the service, sitting back near the door. We were the only white people there, but the congregation didn't seem to mind. They turned to look as we walked in, nodded and smiled. That was it. They were probably surprised, but no one said anything. I took many notes while I was there and used them in "The Prophecy."

Cave originally called his story about that experience, "The White Summons." He did not intend to write it as a pulp tale, but as serious social commentary, hoping to publish the story in a slick paper magazine. Unsuccessful in his attempts, he finally rewrote it as a fantasy tale and sold the story to *Black Book Detective Magazine* as "The Prophecy."

Another significant sidebar of this story is that it is Cave's only pulp tale based largely in fact. With the exception of its typically Cave-esque ending, "The Prophecy" concerns an actual experience, with characters and dialogue drawn directly from real life—including his future wife, Margaret. The story provides us with a window into Margaret's nature, at least from Cave's perspective, which is found nowhere else in his body of work. Possibly, the story afforded Cave an opportunity to vent some of his frustration over their relationship.

The main character is a self-deprecating writer named Peter Hughes.

> Peter Hughes writes stories—not good stories—and sells enough of them to pay the rent . . .[9]

The story's other characters are Swede Corler and Emma Morrisey (Dick and Emily Phelan), Geoffrey Langdon (Ed Long), and his sister, Peter's girlfriend, Meg Landon. Margaret Long's real life nickname was 'Meg,' a not-too-veiled reference.

> She is tall, but not, like her brother, ridiculously so. She has a straight, clear, good-looking face and a body which is beautiful to the hips and over-large from the hips down. She is in love with Peter, but too obsessed with her own importance to admit it. She will uphold Peter's arguments against the others, unconsciously echoing Peter's own voice and believing herself to be strikingly original. Alone with Peter, she will deny his slightest statement blindly and bitterly.
>
> Peter Hughes is slightly shorter than Meg, but exceedingly thin in face and frame. He is dark and wears square-topped glasses which emphasize his over-long features. He smokes continually.[9]

Peter's description fits Hugh Cave like a glove and Meg bears close resemblance to the woman he eventually married. Meg of the story ends up being brutally murdered. Given Cave's conflicting feelings at the time, could this be wishful thinking, perhaps?

Cave did not recall any backlash from Margaret after writing "The Prophesy," which might lead one to believe she never read it.

Chapter 15: A Marriage of Convenience

Cave's career was in high gear by 1934, as evidenced by the following newspaper article about him in the *Providence Journal,* with the headline, "Pawtucket man writes 60,000 words each month."

> . . . Devoting 10 or 12 hours a day to his work he turns out in a month an average of 60,000 words, about a dozen stories. And then he sells everything he writes—has sold everything he has written for the last six years.
>
> Honored by the American Fiction Guild, three of his stories listed in the 1930 O. Henry prize short stories and proclaimed by more than one critic as one of the 10 outstanding writers of popular fiction in the country . . .[2]

Cave wrote so many pulp stories at the height of his career that he used more than a dozen pseudonyms. He first used a pen name professionally (not including the time he wrote "Confessions of a Vanity Publisher's Assistant," "Ah Foo" poems, etc.), with the story "Jailuki Jaws" by Allen Beck, in the June 1931 issue of *Man Stories.*

Another publication, the English *Twenty Story Magazine,* featured four of his stories in a single issue, under four different names—Jack D'Arcy, Maxwell Smith, Geoffrey Vace, and Hugh Cave.

"They picked up 'Jack D'Arcy' for one of those stories ("Watch Your Slip") because Wallace Bamber, editor of *Far East Adventure Stories,* had used that name on a tale of mine in an issue containing two Cave stories. There was, however, a real Jack D'Arcy, I think, unless it was a house name of Thrilling Publications. A story entitled, 'You Hang for Murder,' appeared in *Thrilling Mystery,* October 1936 by Jack D'Arcy, but I didn't write it.

"There was also, I believe, a real Maxwell Smith. That name was used for my yarn, 'Island Ordeal.' Editors in those days were very glib about switching authors' names on stories, causing a lot of confusion for people who today are trying to compile bibliographies!"

The third pen name used in that issue of *Twenty Story Magazine,* was Geoffrey Vace, in honor of his brother's short lived pulp career. The story was entitled, "Too Much Imagination." Geoff Cave had published several stories under his own name before Hugh added it to his stable of pseudonyms. **

The fourth story, under his true name, was "That Monkey of Simms," which appeared in the U.S. a month later in *Far East Adventure Stories,* but under the Jack D'Arcy name.

Other Cave pen names included Carey Barnett, C.H. Barnett, Judy Case, J.C. Cole, William Decatur, Paul Hanna, Carl Hughes, R.T. Maynard, Max Neilson, and believe it or not, John Wayne. While pen names were sometimes appropriated by editors and assigned to a writer's work at their discretion, the practice was perfectly legal. It was not legal, however, for one writer to take another writer's work and assume authorship. That was—and is—called plagiarism.

> "Young Courage" (*Popular Fiction,* December 1931) was not submitted to (editor) Sam Bierman by me. It was copied from a last year's *Short Stories,* in which it appeared under the title "Borneo Brag."

**Three Geoffrey Cave stories are featured in *The Death-Head's March and Others: The Geoffrey Vace Collection,* Black Dog Books, 1998. They are "Four Doomed Men," which appeared first in *Oriental Stories,* summer, 1931; "The Death-Head's March," in *Oriental Stories,* autumn, 1931; and "The Jumping Well," in *Magic Carpet Magazine,* July, 1933. The Geoffrey Cave-authored stories are included in Hugh Cave's bibliography at the back of this book and identified as such.

> Rupert Knowles stole it and sold it to Bierman. Both Bierman and Roy Horn are now hot on the trail of the Knowles fellow, who, it seems, has also sold plagiarized stories to Far East and other magazines.[1]

Probably his most famous pseudonym was Justin Case. "That name came into being in the year 1936 when my agent Lurton Blassingame, telephoned me one day from his New York office. 'Hugh,' he said, 'the editors of the *Spicy* magazines would like you to write for them and they'll pay you more than you're getting from most of your other pulp markets. What do you say?'

"I thought about it and decided I could make some good money, but had concerns about how it might affect my career. At the time, I was working hard to break into higher paying, more prestigious magazines including the *Saturday Evening Post, American Magazine, Liberty, Collier's,* and other slicks. I had a strong hunch that the editors of such publications would not be anxious to use the work of a writer whose name appeared on the covers of magazines with the word 'Spicy' in their title. I had been told that in some parts of the country the 'Spicies,' as they were called, were sold under the counter.

"However, the spicy magazines were paying up to five or six cents a word. The pulps usually paid a penny a word, or $50 for a 5,000-word story. Some of them paid two or three cents a word. I could make $250 for the same length story in the Spicies.

"I contacted Lurton and asked if he thought the spicy editors would let me use a pseudonym. 'I can ask,' he said. They responded, 'why not?'

"Barnett being my middle name, the first thing I came up with was Hugh Barnett. I think I actually put that name on a spicy story when I began writing it. But then I thought of substituting 'Case' for Cave, which made sense, and the first name 'Justin' immediately popped into my mind. The *Spicy* editors loved it and promised they wouldn't make it a house name."

Interestingly, Cave did not make any effort to reveal (or conceal) that he and Justin Case were one and the same until 1983, when he casually mentioned it at Pulpcon, an annual convention for pulp collectors and enthusiasts. (In his 1975 book, *The Shudder Pulps,* even Robert Kenneth Jones refers to Justin Case as a "house name.")

Cave's biographical information used by these *Spicy* publications tended to be as fictitious as the names themselves. "My brother Tom was born in Africa during the Boer War when my mother was an English nurse there and my father a paymaster for the British army. On a couple of occasions, when magazines asked me for biographical stuff, I combined some of his background with my own for added color. This was purely pulp magazine stuff and I'm sure many writers did it. By the time I was asked for biographical material from the slicks, I had some Haitian adventures to use and didn't have to crib from a sibling."

A passage from one of his spicy stories demonstrates why he was sensitive about using his real name and why they were called "spicies:"

> Her whole body begins to tremble most alarmingly. Little ripples of delight course up her tapered legs, and her shapely bosom throbs with new-found ecstasy. And because I am so close to her, gazing down into her adoring eyes, the overflow of her delight filters into me and sends quick little spasms of thrill-fire to my brain.[12]

Cave possessed this uncanny ability to escape into his vivid fantasy world and dwell there for days at a time while he wrote his stories. I asked him where he thought that ability came from.

"Probably from dealing with my father's situation after the accident. In future years, I imagine that was how I dealt with my marriage to Margaret as well."

Cave was a shy soul, inexperienced and naïve about the ways of the heart in spite of his perceptiveness about so much else. Once he fell prey to the love bug, Cave was helpless against the wave of endorphins that washed over him. He also failed to see all the red flags thrown in his path.

Cave had been raised in a loving, nurturing environment thanks to his mother, and before the accident, by his father as well. On the other hand, Margaret's father left home when she was young, leaving her and brother Ed to be raised by a mother who, according to Cave, hated men. He feels that attitude was reinforced by the spinster aunt who lived with them. Margaret grew up as a girl athlete, played on the championship Pawtucket girl's high school basketball team and threw the shot put on the track team. She was also a championship swimmer. Her athletic career ended when she went to college because they didn't have women's athletic teams there. Cave liked sports, but was never that good at them, partly because of his lanky, six foot, 147-pound frame. Margaret was also close to six feet tall, with a muscular, athletic build. When they met at Wesley House, they were thrown together after everyone else paired off, leaving the immature, high schooler with the aloof, athletic college girl.

"We really didn't communicate, right from the start. She never wanted to get into personal things and seemed standoffish. However, she could be charming with people she liked. She had her little circle of friends. Two of them were self-confessed lesbians, which was quite an admission back in those days. I was a romantic young man writing romantic stories and living in a fantasy world, who knew little about such matters."

Over the years between Wesley House and their marriage, Margaret always kept Cave and his ardor at a comfortable distance. However, when he dated other girls, he says Margaret would suddenly show interest. "She was once in Wisconsin taking a physiotherapy summer course and I was dating another girl. Margaret called me once a week. At one point, I told her that maybe we weren't right for each other and we should just break off. She was home a few days later and walked in on me unexpectedly."

He referred to Margaret in his letters to Carl Jacobi, but usually as "the girl friend." It seemed to characterize a relationship at arm's length. An entry in Cave's book, *Magazines I Remember,* amplified his frustration over the relationship:

> 9 July 1932: I'm now sojourning in Boston for the summer. New address for July and August, 118 Riverway, Boston, Mass.*
>
> *(A furnished apartment I rented, to get away from Pawtucket, R.I., for a while.)[7]

Their relationship, with all its flaws and red flags, still led down the path to matrimony. "I think the only reason she got married is because it was the thing to do at the time. By then, I was making good money and I think she viewed me a reliable provider."

He still maintains that love was his primary motivation for getting married. Whatever the true reasons, Margaret and Hugh were willing partners in the decision. As their wedding date approached, they rented a house in Cranston, Rhode Island, one block from Blakemore Pond, and moved in before the marriage. "We lived together platonically; in those days people didn't just live together physically as man and wife unless they were married."

Hugh and Margaret were married at the Congregational Church in

Providence, on July 11, 1935, also his 25th birthday. She had been raised as a Congregationalist and chose this small church on a hill below Brown University. Neither of them went to any particular church at the time. He wore street clothes; she wore a white suit.

"The wedding party was small, maybe ten people. Margaret's friend, Rosemary Dunn, was her bridesmaid and her brother Ed was my best man. I don't recall any members of my family being there, although Geoff may have attended. The day is very hazy now, but I can't remember being very happy about getting married."

After a simple ceremony, they left for their honeymoon. "I had bought a brand new silver gray Dodge to take on our honeymoon. We went to a little hotel at Lake St. Catherine in western Vermont. The summer before, Margaret taught fencing and horseback riding at a girl's camp across the lake. I came up and stayed at this hotel for six weeks while she was there. I could live anywhere; I just had to bring my typewriter. We met in the evenings. Once in a while, she paddled across the lake in a canoe to see me.

"We arrived around four in the afternoon to start our honeymoon and she insisted on walking around the entire lake—eight miles—before we went to bed to consummate our marriage. She hoped I would be too damn tired for anything but sleep, I suspect."

As mentioned before, sex was apparently an unwelcome subject in the Long household. Cave says Margaret's mother and aunt spoke of it negatively. He should not have been surprised then, that Margaret might feel the same way.

According to Cave, their love life went downhill after the honeymoon. "Margaret didn't like to be touched. She discouraged affection and I was an affectionate man. She insisted on twin beds because it wasn't sanitary to sleep together and breathe each other's breath all night long.

"I believe she didn't want marriage, but in those days, to be respectable, you did it anyway."

Another source of information about the marriage, though understandably biased, came from Peggie, the woman who became the love of Cave's life. She told me she came to know Hugh's brother, Geoff, in the years before his death, and had talked with him about the relationship between Hugh and Margaret. According to Peg, "He (Geoff) said that Margaret was very cold, sarcastic, and put Hugh down a lot. Geoff and his wife didn't want anything to do with her."

Hugh and Peg both feel that while the marriage wasn't successful, it did have one major benefit—it gave him the time, the energy, and the excuse, to become a good writer. They led separate lives, except for vacations and later adventures in Haiti and Jamaica. To write for a living, Cave needed to be at the typewriter most of his waking hours. Had the marriage been good between them, he might have spent less time writing.

Chapter 16: Live to Write

> A more careful craftsman than many pulp scriveners, Cave maintained his prodigious output by dint of long hours. He would stack jazz and classical records on an old Orthophonic Victrola and write all day and long into the night—often as late as 2 or 3 am—and begin again at the crack of dawn. Usually he wrote his stories first draft but would often retype them later, making minor corrections as he proceeded. In the trade he was famous for producing clean, printable copy—a boon to word-weary editors and typesetters.[12]

With their honeymoon over, the newlyweds returned to their separate lives, this time under the same roof. However, the rental home they shared quickly became too small for Cave to carve out a writing space. "I didn't think my new bride would like the clickety-clack of a typewriter all day long and then be shut up in another room so she couldn't talk to me either."

A month later, in August 1935, he rented an office on the eighth floor of the Old Industrial Trust Bank Building in downtown Providence across the square from city hall. The office was small and Spartan, but sufficient for his needs. The New Industrial Trust Bank Building was more modern, but the rent would have been much higher than the $50 per month he paid.

Hugh arrived at the Old Industrial Trust Building just before nine o'clock, as he did every morning. He walked purposefully through the small lobby and into the elevator, nodding hello to a few other commuters, talking to no one.

From the elevator, he walked directly to his small office and unlocked the door. The clatter of metal key in metal lock reverberated down the quiet hallway. As he opened his door, a hinge squeaked to announce him, stirring the tomblike silence of his modest office. The door clicked shut behind him, engulfing him in delicious solitude. He switched on the stark ceiling light although it was not yet needed.

A large, oak executive desk faced the door, dominating his 9x12, beige plaster-walled room. The desk bore generations of scratches and scars on its worn surfaces. A much newer straight-backed wooden chair snuggled up to the desk in front of Hugh's black manual typewriter. He placed a vertical rotary telephone with its trumpet-like mouthpiece to the right of the typewriter, ready to accept a call if he should receive one during the next eight hours. A brass floor lamp stood vigilant by the desk, waiting patiently for one of Hugh's late evenings or dreary black days.

Light streamed in around the window shades, signaling the start of another hot, stuffy summer day. Hugh walked across the creaky floor and opened both windows, letting in the morning rhythms of downtown Providence along with a wisp of warm air. Then he tossed his newspaper on the overstuffed easy chair, its only use except to seat an infrequent visitor. A coat hook hung on the wall to remind him of the coming winter when his overcoat would rest there. Underneath it, sat a small, two-drawer file cabinet, olive green and rusted around the edges. Hugh kept an old Victrola on top of the cabinet, like the ones he had as a child. Next to that was the door to his modest bathroom.

He pulled out the desk chair, sending a shudder through the room, then sat on the small cushion he brought from home after one day on the unforgiving wood seat. He glanced at the framed picture of Margaret, quiet and unyielding as she was in life. Then he opened the middle desk drawer. He pulled out a clean sheet of white paper, placed it in the typewriter, and clacked out a sentence. Displeased with the results, he removed the worn typewriter ribbon and tossed it into the waste paper basket. He then opened a second drawer that contained a razor, scissors, pencils and several new typewriter ribbons. He grabbed one of the ribbons, installed it in the typewriter and clacked out another sentence. Nodding approval, he reached in to a third desk drawer and grabbed a handful of typewritten pages. He stacked them neatly on the desk, reading only the last page. After returning it to the stack, be began clacking away at the keyboard, ten fingers flying.

The typing continued almost non-stop except for a quick visit to the bathroom, or to step outside his office and walk the halls a few minutes for exercise. Then at noon, he stopped, washed his hands, grabbed the newspaper, and walked out of his office, locking the door behind him.

Hugh rode the elevator alone. A "ding" sounded announcing his exit and as the doors opened, he heard the din of conversation and purposeful footsteps on the marble lobby floor.

He stepped outside the building, wincing in the bright sunlight and street noise that assaulted his senses. He walked briskly around the corner to a small neighborhood bar in the building.

Hugh said hello to the bartender and a few regular customers he recognized, then sat on a barstool and immediately found a glass of draft beer in front of him. Without saying a word, the bartender then slid jars of pickled eggs and ham hocks toward him, and asked if he wanted a sandwich. Hugh ordered tuna on whole wheat, then began to read the paper.

After eating his fill and hardly saying a word to anyone, Hugh reached into his pocket, plunked 50¢ down on the bar and walked out, returning to his office. He often took walks after lunch, but needed to get back and complete a story that was promised the next day.

After half an hour of furious typing, he became drowsy. Clearing a spot on the desk next to his typewriter, he lay his head on his hands for a short nap. After twenty minutes, he awoke refreshed, went to the bathroom, then cranked up his Victrola, playing a stack of favorite Paul Whiteman tunes. He sat down at the typewriter, rubbed his hands together, and began clacking away.

I asked if he ever ran out of ideas, writing such a prodigious amount of copy.

"That didn't happen very often, but one way I kept the ideas coming was by talking to myself at the typewriter. I would sit down and say 'if he does this, then what will happen when she finds out.' I talked myself into the story, making notes directly on the typewritten page, free forming, typing whatever came into my head. Then I looked through the notes and pick a story out of it.

"I was always looking for story possibilities, and if you make a practice of it, you can find them in all sorts of places. Once I received a series of letters from a guy named Olson, a total stranger and a real nut. His letters rambled on and on about every subject under the sun. I wasn't the only writer to receive his letters, and he was considered a nuisance. But I thought they were filled with ideas for stories, titles, characters and more.

"I also had this one trick I used for short story ideas. In the mornings, I had a five or ten minute walk from the parking lot to the building. I would pass a newsstand and buy a racing form.

Sometimes the horses ran at Narragansett Park at noontime, so I might place a bet on one when I went to lunch. On days when I needed to start a new story but didn't have any ideas, I opened the racing form, looked at the horses' names, and combined them. For instance, 'Shady Lady' and 'Discovery' and 'Woodland,' to suggest a story line, possibly about a mysterious woman, engaged in some shady enterprise, making a life-shaking discovery in the woods. Then I would ask what it was? Who was there? And so on. I'm sure it would work for me today were I still struggling to turn out stories at such a pace. Of course, with such a method you only ended up with a bare-bones plot. You had to people it with believable characters, atmosphere, convincing locales, and so on. But you have to do that with any bare story line. The big thing was, by using the horse names you sent your imagination down all sorts of different byways to many unexpected destinations.

"I sold about 50 stories to *Detective Fiction Weekly,* and many of them came from my racing form creative process. I would do just about anything to avoid sitting there and staring at a blank piece of paper, asking what the hell am I going to write about.

"There was a book in existence at that time called *Plotto,* written and published by a pulp writer named William Wallace Cook. It cost, if I remember rightly, $25, a lot of money in those days. I'm sure many pulp writers used it. Cook had reduced every story he had ever read—and he seemed to have read almost everything ever written—to a paragraph or so, using symbols for characters. Thus an entry in *Plotto* might read something like, 'A-1 and B-1 marry and have to spend their honeymoon night in a haunted house when their car breaks down.' There were dozens of symbols for different kinds of characters. You were supposed to interweave these nuggets in such a way that you would come up with an original plot of your own. The book had sections for mystery stories, love stories, adventure, etc. It was a very clever book, and I'm sure it helped many writers come up with plot ideas. But after trying a few times to use it, I came up with a better way of thinking up plots. Better for me, anyway. That was using racing forms."

How about developing new characters; wasn't that difficult with so many stories?

"Here's a trick I worked out for getting realistic characters in my stories. I saved pictures of interesting-looking people from papers or magazines. I kept these photos in a folder for use when needed. Having decided on, say, a story character to fit a plot, I'd give him a name, then find a photo that seemed to fit the sort of person I had in mind. I would slap it down beside the typewriter, and refer to it every time I had to describe that character or show him in action.

"Of course, real life situations always produced characters and circumstances that could be used for stories. For instance, I once had a friend named Dempsey, who was an undertaker. He and his wife were at our house one evening when he got a call that someone had died and he had to go get the body. He took me with him. We went into the house, retrieved the old man's body, and took it to the funeral home. I helped him embalm the body, which took half the night. He worked in sort of a shed. We went through the entire process of draining fluids and waste, then filling the body cavity with embalming fluid. I guess that had something to do with my dislike of funerals, but it sure provided me with new material."

Did you have a problem with interruptions—too many visitors or phone calls?

"I had friends in Providence and they might drop by, but they wouldn't stay long because they knew I needed to write. Even Margaret didn't come by very often. Remember, I loved the writing life. When you really love to do something, you find a way to get it done regardless of what goes on around you."

Editing a story can take longer than writing one. How much of your time did you spend editing?

"I would write a story in rough draft straight through, no editing or reading until it was completed. I learned early in the game that if you kept revising what you wrote, you never got to the end of the story. One of Carl Jacobi's great faults was that he could never get away from that habit. He went to work in the morning with eight pages of a story written and would read the eight pages and decide he needed to rewrite them. So he ended the day with maybe nine or ten pages. It took him forever to get through a story. I would do it in rough draft, then go through it with a pen or pencil, word by word, make corrections, then retype it once clean and mail it out. Everything I sent out was ready for the printer. Karl Wagner wrote everything out on a yellow legal pad, then edited and rewrote it at the same time on an old manual typewriter. He worked that way right up until the time he died. Manley Wade Wellman once said that I talked 'as if I were accustomed to using a dictating machine.' Actually, I was experimenting with a dictating machine at the time we met, but I gave it up because I had to see the words in front of me as I typed them, or I got lost."

Did you have objectives for a day's effort?

"I would get up in the morning and go to the office. If I didn't have a story in progress, I'd start out by saying 'who am I going to write for today and what am I going to write about?' I always had a notebook filled with scraps of ideas about an inch thick that I called my 'idea book'; I still have it. I went through the idea book and found what appealed to me at that time. Maybe it didn't yesterday or wouldn't tomorrow, but at the time, it did. When I've used an idea from my idea book, I tear the page out and throw it away. Some of my ideas are just that. Others might become good opening paragraphs. Others are oddities such as: 'story idea embracing music and color.' 'Color hearing' is described in my encyclopedia of music. Seems certain persons 'see' music in color. Why not a fantasy worked out along these lines, with a certain piece of music seen as 'all black,' meaning it is death music. Also, some of the entries in my idea book are titles, such as 'Professor Heller's Cure for the Woes of the World.'

"Anyway, I took one of those ideas and started to elaborate on it by talking to myself at the typewriter. Might do a page, two or three. By the time I finished talking to myself, the story was in my mind, how it began, where it was going. Then I would wing it.

"I never worked out a story all the way through, didn't plot it out, develop characters, and so on. I found out early that all the fun was gone if everything was written out and the only thing left was to weave words around the notes. I wasn't surprising myself and not having any fun. Once I knew what the story was about, where it was going and how it would end—which you must know or you will never get there—I just wrote it; took some characters, put them into some action and let it go.

"It's the same process with a novel. I have never completely outlined anything. The only time I took complete notes was when I did war books and listened carefully to someone else, taking detailed notes. Even travel books were winged. Whatever was interesting to me, I wrote about it. In my notes I might say, 'now wait a minute, if Joe goes to Boston at this point when he is supposed to be in New York, how am I going to explain his absence? I asked myself questions an editor might ask if I gave him the idea in a conversation. I learned how to ask myself those questions and get them straight in my mind. I did it all on the typewriter rather than just staring into space and thinking. You have to work at it. The seed for that session might have begun as something I read in the newspaper, or read by someone else and thought I could approach it differently or better.

"I tried to write a story a week. Many were novelettes, 10–20,000 words for pulps. Whether a day was successful or not depended on how many pages I finished; 2,500–3,000 words a day was good, ready to go to the editor, 250–300 words to a page, that's about ten pages of copy. But remember, this was on an old manual typewriter. It was hard work pounding on those keys all day. Imagine how much I could have written if I had a computer back then.

"I didn't do research during day hours. I didn't research detective stories, but did on adventure and westerns. I had plenty of information on the South Seas. I read books at home and researched westerns, new adventure locations. During the day I never read. When I went to lunch at noon, I just sat there. I didn't read or carry my work down with me. I would talk if I knew someone there. Then I might take a walk for some exercise before going back to the office. Then I wrote the rest of the day, until 4:30–5:00."

What did you do for recreation when you weren't writing?

In the evenings we ate dinner and then sat around listening to the radio. I did quite a bit of reading every evening. Friends came over often, mostly Margaret's. Mine didn't come around much because they weren't too welcome."

The use of recurring characters and themes was commonplace in the pulp days, much like movie sequels are today. Popular characters at the time included Sam Spade (Dashiell Hammett), The Shadow (Walter Gibson), Conan the Barbarian (Robert E. Howard), Doc Savage (by Lester Dent as Kenneth Robeson), Zorro (Johnston McCulley), and Phillip Marlowe (Raymond Chandler). Hugh Cave had a handful of these characters who have remained fresh through the years and have been reproduced over the past decade in Hugh B. Cave anthologies.

His first series, and probably his most famous, was Tsiang House, the fictional British outpost in Borneo that captured the public's imagination. "The Shadow of Tsiang," one of Cave's first pulp stories, launched the series in the October 25, 1929 issue of *Short Stories* magazine. It represented the kind of escapist fiction that helped Americans through the Great Depression. Coincidentally, the Depression began with the stock market crash, a few days after that first story appeared.

Detective Peter Kane, another Cave creation, made his debut with "The Late Mr. Smythe," in the August 1, 1934 edition of

Dime Detective. Another durable Cave character was The Eel, first appearing in a story called "Eel Trap" published in the June 1936 issue of *Spicy Adventure Stories*.

> Removing her wet clothes from the chair, I seat myself there and draw their owner gently into my lap. "When this trembling little body of yours is warmer," I murmur, "you shall have dry clothes to wrap around it." And she does not protest when I stroke her in an effort to restore some heat.
>
> "Also your lips are cold," I declare, and proceed to warm them with my own.[11]

"When I wrote the first Eel yarn I had no idea there would be others. I must have been reading Damon Runyon stories at the time. He wrote in present tense and a first person style, the same as I used in my Eel stories. Anyway, the editors at Culture Publications liked "Eel Trap" and suggested I use the Eel character in other spicy tales."

One more series character, Officer Coffey, appeared in just three stories during the 1940's. All three characters would be reprised in their own collections: *The Dagger of Tsiang*, copyright 1997, by Tattered Pages Press, Chicago, IL; *Escapades of the Eel*, copyright 1997, Tattered Pages Press, Chicago, IL; *Officer Coffey Stories*, a chapbook featuring two stories, copyright 2000, Subterranean Press, Burton, MI; and the third Coffey yarn, "Loose Loot," in a chapbook of that name, published in 2001 by The Sidecar Preservation Society.

Looking back at the 800-plus stories he wrote during his pulp days, one has to be impressed with the fact that with these few exceptions, every story had a different setting, characters and plot line. The catalyst for that creativity was, and still is, uniquely Cave.

In June of 1938, Cave decided it was time to take care of some unfinished business. Unlike his father, Cave had always considered himself an American, not a British subject. However, he had never officially become a U.S. citizen. It was time to change that. Obtaining citizenship was merely a formality at this point in his life, but one he considered important nonetheless.

Cave's ability to lose himself in his writing proved to be a double-edged sword in at least one case, during the summer of 1938. Hugh and Margaret had moved to a second rental home on Witmark Street. The combination of a passive marriage and the cocoon of his downtown office, enabled Cave to enjoy the most prolific years of his career. In two years, 1937 and 1938, he published a total of 119 stories, from shorts to novelettes. The results were a tribute to his creativity, imagination and sheer tenacity. His writing provided a successful escape, but also left him oblivious to the events around him, especially on September 21, 1938.

Hugh pounded away at the typewriter, his head filled with images he raced to capture on paper before they flitted away. The room grew dark, so he turned on his floor lamp, unaware of the reason he needed it. Outside his office, storm clouds gathered. Wind gusts blew the first rain against his windows.

He finished a page, ripped it out of the typewriter with one hand as he reached for a clean sheet of paper with the other. A strong gust rattled the windows. He continued to pound away, the keystrokes growing more furious as the story in his mind raced to a climax.

Hugh did not hear the voices outside his door or the footsteps rushing to the elevator. Heavy rain now pelted his side of the building. The windows rattled almost constantly.

Hugh stopped typing and glanced at the darkened windows just as a huge gust shook the entire building. He picked up the phone and tried to call Margaret. The line was dead. He had no radio, either.

Hugh opened the door to his office to see an empty hallway.

"Hello?"

No response other than the echo of his voice.

"Is anybody here?" His voice cracked.

He was alone and this was no ordinary storm. He swept everything off his desk into one of the drawers, then rifled through the desk until he found a typewriter cover. He set his typewriter under the desk, grabbed his raincoat, and ran out, locking the door behind him. He rarely brought his raincoat but the weather report this morning had warned of showers. Showers, indeed.

Hugh repeatedly pushed the elevator button, annoyed that no one on the floor had knocked on his door to warn him. Then he reasoned that someone may have knocked and he was too involved with his writing to notice. He cursed his 'til-now superb powers of concentration.

At that moment the lights began to dim. This is no time to be trapped in an elevator, he thought to himself, then ran for the stairwell.

A handful of people scurried around the lobby, others stood at the building entrance, donning raincoats and opening umbrellas. Hugh saw people running on the streets, umbrellas inside out, hats flying. Traffic was surprisingly light as he realized most people had already gone home. He looked at his watch. It was 1:30 and he had forgotten to eat lunch. Food was the last thing on his mind now.

Someone opened the door to leave. A gust of wind-driven rain whipped through the lobby. A few remaining people ran for the open door, one of them falling on the rain-slicked floor. Hugh pulled the collar of his raincoat tight, bowed his head and followed the others outside.

He was unprepared for the wind's strength and almost lost his balance. Fighting wind and rain, he headed towards his parking lot down by the Providence River.

Looking up to cross the street, he felt the sting of wind-borne rain. From there he kept his head down, only occasionally looking up to get his bearings.

Hugh had never experienced anything like this and wondered if he was in a tornado or tropical hurricane. How could a vicious storm like this happen without warning?

Debris flew through the air; trash cans rolled in the street. Two cars sat in the middle of an intersection, abandoned right where they had crashed into each other.

By now the streets were becoming flooded. He approached the parking lot to see that the river had already risen above its banks. Hugh didn't think he could get anywhere by car and decided to walk home. It was a tiring three miles in normal weather; under these conditions, it would test his survival skills.

He struggled against the wind and stooped lower as he saw people being blown off their feet. His face was numb from the pelting rain that seemed to come from every direction. Already soaked to the skin, he pulled off his raincoat and held it over his head. As he walked along in the middle of the street, Hugh heard a car coming up behind him. He moved a little to the side, but not by much. He was unwilling to walk through water now rushing along the edge of the street into overflowing drains.

The car came to a stop next to Hugh and he heard someone beep the horn.. He looked up to see a fairly new Ford with four men riding in it. One of them rolled down the window enough to yell, "Want a lift?!"

Without hesitation, Hugh ran for the rear car door as it opened and jumped in, slamming the door behind him. "Thanks," he said, trying not to soak the man cramped up next to him

"Isn't this unbelievable?" shouted the driver.

"Where did it come from?" asked Hugh.

"It's a hurricane," the man next to him said, "A bad one. First ever to hit Providence. They say the winds might reach 100 miles an hour."

"No," said Hugh, annoyed that he knew nothing about it. He vowed to buy a radio for his office tomorrow.

The men sat in silence, watching the driver as he struggled to keep his car going in the fierce wind gusts. They crept up Broad Street and as he turned on to Witmark, a huge gust shook the car. The driver swung his steering wheel back and forth as the car began to tip. "Watch out!" he yelled.

The car rolled over on its side, tossing the occupants around. Hugh winced as he was struck on the forehead by someone's shoe. He struggled under the weight of at least one man and could not see a thing. He heard the others struggling to open one or more doors, then felt a torrent of rain that told him they were successful. One by one, the men scrambled to get out and by the time Hugh climbed out of the overturned car, the others had already scattered for cover at neighborhood houses.

He decided to continue walking though, since he was now less than a mile from home and concerned about Margaret. She had probably tried to call and warn him but the phone was dead. Hugh saw downed phone and electrical lines everywhere.

Within a block of his house, downed trees and live electrical wires danced in the wind preventing him from continuing. He ran from the street to a neighbor's backyard, sloshing through calf-deep water and skirting debris, constantly on the lookout for fallen power lines. He no longer had a raincoat and used his arm to try and shield his face from the driving rain.

He finally made it home. Margaret opened the back door and yelled to him, gripping the screen door handle to keep it from flying off its hinges. His heart pounded as he ran inside the house.

"I tried to call you!" Margaret screamed as she pulled the door shut.

* * *

"It took almost four hours from the time I left my office until I reached home. I knew we were in the middle of a major storm, but I didn't realize the devastation it caused until later."

Known as the Great New England Hurricane of 1938 (this

happened well before storms were given names), it had crashed onshore moving at the incredible rate of 60 miles per hour. Rhode Island weather stations recorded sustained winds of 100 mph with peak gusts of 125 mph. Downtown Providence was submerged under a storm tide of nearly 20 feet. A total of 564 people died and 1,700 others were injured in Southern New England; almost 9,000 homes and buildings were destroyed and 15,000 more sustained damage.[23]

"There were water marks on the sides of buildings eight feet above street level. Damage was in the millions. Nothing like it had ever hit Providence before or since. I didn't go back to the office for three days, but stayed home to clean up the mess. We were pretty shook up, too. My car made out, in spite of being covered by water. And the windows to my office held, so nothing was damaged there. I did make it a point after that to talk with some of my neighbors on the eighth floor. If something like that ever happened again, I didn't want to be left behind because no one knew that I was there."

Cave kept his downtown office for another year, until he and Margaret built their own home on Groton Pond, complete with a study that would become his new office.

Chapter 17: Family Man

After their marriage in 1935, life for the Caves quickly settled into a routine that sent him to his typewriter every day and left her as lady of the manor. However, as the cold weather settled in that first winter, Cave decided they should go to Florida for a break. They certainly had plenty of money to do it, and Cave could park himself anywhere without missing a keystroke. He consistently earned around $5,000 per year, a good living at this point in the Depression. To put it into perspective, a new car still cost only $600. Even though they owned their home, they could easily afford a few months in Florida.

Cave decided to vacation in Delray Beach, a small seaside town near West Palm Beach. "I'm not sure why we decided on Delray Beach. I did know a man in charge of the Mackie Radio Station in Jupiter, a ship-to-shore outfit, because he knew my brother, Tom. We may have gone down to see him, I don't recall. Whatever the reason, we rented a house and spent several months there, probably January and February. The weather was great. I spent my time writing and Margaret liked it, too."

Their first child, Kenneth Long Cave, was born three years later, on January 19, 1939. "I'm not 100% sure on this, but as I recall, I named him for my good friend, editor Ken White."

They moved to a large rental home on Wheeler Avenue, but soon began planning a home of their own to accommodate their growing family. The two-story, split-level ranch home, at 281 Gorton Lake Boulevard, would be completed in a year. It was located in the Greenwood section of Warwick, Rhode Island, on a hill with a backyard that ended at the edge of Gorton Pond, a half-mile long lake. "You walked in the front door and went upstairs to the kitchen, living room and bedrooms, straight ahead to the game room and my study."

The home was even featured in a pictorial spread about Cave in the July 21, 1940 *Sunday Providence Journal.*

"Margaret loved to sew; she was very good at it. She made clothes for her and Ken. She sat in her sewing room hour after hour; I would be down in my study."

Cave noted that both rooms faced the lake—they shared this beautiful view from their home but not with each other.

After Ken was born, Cave hired a full-time nurse to stay with Margaret and the baby after she came home. Cave later wrote a story based on their newborn experience called "The 75th Baby."

Margaret adapted effortlessly to the role of mother and homemaker. However, life didn't change much for Cave. He spent long hours in his study grinding out copy as he did before.

I asked him if he felt additional pressure to produce with another mouth to feed.

"No, I didn't feel more pressure because I always worked to capacity. The pressure comes from magazines looking for stories. There was also pressure to keep a writer's work in front of an editor. I felt pressure to send the next story to an editor who was consistently publishing my work because if I didn't, the editor would find someone else who could.

"In fact, I had wanted to take trips several times during the 30's, including one to fulfill a lifelong dream and see the world, but my work prevented me from going."

He described one near-adventure to Carl Jacobi in a letter dated January 4, 1933:

> Mister, I'd go to Singapore, Sandakan etc., tomorrow if I had sufficient money. As a matter of fact, I came very close to taking a long trip two years ago. Had it all mapped out—Boston by freighter to Algiers, inland through Morocco for three weeks, Mediterranean to the Suez, etc. Bedford-Jones gave me some pointers; so did Roy Horn. Douglas Dold squashed the idea by telling me I'd be the damndest damned fool if I left the U.S. at that particular period of my development. Said I'd lose contact completely and would have to start all over again on my return.[1]

In the years 1939 and 1940, as Cave settled into his role as father and then homeowner, Cave published a total of 73 stories. The market was changing and his work became much more focused. "By 1937 I think I more or less abandoned the adventure genre and concentrated on detective story publications. My success with *Detective Fiction Weekly* probably had a lot to do with that."

Through 1941, the overwhelming majority of his published stories were of the detective variety, eventually selling to 39 pulps that used detective tales.

One thing had become increasingly obvious—pulp magazines were disappearing from the popular cultural scene. They had served their purpose through the 1930's, helping millions of Americans through the Depression. Competition was now increasing from other sources. Comic books, which had originally been merely reprints of newspaper strips, now came into their own with the arrival of Superman from Krypton by way of *Action Comics*. Comic books captured the imagination of youthful readers with simple story lines and colorful illustrations.

Radio had also become popular, with actors reading stories to listeners complete with sound effects and laughs. Paperbacks were soon coming on to the scene, top quality novels in an inexpensive, portable format. Television would not be far behind.

The single event most responsible for bringing the pulp era to an end though, was also the event that radically changed the course of Hugh Cave's writing career. That event was World War II.

"When they announced the attack on Pearl Harbor, Margaret, Ken and I were driving to Pawtucket to visit Meg's mom. We had the Dodge I purchased when we were married. My reaction to the news was that I thought I would be drafted. Margaret was probably concerned, especially with a two-year-old baby."

He was not drafted though—at age 31, Cave had outlived draft age. However, the war still played an important part in his life. A decision he made earlier that year not only kept him out of uniform, but sent his writing career off in an entirely new direction. It all began with a fishing trip.

From an early age, Cave loved to go fishing. Not much of an athlete once he left high school, Cave preferred the sport of fishing throughout his adult life. It was a fishing trip that resulted in his first book-length pulp story, "The Midnight Horde," and his most memorable weird menace tale, "Murgunstrumm."

"As I grew older I developed a fondness specifically for fly fishing; I tied my own flies. There were some nice trout streams in Rhode Island. I would go trout fishing two or three Saturdays a month with my fishing buddies, Ted Martin, Larry Dunn and Sam Engdahl. Ted and his wife rented the upstairs part of our two-decker house in Providence. Margaret and I rented the lower part. Larry's wife, Rosemary, of course, was Margaret's best friend. She was Maid of Honor at our wedding, and like Margaret, she was a school teacher. I can't remember what Larry did for a living; I do know he worked in an office somewhere in Providence and graduated from Rhode Island State University. Sam was a good friend of Larry's. He worked for the state of Rhode Island designing bridges.

"Often I went fishing alone. One of those solo outings is, of course, how 'Murgunstrumm' came about. I even talked my oldest brother, Tom, into joining me on a fishing trip to Canada once. Later, my friends and I began traveling to Maine and New Hampshire every year, usually Memorial Day and Labor Day weekends. After a while, my agent at the time, 'Count' Lurton Blassingame, and his buddy, Ken White, began going with us. Ken was a small guy, about 120 pounds, and sported a beard. We dubbed him 'Dr. Livingstone.' By the way, my nickname was 'Trailblazer.' I earned it by getting the guys lost on a prior fishing trip to Maine.

"I first met Ken White on my brief stay in New York. He had been an agent before, but now worked as an editor for a Boston publishing house. Lurton and Ken would come to the house and we took my car to go fishing. By the time we built our house in Warwick, I had already thought about leaving Count, but we remained good friends, even after severing our professional relationship.

"We went to Sebago Lake, or the Ripogenus Dam country above Moose Head Lake and Frost Pond, or Sourdnahunk Lake in Maine. Usually we would go to fishing camps because they had cabins. Then in 1941 we went up to New Brunswick, Canada, to the Miramachi, for Atlantic salmon. It was there that the boys cooked up this Canadian wilderness trip."

For Cave, and his friends, the Canadian wilderness trip became their greatest adventure together.

"One summer day, the four of us—Lurton, Ken, Larry and I—drove to a little town called Iron Bridge, Ontario, on the north shore of Lake Huron. We rented two canoes, hired a couple of guides and spent the next six weeks alternately canoeing and portaging through the Canadian wilderness between there and Hudson's Bay. We never saw another soul, but did we catch some fish!"

Cave and Blassingame had talked or written back and forth numerous times about Cave's future direction as a writer. Cave had started making inroads with the slicks, which paid much more money, but felt if he was ever to achieve popular status with the general public and make the big bucks, he needed to start writing books.

"Lurton lived in New York and I received a letter from him at least once a week. We never discussed going into the slicks because he was against it. 'Tough market—won't sell as much. Why start over again when you're getting top dollar rates and you're well known in the pulps.' However, Lurton knew I wanted to move up and we had discussed the possibility of writing books.

"He must have been looking for opportunities; maybe he convinced some editor who had been following my pulp stories and recognized me as one of the better writers. Then one day, Lurton approached me about doing a book on our Canadian adventure, but targeted to young adults. Turn the four of us into four kids and put in a mystery of some sort. He had approached Dodd, Mead and they agreed to publish it as long as it was laid in the U.S. and not in Canada.

"So I took some of our fishing adventures and made a story out of it. I set the story in Minnesota after studying many maps about the lakes there."

Fishermen Four (Dodd, Mead and Company, 1942) became Cave's first book. The master of shudder pulps had written a wholesome book for young adults. "It earned good reviews and was recommended by the Boy Scouts of America."

Before the book was published, Cave received some bad news. Within months of their Canadian fishing adventure soon to be immortalized in the new book, Larry Dunn suddenly died. That broke up the fishermen four. "Count and I never went fishing again. We kept in touch with letters and Christmas cards, but I didn't see him much except when I went to New York on business and called on him."

Their business relationship didn't end though. Cave stopped using Blassingame for pulps—that market had begun to dry up with paper shortages and the popularity of radio—and he never did use him for slicks. However, they continued working together on books. Blassingame still went on fishing trips and ended up specializing as an agent for writers in the book field.

"Lurton had always operated as a one-man agency, but years later he went into partnership, I think, with Eleanor Wood. They all worked out of the same office for a time."

Cave would eventually work with Eleanor Wood as well as another New York agent, Kirby McCauley, who gained fame as Stephen King's agent.

Cave and Blassingame continued their professional relationship until Cave's book, *Haiti: High Road to Adventure,* came out in 1952. Eventually Lurton gave up his agency and moved to Florida. "His brother, Wyatt, a well-known writer himself, lived on the same island near Tampa where my brother Tom had retired. The last I heard from Lurton was a Christmas card in 1985; he died, I believe, in 1988."

Cave had been the youngest of the four fishermen who made that trip to Canada. Although the book, *Fishermen Four,* was based on their adventure together, Cave was forced to change the characters and locations to suit the publisher's youth market.

He finally immortalized that special memory in his life with another book, *The Dawning,* released on July 11, 2000 in honor of his 90th birthday. The book, an end-of-civilization-as-we-know-it horror tale, traced their 1941 trek and included the actual locations. The book's dedication reads: "For Peggie; this novel is also dedicated to the memory of Ken White, Larry Dunn and Lurton Blassingame, who traveled these wilderness trails with me."

Chapter 18: Writing for Victory

The nation was now at war, but its initial impact had little effect on Cave's income. His writing had become more diverse; of the 38 stories he sold in 1942, only 14 were detective/mystery yarns, nine of those appearing in *Spicy* magazines. He also published five stories in slick publications and one came out in *Scholastic Magazine*. Four of his sales were reprints. The *Scholastic Magazine* story, "Two Were Left," would end up becoming Cave's most reprinted tale, appearing 73 times over the next 59 years in school-oriented publications and still in demand.

"The story concerned an Eskimo boy named Noni, and his husky dog, Nimul, both stranded in the Arctic on an iceberg with nothing to eat. They eyed each other hungrily, but in the end, their love for each other won out and they worked together to survive and reach land."

Cave's first major accomplishment of 1942, was his novel *Fishermen Four.* It received good reviews and sold moderately well, but the book's greatest impact was not on the youthful readers it targeted.

"At the time, the U.S. Government was encouraging publishers to put out books about the war effort in order to intensify public support. Something about *Fishermen Four* caused the publisher, Dodd, Mead, to contact Lurton and suggest I write a war book. If it turned out to be successful, I might have a chance to do more."

Cave accepted this new opportunity without hesitation. The book was to highlight the exploits of a daring PT boat crew and their heroic deeds early in the war. "They had been a cover story feature in an issue of *Life* magazine and I had just finished reading the popular book, *They Were Expendable.* So here was the same situation and I would write about it through the eyes of the participants."

The publisher paid his way down to Miami where the PT boat crews were in training. "I took a train and it was packed, so I stood up a good part of the way or sat on a box between cars. There were fewer trains available during the war and people didn't drive much because of gas rationing. However, I did get to stay in a decent hotel once I arrived.

"The Miami base was only used for some of their training. They also trained in Rhode Island and most of the time, in Panama. The crew I was chosen to interview had been the first into battle and first to return from service in the Pacific. They now trained new PT boat crews. People didn't know what PT boats were at that time, which was one reason they were selected as subject matter."

After arriving in Miami, Cave met with his three subjects. The three officers were Ivy League lieutenants, Lt. Robert L. Searles, Lt. (JG) Leonard A. Nikolorik, and Lt. Commander Alan Montgomery. Montgomery was an Annapolis man.

"They liked the idea, and they seemed to like me personally, but I'm not sure how they felt about Hugh Cave the writer who had never written an adult book before. I promised to show them every chapter as I wrote them before sending my completed manuscript to the publisher."

Cave spent several weeks with the crew, talking with them individually, and joining them on training exercises in Biscayne Bay. "I learned first hand what it was like to live and work on that small a boat. I just sat in the background and observed, taking longhand notes. I had to learn quickly because the boat and crew were due to head back to the Pacific."

He started writing as soon as he returned home to Providence. "I worked day and night on the book; I was keen on it. These guys had helped turn back the big ship from the Japanese navy and saved Guadalcanal for us."

Cave would spend a few days writing each chapter, then mail it to the crew. They made corrections or added other ideas and mailed it back.

He completed the book in two months. "The entire project from start to finish took about three months, the same amount of time it would later take me to write a novel."

The book was published soon afterwards with the title, *Long Were the Nights*. "It told the story from the crew's perspective, beginning with their training days, how they made it to the Pacific and ended up at the Solomon Islands. We didn't have a big ship navy at the time; most of them were sunk at Pearl Harbor. The Japanese big ship navy was in the Solomons. They had taken Guadalcanal and we had just retaken it. They would come down through The Slot as they called it, between the Solomons, a string of islands on either side with Guadalcanal at the bottom. Night after night they shelled our Marines on Guadalcanal in anticipation of recapturing it from us. All we had for a while was a squadron of PT boats.

"The boys in the book were based on Tulagi, a small island across Iron Bottom Sound from Guadalcanal. Iron Bottom got its name because of all the sunken warships in the area. Savo Island was right in the middle of The Slot. They had a YP, or "Yippy" boat that went back and forth to the Marine commander on Guadalcanal with messages."

Cave couldn't give the boat's actual name, so he called it *The Nameless*. "The Navy censors then eliminated the word 'nameless' with a note saying you couldn't use actual ship names."

That wasn't the only change forced by Navy censors.

"I had been using the actual boat numbers when I wrote the book, but Navy censors told the publisher to remove all boat numbers. The book had already been typeset with the pages arranged in order. Dodd, Mead made the changes right in their office; I pity the poor guy who had to do it. You couldn't change the length of any lines or it threw off the pages and they would have to reset the entire book. There was an awkwardness to the book because of word substitutions and line constraints that made me weep when I read it. A few reviewers picked up the problem and one actually figured out what had happened. Censorship was so strict at that time."

The book was released within a few months of the decisive campaign at Guadalcanal. "Reviews were good and the *Saturday Evening Post* immediately wanted to publish part of it. The book did terrifically well, spending six months on the *New York Herald Tribune* bestseller list."

A sample of the reviews confirmed the book's success:

> This book is living history that throbs with the thrills, chills, and plain terror of actual combat.—*Chicago Tribune*[1]

> At last we have a comprehensive account of the operations of PT boats in the South Pacific, and it makes a dramatic and intensely interesting story. The narrative is vigorous and straightforward, and the picture comes out with startling clearness.—*N.Y. Herald Tribune*[1]

Cave had time to spend on this book because he wasn't writing many new stories. "I don't remember how much I made from it, but I split the royalties fifty-fifty with the four officers."

Management at Dodd, Mead and Company soon offered him the opportunity to write another war book.

Cave was riding high on the popularity of *Long Were the Nights*, but his income had suffered. "The book didn't sell that many copies because they couldn't get the paper. Paper shortages also killed the pulps and hurt books in general."

It wasn't all doom and gloom, however. "Our home, which cost $18,000 to build, was already paid for, as was our car, a red

Chevy I had purchased new. We weren't hungry by any means."

In 1943, Cave sold only 28 new stories, his lowest output in 13 years. This happened for a combination of reasons, most notably the months he took to write each book and the disappearing pulp market. His 11 reprints were a new high, though, and the diversity of publications—25 separate magazines, 11 of them outside the U.S.—also spoke well for the future. Pulps only accounted for a small percentage of his sales now, reflecting the death throes of the literary form that had fed and clothed him from the days he began his career as a writer. He only published a single spicy story in 1943, the last year spicies were published. They were succeeded by "speed" magazines. Cave published two stories in *Speed Mystery* that year and six more in *Speed Adventure* over the next two years.

One of his last pulp stories would add to the already established Cave legend. "I received a call from the editor of *Dime Detective* who told me they had some great cover artwork for their next issue, but no story to go with it. He mailed me a blueline of the cover, which showed an underworld bakery and the baker held a huge wooden peel with a dead body on it, shoveling it into the furnace. The editor told me he needed 10,000 words by the following Wednesday."

Cave responded with the novelette entitled, "This is the Way We Bake Our Dead." It would be his last story for that publication.

Another incident demonstrated the bumpy transition he experienced between pulps and slicks. "I wrote a story called 'Tomorrow Is Forever' about a German soldier who is killed in combat and must spend eternity wandering through the Czech town of Lidice. The town and its people had been wiped from the face of the earth after a resident killed an occupying German officer.

"I submitted it to several high paying slick publications—*Collier's, American Magazine* and *Atlantic Monthly*—but they rejected it with nicely worded apologies. The pulp magazine *Adventure* then picked it up and paid me $40."

He was now writing regularly for the slicks, so his higher income per story helped compensate for the dearth of markets available to him. "I could write short shorts for *This Week,* the Sunday magazine of the *New York Herald Tribune* newspaper, usually about 1,500 words, and get paid $700–$1,000 each for them. That was good money at the time."

However, not good enough for Margaret Cave. "She wasn't

particularly happy with my decision to write books because they didn't pay as well as short stories. Lurton Blassingame, on the other hand, recognizing the demise of pulps and because of his own disinterest in slicks, encouraged me to write more books. Consequently, my professional relationship with Lurton soured."

Most of his attention that year centered on war books, his reputation assured by the success of *Long Were the Nights*. He wrote two of them in 1943, *The Fightin'est Ship* and *We Build, We Fight*.

"I don't remember which one was written first, but for *We Build, We Fight,* I began my research at Quonset Point, the Navy Seabee training base, which was just a few minutes down the road from my home. I would drive down and watch them go through their training, talk with the men, even participate in some of the training with them. I went through obstacle courses and so forth, to see what it was like.

"Then I took a train to Washington— believe it was the Pentagon—to look at archive reports and files about mostly Pacific actions. I'm not sure how many times I visited Washington for this book because I did go back there to research subsequent war books."

The Fightin'est Ship was also written that year. "Lurton said that Dodd, Mead wanted me to get together with this man, Lt. Colton G. "Chick" Morris, who served on the U.S.S. *Helena.* The ship had a great combat record before it was sunk by torpedoes in Kula Gulf. Morris was the ship's radio officer and came from Boston. He spent a great deal of time with me putting this book together. Chick came to my house many times and we talked about his Navy career. The book became more of a personal account about his time served aboard the Helena as a drafted seaman. He survived after the ship went down. Chick's brother worked for the *Christian Science Monitor* and reviewed the book when it came out."

> From the opening paragraph to the end, "The Fightin'est Ship" is clearly, crisply, vividly, honestly written.—*Christian Science Monitor*[1]

> As personalized and human as a letter from the battle front. One of the great stories of the war.—*N.Y. Herald Tribune*[1]

Both books were published in 1944. They did well, but not well enough to make up for the income he had lost from his short story markets. Besides the two books, he published 27 original fiction and non-fiction stories and seven reprints. The most significant new publishing relationship that year was with the *Saturday Evening Post.* An excerpt from his new book, *The Fightin'est Ship,* appeared in its January 22, 1944 issue. It became the first of 43 stories he wrote for the magazine over the next 50 years.

Cave returned to Washington for research on his next book, *Wings Across the World,* about the Air Transport Command. However, not all the military brass in Washington were aware of his literary efforts. "I never thought of writing war books as a way to beat the draft. I didn't really write as a way to help the war effort either. I wrote those books because they were interesting and I was getting terrific experience as a writer.

"It never occurred to me, at age 35, that I might be drafted, but that's what happened. So, my draft notice arrives and I am ordered to come in for a physical, which I did. I wore glasses at the time and the guy giving me an eye test asks if I can read the 'E' on the top line of the eye chart without my glasses. I answered no. Then he says, 'Why don't you walk toward it until you can tell me what's there.' So I did that and told him I could see the 'E' now. He said, 'Fine,' and completed my physical without even looking at me."

Cave now faced the prospect of military service in a savage war. It also came at a time when his career was already drifting. With the pulp market all but dead, he had been handed this book writing opportunity that could lead to bigger and better things in the future. His family depended on him for an income, especially with the newest family addition, Donald Hugh Cave, born on June 15, 1944.

Once again, Cave averted a potential disaster when the Navy intervened on his behalf. "I had been on loan to the Army to do *Wings Across the World* when they drafted me. The Navy stepped in because they wanted me to do a book about Commander Norman M. 'Bus' Miller, the most decorated Navy flier of World War II. They didn't want to lose me because they liked my books and the men liked them too."

Relieved that he would not be drafted, he focused on his new war book, *I Took the Sky Road.* "Bus Miller was in Florida, either Jacksonville or Pensacola. I took the train down and stayed at a hotel near his home. He reported for duty every day and went home every night during our days-long interview, then we corresponded. I ended up taking 150,000 words of notes for an 80,000-word book."

It became his last war book and was also well received.

> It is an exciting, solid account of the way brave men wage war, and the way one fitted himself for the job.—*N.Y. Times* [1]

> A thoroughly good tale. Should take its place among the best stories of the war—*San Francisco Chronicle* [1]

The war books were a far cry from his creative fiction, more journalistic in style, but he had a way of presenting facts so they contained the same storytelling elements that made his fiction so readable. The experience would help him shape his later nonfiction books, also quite successful.

Chapter 19: Hugh B. Cave, War Correspondent

As World War II dragged on, consuming American lives and resources, it impacted virtually every man, woman and child in the country. This came on the heels of the Great Depression, and both experiences would go on to shape the character of what would become known as "America's Greatest Generation." For Hugh B. Cave, whose adult life now spanned both generation-defining events, his writing career provided an economic and emotional cocoon.

His once lucrative pulp market had now dried up. He struggled to establish himself in the slicks, but the war affected that market as well. Writing war books enabled Cave to bridge the gap.

By 1945, with his efforts devoted primarily to books, he published just 22 new short stories, all but two of them in slick magazines. One of those stories as described before, "The 75th Baby," was written about Margaret's experiences with their newborn boys—two weeks in the hospital, then home with a full-time nurse for two or three weeks more. Apparently Margaret did not appreciate the story, so he sold it under a pen name, C.H. Barnett. It appeared first in *Women's Home Companion* (March 1945), then as a reprint in an anthology, *Babies Keep Coming* (Whittlesey House 1947).

He started writing for *Boy's Life* towards the end of the war, a relationship lasting for 21 stories over 21 years. Many of his earlier stories for the magazine featured two characters, a white boy named Joe and an island boy named Oerar.

"Joe had served on a PT Boat during the war. He and Oerar owned a trading schooner and the stories covered their adventures with it in the South Seas. Many of those adventures were inspired by incidents I remembered from writing *Long Were the Nights*. At one point a publisher considered putting the stories in book form, but the project never materialized as so often happens. Some were later reprinted in anthologies, and nearly all of them appeared in the magazine's English counterpart, *Boy's Own Paper.*"

Many of Cave's stories were non-fiction pieces about the war. Focusing on this grim reality did not dampen his imagination which is so important for fiction writing. However, his worlds of fantasy and reality were soon to merge.

"My agent, Lurton Blassingame, contacted me to say the Army had offered, through my publisher, a tour of duty as war correspondent in the Pacific. I believe this opportunity resulted from my successful war books. He told me I'd be a damned fool to go, that I could be killed.

"But I said sure, I'd like to go. I've written about these places and I wanted to see them. It took me about ten seconds to decide. I had a fascination with that part of the world since my childhood, and I had a strong feeling that if I got to see the South Pacific first-hand, I could write some damn good fiction. Besides, Margaret and I weren't hitting it off at the time."

Cave jumped at the chance for this, his greatest adventure. First he would have to get his uniform, shots, orders and ID. The Army sent him a few minutes from home to Quonset Point, where he had gone to research his book about the Seabees, *We Build, We Fight.*

"They gave me about eight shots, all in one afternoon, and my arm swelled up like a football. I could hardly lift either of my arms for the next few days. Then I had to get a war correspondent's card. This guy said I have to represent somebody and he named the major magazines, but they all had correspondents. He finally said that no one was assigned from *American* magazine so that's the one I used. *American* had published two stories of mine three years earlier. It was a magazine like *Redbook*. I didn't write for them again until the early fifties and they eventually went out of business. Anyway, I was now a 'recognized news correspondent,' according to the ID card, which I still have. The card has two photos, one civilian and one in uniform, with 'Cave, Hugh B., War Corr.,' printed under it.

"I was fitted with a uniform that included a tag on the shoulder, 'WC,' for war correspondent. I wasn't allowed to carry arms and they gave me the rank of captain in case I was captured by the enemy."

He went home to say his good-byes, then boarded a train, first for Washington D.C., then to Orlando, Florida. "I had to spend a week in Orlando for some basic training about the Army way of life. There were ten of us correspondents. I can't remember everyone, but our group included J.C. Furnas, who wrote for *Reader's Digest,* David Sarnoff, Jr. of RCA fame, George Harmon Coxe, a mystery writer, and screenwriter Dalton Trumbo (*Thirty Seconds Over Tokyo, Spartacus, Exodus*) who ended up in jail after the war during the McCarthy witch hunts."

"We then flew to San Francisco in a small ten-seater plane—a DC-1 or DC-2. We made stops in Dallas and Albuquerque along the way. It was a rough trip—we were tossed all over the sky—and my first time cross-country. The ten of us became good friends by the time it was over.

"From San Francisco, we flew to Oahu, Hawaii for a week-long jungle survival course. We had to live off the jungle by ourselves. Then we went through this graduation exercise in a Quonset hut, where they had tables covered with platters of food. Each platter had a number. We were obliged to taste something from each platter and write down a description of what we thought of it. Two hours later, they handed out a sheet that indicated what we had eaten. It included fried termites, grubs, lizards, crocodile, monkey brains and more."

After the week of training, the correspondents took off on a flight to the South Pacific. Cave still has a map of his circuitous route that took him from Hawaii to Kwajalein in the Marshall Islands, Kwajalein to Guam, Guam to Saipan/Tinlan in the Marianas Islands, Saipan/Tinlan to Iwo Jima.

"We were right behind some of the invasions. For instance, we were on Iwo Jima a week after it was declared secure. Of course, it wasn't secure at all; Japanese soldiers were still hiding in all those caves."

Then they flew back to Guam, Guam to Manila. "We arrived in Manila just a few days after it was secured. From there, we went to New Guinea, where natives would turn in captured Japanese soldiers or their heads for bounty."

An Army captain named Robert Reeves led their group of correspondents at this point. "Bob had written for *Black Mask, Saturday Evening Post,* and did some detective novels. We became friends on the trip. While we were in Manila, waiting to continue on our trip to Borneo, Bob told me he would make arrangements for me to go with him on a bombing mission over Formosa. I was to fly in the squadron leader's plane with Bob as the wing man. We set the date for a few weeks later. Needless to say, I was excited over the prospect."

But first it was on to Borneo, land of Cave's childhood dreams. "I had been given the opportunity to join a combined Navy and Australian Army force planning to recapture Borneo. I really wanted to see Borneo ever since I was a child. So I volunteered—begged—to go along with the other correspondents."

They flew from Manila to Tawi Tawi in the Sewall Islands, then boarded a ship, an LCI (Landing Craft, Infantry), from there to take part in the Australian invasion of Balikpapan, an oil port and refinery on Borneo.

Borneo is the third largest island in the world. It is a predominantly mountainous, lush, tropical island, very humid, with many rivers running through it. The varied wildlife includes elephants and rhinoceroses and the main export is petroleum. The latter resource made Borneo a major target for Allied invasion.

One evening aboard ship, while playing cards with some of the other correspondents, an incident occurred that would later become embellished as part of the Hugh Cave legend.

"I was playing poker with David Sarnoff, Jr., who had come to investigate the oil fields at Balikpapan, George Harmon Coxe and J.C. Furnas. A Navy man comes into the room and asks, 'Is Hugh Cave down here?' I said, 'I'm Cave.' He then told me, 'There's a PT boat alongside and some officer wants to talk with you. It was one of the boats featured in my bestseller, *Long Were the Nights*. I'm not sure at this point, but I think it was Stilly Taylor's boat (Lt. Henry S. Taylor) and they were back in action.

"I went and spoke with him. Stilly asked me if I had received the book he sent me. Each of the crew members had autographed a copy of the book and mailed it to me in Providence. I think my son has that copy now in his possession. We talked a little while longer, both our boats heading into battle on that dark night."

Later, Cave altered the story a bit, indicating that Stilly Taylor handed him the autographed book ship-to-ship as they headed to battle. That version of the story was repeated (or misquoted) in the press, a little bit of literary license to help the war effort back home.

Cave eventually joined up with the troops a few days after they began their assault on the beaches of Balikpapan in what became known as the Battle of Amana Ridge and the final amphibious assault of World War II.

"I was assigned to an Australian unit, the Silent Seventh Division, part of a cooperative effort between the Americans and Australians. These guys had stopped the Japanese in the Owen Stanley Mountains in New Guinea and saved Australia. They hadn't been back home for several years and were a tough group—every second word was a four letter expletive.

"Balikpapan was an oil port and refinery with a white sand beach, about one and a half miles long, and a huge mountainous sand dune behind it. On top of the dune, known as Amana Ridge, the Japanese were entrenched with heavy artillery they had captured from the Allies in an earlier battle. They would fire at Allied ships from that position as they came in. We had to take out the three-inch guns on top of Amana Ridge before our ships could unload Aussie army troops.

"One shell went screaming over our ship and took out the radio mast on the ship next to us. Shells were landing in the ocean all around us and exploding, sending up geysers. I was never so scared.

"At dawn the next morning, the first wave of troops went ashore. I went in with the second wave along with the other correspondents. We hit the beach and dove into foxholes dug by the first wave of Aussies. I had to stay there a couple of hours, unable to move, shells whizzing all around.

"All of a sudden, this PBY aircraft lands in the water. A rubber boat comes off with three or four men in it and motors to shore. The men get out and start walking up the beach. One Aussie puts his hand on my shoulder and says, 'Holy Mother of God—it's the Messiah himself!'

"Sure enough, there was General Douglas A. MacArthur, tall and slender, with a cigarette holder clenched in his teeth, striding down the beach—and I mean *striding* down the beach, as if on parade—while everyone else in sight had his head down! He walked through enemy fire as though he couldn't be touched—like a god!

"We stayed in our foxholes as Aussie troops battled their way up the ridge to silence those guns. Tanks and other vehicles had already gone up. The guns were finally silenced.

"I went up with an Aussie soldier. We saw the body of a dead

Japanese infantryman. He had been run over by many tanks and was hardly recognizable as a human being.

"We reached the top of another ridge, Parramatta, by early afternoon. I was walking along with this same Aussie soldier and we came upon an abandoned Jeep. All of a sudden, Zing! Zing-zing! Bullets went flying past us. We both dove under the Jeep which was the only cover around. The Japanese kept firing at us, shells pinging off the top of the Jeep.

"We spent at least an hour under that Jeep, trapped by a Japanese sniper. We didn't know he was there because he came out of a spider hole, something the Japanese used when defending mountains and ridges. They dug vertical shafts down with rope ladders and covered by boards so no one could see them. Then when soldiers walked by, they lifted the cover and popped up with a machine gun, raking the top of the ridge and often killing many people.

"This sniper was high above us and couldn't depress the gun enough to get under the Jeep where we hid, so he shot it to pieces. We were scared shitless and the Aussie soldier with me started weeping. Someone finally shot the sniper and I walked the soldier back to the beach with my arm around him. I left him with his buddies and came back to the ridge later.

"Aussie soldiers dug trenches on the ridge overlooking Balikpapan. The Japanese had set the refineries on fire and the entire valley was ablaze, red flames dancing in a monstrous wall of black smoke, just like the Iraqis did in Kuwait a few years ago.

"Later that same day, we were on top of the ridge looking down. I had jumped into a trench with four or five soldiers. To see better, I hitched my ass up the back side of the trench and knelt on the front edge looking down at the fire. Suddenly I heard Phtt! Phfft-phfft! going right past my ear. One of the Aussies grabbed my leg and pulled me down. He yelled, 'Get yer fuckin' 'ead down, mate, or you'll bloody well get it shot off!'

"We eventually walked down into the town. We found an old schoolhouse with books written in the Malay language, and also came upon a dead Japanese soldier. The Aussies searched him—they always did that to see if he had anything. He was carrying a little notebook. The Aussie who found it handed it to me and said this isn't anything, but I kept it all through the trip and brought it back home with me. I later found someone at one of the local colleges who taught Japanese and he offered to translate it for me. I told him I wanted to know what that dead Jap was doing in Balikpapan. The fellow gave it back to me some time later and said the book contained notes about how much he loved his wife and words to their favorite songs."

While in Balikpapan, Cave bumped into another correspondent, Coles Phillips, who served as editor of *Elks* magazine back home. "We became instant buddies as so often happens in times of fast action and stress."

However, this was a fast friendship that would once again save his life. "Coles came down with 'cat fever'—dengue fever—and he said, 'You don't have to go to Manila just yet, do you?' I said no, I just had a date to go with a bombing mission over Formosa.

"So instead of flying back to Manila as I had planned to do, I accompanied Coles aboard a hospital ship. The ship carried us to Morotai, a little island off the north coast of New Guinea. The Australians had recently kicked the Japanese out and taken over.

"We were put ashore in an Aussie camp, a sprawling place, not compact, half of it out in the jungle. They gave us a tent near the perimeter where one of them had been knifed the week before. Japanese soldiers were still lurking in the jungle.

"After we settled in on our cots that night, a few guys started talking about their buddy who had been knifed when some Jap had sneaked up in the dark and stole his shoes. Their own shoes had worn out from living in the jungle. The guys told us to be very careful following jungle trails and don't go out by ourselves. Of course, we had to go out there to relieve ourselves. They had built latrines in the jungle that consisted of one-inch metal pipes driven into the ground with funnels at the top. For anything else, you just went out into the woods."

Cave not only took the inconveniences in stride, he enjoyed himself. Here he was, living this primitive jungle life at ground central of his childhood imagination. He could only have come here if he wasn't a writer—or as a frontline soldier, which is what would have happened if the Navy hadn't rescued him from the draft!

As he absorbed these experiences into his consciousness, he delighted in one notion. He knew whatever fiction he wrote from now on, would be based on his actual experiences, not from books he had read or second hand information through patrons like Dr. Douglas Dold.

Cave still had not seen New Guinea and he was now so close, he would be terribly disappointed not to go there. Who knows when or if he could ever again have the chance?

"After about a week of experiencing the primitive jungle life, some Aussies came to me one day and said they were flying to Darwin, Australia to get beer. They asked me if I wanted to go and, of course, I did—our route was to take us over New Guinea.

"So we flew right over the jungles of New Guinea. There was little sign of human habitation, just ancient forest."

Cave had another opportunity for a closer look. "I had flown over to Hollandia on the north coast of New Guinea one day. I began talking to a small plane pilot there and he asked if I would like to see the interior, where it remained unchanged from the Stone Age.

"So we went up and spent several hours in the air, flying along the Sepic River route. I already knew more about New Guinea than most of the other guys who were there; now I could tell them what was back there over those mountains and none of them knew it. The same with Borneo. That trip inspired me to write stories about the South Pacific afterwards that were truly factual."

They stayed on Morotai long enough for Coles Phillips to recover from his dengue fever, then Cave headed back to The Philippines.

"By the time I reached Manila, I had missed by two days my previously arranged date with Captain Bob Reeves on the bombing mission over Formosa, now Taiwan. I went to the officers' club at Clark Field one evening and met up with four or five correspondent friends having a drink. I asked them if they had seen Bob. They gave me a funny look and told me that his plane had been shot down during the mission. Witnesses on another plane saw it go down in flames and crash into the sea. There were no survivors.

Coles Phillips' illness, and Cave's decision to stay with him rather than experience firsthand an actual bombing mission, saved his life. Had he taken that flight as scheduled, Cave would today still be remembered as a great pulp writer. However, we would have been deprived of his huge postwar body of work, from a reenergized writing career that was to take him in directions he never imagined back then in 1945.

Cave spent about two months in the South Pacific but enjoyed a lifetime of experiences. That included crossing the international date line once coming over (June 30, 1945) and a second time going back (July 19, 1945). The second time was more notable. "We actually crossed the equator and the international date line at the same place, which warranted an initiation ceremony."

He also had the opportunity to meet General Douglas Mac-

Arthur at one of his stops in Manila. "Three or four of us correspondents were in his office getting a lecture from him on the potential dangers of atomic energy. He wasn't about to tell us they had the bomb right there, but they did, and they were about ready to use it. After the briefing, we asked him to sign our 'short snorters,' which were different island currencies stapled together with autographs on them. Instead, he reached in his desk and pulled out fresh new Philippine pesos and signed one for each of us. I still have it."

Cave spent the last days of his South Pacific adventure in Guadalcanal. Then flew back to Hawaii on a plane with only three working engines. His homeward route took him to San Francisco, Cheyenne, Chicago, Washington and Providence.

I asked him to reflect on his brief, but exciting tour of duty.

"I never went there for any reason other than the fact that I wanted to go. If I'd been able to, I probably would have tried to see more of Borneo than merely Balikpapan. I loved the islands and their beautiful tropical settings, but I hated the war. I even hated to see Japanese soldiers in prison camps, even though they were nicely treated, much better than they treated our guys."

What are your feelings about the Japanese?

"I still remember the unnecessary cruelty, the way they treated our people. I visited Allied prison camps and the Japanese prisoners didn't appear too unhappy; they seemed glad to be out of the war. But the Aussies told stories of how, in the middle of the night, the Japs came to the edge of their camp in the Owen Stanley Mountains and pushed naked prisoners into the camp who had been castrated, or had their eyes gouged out. They put prisoners in tiny bamboo cages, too small to lie down or move, and left them there for weeks at a time. It was just unbelievable cruelty. There were stories that would turn your stomach."

Cave cannot understand why they have never even apologized for the war.

"Who the hell do they think started it? What were they on the defensive against? We didn't want them or anything they had. I guess I've gotten over it though. I drive a Japanese car and watch a Japanese TV.

"Of course, our side wasn't completely innocent when it came to cruelty, especially with our own men. During basic training at sea, Navy initiates stripped down to their shorts and were forced to crawl through this small canvas tunnel filled with days' old garbage. Sailors lined up with paddles and as a bulge in the canvas went by, they whacked it.

"I went through a lighter form of hazing myself when we crossed the international date line, but we were on an LCI, which was an intimate ship, so the hazing wasn't so bad. But on the bigger ships, I saw men deliberately hurting each other. I was asked to write an article in the form of a letter to the Secretary of the Navy about the practice and why it should be stopped. The article was entitled, 'It's Not Funny' (*Elks* magazine, September 1946)."

The editor at *Elks* magazine was his fellow correspondent, Coles Phillips. "I had never tried selling to *Elks* before meeting Phillips; they only published one short story per issue so I figured it wasn't much of a market. Yet, Coles asked me to send in stories. I only saw him once after the war, when I brought him one story on a visit to New York. I can't remember when I sold my last story to the magazine, but he resigned as editor at some point and I never spoke or wrote to him after that."

The first story Cave did sell to Coles Phillips after the war was never published. Enthusiasm for war-related fiction had quickly waned. The same was true for his non-fiction war books. However, he did find willing buyers in the slick magazine market, and it is there Hugh Cave began to rebuild his writing career.

Chapter 20: Coming Home

After returning home, he began to sell stories about the South Seas, all of them to slick magazines, often Canadian publications. His stories were particularly popular in Canada. He had sold 23 stories north of the border between 1943 and 1946, his first back in 1932 to *Canadian Magazine*. Between 1938 and 1966, the *Toronto Star Weekly* published an incredible 92 Hugh Cave stories, the first being "The Midnight Horde," printed as a condensed novel.

Cave's popular war books yielded numerous ancillary publishing credits. Excerpts or condensations from the books were reprinted in magazines as diverse as *Adventure,* a pulp magazine, *Liberty,* the *Saturday Evening Post* (his first sale to them), *True Magazine* and *Yachting Magazine*. They also appeared in books, including *This Is the Navy* (Penguin Books, 1944), and *The U.S. Navy in World War II* (William Morrow & Co., 1966). The latter featured excerpts from three of Cave's war books and was a Book-of-the-Month Club selection that year. His war books were also re-released in their entirety, first by The Zenger Company in 1981 (with all the previously censored copy and photos reinstated), and recently by Wildside Press books-on-demand.

Cave had been gone from home almost three months, but now that he was back, life picked up right where it had left off. His relationship with Margaret remained the same, but there were new dynamics in the family with two sons to raise.

Cave enjoyed his time with Ken, now seven years old. "I had bought a huge balsa wood raft with canvas webbing. These rafts were found on the decks of warships so in an emergency, they could just throw them over the side and jump in. I purchased one from Quonset Point when I was there working on a book, cut out the webbing and dropped it in the pond behind my house. The kids played on that raft for hours at a time. I also took Kenny with me to Sebago Lake to go fishing."

On the surface, it was a typical happy family, but there were problems, not just between Hugh and Margaret, but between Margaret and the kids. "From the time Kenny was born, Margaret imposed very strict discipline on him. I objected, but to no avail. Even her own friends criticized her for it. Then, from the time Donny was born, she treated him entirely the opposite, showering him with love and attention. She babied him to death and spoiled him. He could do no wrong; Donnie was obviously her favorite. That pattern continued all through their childhood."

By 1947, Cave's writing career again flourished, only this time in slick magazines. A total of 68 original stories and reprints were published, numbers that approached his best pulp years. The *Boston Globe Sunday Magazine* carried 13 Hugh Cave stories that year; 11 appeared in Canadian publications. The bulk of his stories were mainstream, very different from the pulp style he had mastered. The subject matter often came out of left field.

"An acquaintance of mine in Maine called and suggested that I come up for a bluefin tuna tournament. He offered to take me out on his boat for a free fishing trip and I could then do a story. So I went, took photos, and wrote a story for the *Saturday Evening Post* ("Bluefins are Bedlam," December 20, 1947).

"I loved to play table tennis; I once knew and had played with the New England state champion. So I wrote an article about it entitled 'White Lightning' (*Elks* Magazine, January 1948).

"The best paying and most prestigious magazine back then was the *Saturday Evening Post.* I tried a few more articles after 'Bluefins are Bedlam' but they were rejected. Then I received a letter from Stuart Rose, one of the top three editors for the *Post,* asking me to come down to Philadelphia and talk with him. We met one day and he told me, 'Hugh, we can get non-fiction with no problem, but you are a fine fiction writer and we would much rather have you submitting that. It's hard to find good stories, so if you want to make money and continue selling to us, write fiction.'

"I submitted a fiction story set in New Guinea, a subject I could now write about from firsthand experience. But they rejected it and asked me to do a rewrite. I was so set on writing for the *Post* that I even signed up for a correspondence course on writing fiction.

"After rewriting and resubmitting that story a total of four times, I went to see Stuart Rose again. He told me where I was right for the *Post* and where I was wrong. He said my thinking and plotting were a little too 'pulpy.' If I had one more go at the story, he was certain they would buy it."

They did. The story, "Fool's Courage," appeared in the June 18, 1949 issue. "I received $800 for that story, the first of 40 I was to write for the magazine. Towards the end I was making $3,500 per story."

The postwar boom provided plenty of writing opportunities and they paid good money. He sold 51 stories and reprints in 1948 and another 34 in 1949. Radio rights were sold for two of the stories, but neither of them was broadcast. Cave still sold a few pulp stories as well, two to *Argosy* and four to *Short Stories,* which had been cut back to a monthly by 1949. Over the two-year period he sold 11 stories to the *Toronto Star Weekly* and ten to the *Boston Globe Sunday Magazine.* He ultimately sold 84 stories to the latter publication between 1931 and 1955. As mentioned before, that newspaper was the one that ran Hugh Cave's first two published stories back in 1925 and 1926, when he was a starry-eyed lad of 15 with vague notions of becoming a writer.

While his career flourished and his family life had stabilized, something nagged at Cave's consciousness. Because of the war, he had left behind his life as a pulp writer. Yet the war had given him a new life, as a slick magazine writer, a book author—and as an adventurer. He had finally experienced a taste of what, up to that

Hugh B. Cave's birthplace, Ways Green House, England.

Hugh B. Cave (seated on car's bumper) on one of his numerous fishing expeditions. From left to right: Larry Dunn, Ken White, Burton Blassingame (Cave's literary agent) and Sam Engdahl. Maine, 1939.

Hugh B. Cave (fourth from right) with fellow war correspondents in the South Pacific during WW II.

Family passport photo for first trip to Haiti, 1949.

Cave with two sacred voodoo govi urns acquired in Haiti, 1950.

Hugh B. Cave in 1952 with book, *Haiti: High Road to Adventure*.

In Vallieres, Haiti, 1958.

Hugh B. Cave on his Jamaica coffee plantation, early 1960s.

At the World Fantasy Convention with Ramsey Campbell, early 1990s

With his brother Geoffrey Cave, 1991.

With his Haiti book 44 years later, 1996.

Hugh and "Peg" Cave, 1998.

point, he only dreamed about. The booming economy fostered many markets for his writing, but nothing in his postwar life at this point satisfied his need for adventure. That would soon change in a most peculiar way.

Chapter 21: Visions of Spiders

Hugh Cave had always been an adventurer in his imagination, but visiting the epicenter of his youthful dreams did not leave him fulfilled. Instead it was a revelation. He had found a way to transform fantasy into reality: use your imagination to write; use your reputation as a writer to earn opportunities for adventure. Like a powerful drug, his wartime experiences only fueled the desire for more of the same. He must travel again

"I really wanted to go back to the South Seas, but I couldn't justify going alone nor could I afford to take the wife and two kids there. So I began thinking of other potential destinations."

One of those destinations was relatively close. "From the time I read *The Magic Island* by William H. Seabrook as a young boy, I had a yen to visit Haiti. Seabrook had only been there a few weeks, yet he wrote this book about Haiti and voodoo. From then on I wanted to go there. After being overseas in the South Pacific, my interest in exotic destinations became a real desire. I had fallen in love with tropical islands."

However, he did not have anyone willing to pay his way this time. After all, what could he possibly do of value to the U.S. government in a backward country like Haiti? And why would a publisher finance his trip when he had been so successful writing stories about places he had never seen? Even if an opportunity presented itself, he would have a difficult time leaving his wife and kids behind. "Margaret accepted our financial sacrifices while I was writing war books because everyone made sacrifices during the war. She didn't mind that I left for three months to the South Pacific for much the same reason. Now I had to think of our growing family's financial situation first."

Cave had been writing short stories on a regular basis for *This Week* magazine, a Sunday supplement like today's *Parade Magazine*. "The editor's name was Mary Day Wynn. She was in New York and knew a couple named Bill and Peggy Krauss. They had written an article about Haiti which put it on the tourist map. She also knew of my interest in Haiti and recommended that I come down to talk with them. We ended up meeting at a party."

The Caves drove down from Providence and the Krauss's came in from New Jersey. Another friend of the Krauss's also came to the party. "Father Henry J. 'Harry' Smith was an English-born Catholic priest who lived in Haiti and taught at the Collegé St. Martial in Port-au-Prince. Our evening together lasted well into the night as we all talked about Haiti."

At this point, his plans to visit Haiti were still in the fantasy realm. He had to convince Margaret why they should go there and bring the kids, not for a vacation, but for a winter. "I was convinced that no one could learn about a country just being a tourist."

Then there was the matter of earning a living. Cave had always said a writer can live anywhere, but now they owned a home and did not need the expense of another one thousands of miles away. It was a tough sell, but fate unexpectedly walked—or crawled—on the scene.

"My son Ken, who was ten-years-old at the time, had taken strangely ill. He ran high temperatures every afternoon around five o'clock, then have visions of spiders and other curious things crawling on his bedroom walls. We took him to several doctors and they tried all sorts of antibiotics on him, but no one could diagnose the illness. Finally, his fever subsided and the doctor told us to get him out of town, that the cold Rhode Island winter would not be good for him this year. We ought to take him someplace where it's warm."

Cave couldn't remember how quickly he thought of Haiti once the doctor made that suggestion, but it must have been as close to immediate as you might measure. Then he floated the idea of Haiti past Margaret. "She probably had an adventure fantasy life just like me; she was a horseback instructor at summer camp, not an office gal."

Margaret agreed. Still, the West Indies was a compromise for Cave. He really wanted to go back to the South Seas, but Margaret might interpret that as more of a self-serving decision. The same might be said for Haiti, since Florida was a more convenient destination that they both enjoyed. Fortunately for him, "The idea of a primitive country at our doorstep had its appeal."

Cave then contacted Father Harry Smith and took him up on his offer to find a rental house for them. The entire family became excited about their adventure, but none more than Hugh Cave.

"I bought a secondhand Jeep and drove it down to the dock in New York for shipment to Haiti. I stood and watched them load it. Then I took either a train or plane back to Providence, I can't remember which."

The boat, a French freighter called the *Bresle,* not only carried their Jeep to Haiti—it would carry them as well. "A week or two later I put the car on blocks, closed up the house on Gorton Pond in Warwick, turned off the hot water, drained all the radiators and emptied the pipes. Someone drove us to New York and we were off."

Hugh, Margaret, Kenny, age ten, and Don, age five, began their first family adventure in September 1949. Cave doesn't remember Margaret's reaction to their shipboard accommodations, "but she wasn't very happy about it. There were only 12 passengers on board, five of them from Haiti and three from St. Maartens, plus the four Caves. We were the only white people on board. For meals during the trip, we ate every part of the cow except the steak—tripe, liver, kidneys—and had nothing but red wine to drink, even the kids.

"We became friendly with the Haitians on board. We all played poker for matchsticks every evening, and while playing, the Haitians taught us Creole, their local version of French. By the time we landed in Port-au-Prince six days later, we spoke enough Creole to get by, even five-year-old Donnie. One of the Haitians on board, Lionel Elie, traveled alone. He was the son of the Port-au-Prince fire chief and we looked him up once we settled in. I have pictures of our two kids sitting on a fire truck at the station."

As they approached their destination, the entire family grew excited. For Hugh B. Cave though, this was far more than exciting—it was another childhood dream about to become reality.

PART FIVE: THE MAGIC ISLAND

Chapter 22: An American in Port-au-Prince

THE CAVE FAMILY, HUGH, MARGARET, KEN AND Donnie, were delighted when their boat dropped anchor in the Port-au-Prince harbor. No doubt, some of that delight had to do with getting off the boat, but they were also happy to see a familiar face waiting for them. Father Harry Smith, the man Hugh and Margaret met in New York with Bill and Peggy Krauss, welcomed them to their new home. "Father Smith told us about the house he rented on our behalf. It belonged to Georges Leger, a local political figure who later became Haiti's ambassador to the U.S."

Once they collected their baggage, the Caves climbed into a taxi and rode to their rental home. "It was five uphill miles from Port-au-Prince to Pétionville and our first trip in a Haitian taxi. I only saw blind curves rushing toward us, the descending curves hurtling past and an ever more picturesque view of the city and bay spreading out below.

"The house was very pleasant, two bedrooms, colorful tile floor and mahogany furniture. A couple of days later, we met the home's owner, Georges Leger, who became a friend and an enthusiastic student of photography once I showed him how to use the camera."

The first hurdle they faced in this new country was processing their Jeep through customs. "They impounded the Jeep and kept it in the customs yard for a few days. We soon found out that everything was difficult in Haiti. I once spent an entire morning trying to get a package out of customs that someone had sent to me. It turned out to be a carton of cigarettes, which I could have bought right there in Haiti. I got a lecture from a customs officer in broken English that it was very good for Americans to learn to be patient; we were always in too big a hurry."

Taking their boys out of school for several months in the middle of the year meant the Caves had to arrange formal schooling in Haiti. "We enrolled them in the Union School for English-speaking children. I believe it was sponsored by the U.S. embassy and the teachers were all foreigners. The Haitian elite sent their kids to school there, too, because Union School was superior to the Haitian schools.

"High schools were called collèges in Haiti, and there were no schools out in the country, only in the cities. Father Smith taught at the Collège St. Martial, a Catholic school. I took the boys to Union School in the morning and picked them up afterwards. They received an excellent education and were not behind in their studies when we returned to the States."

His boys quickly earned nicknames with the locals because of their very different personalities. Ken was "The Worry Wart," always concerned about the consequences to his family of any activity they might undertake. They dubbed Donnie, five years younger, "The Character," for constantly finding ways to get into mischief.

Cave spent much of his time writing, but not yet about Haiti. As the family settled in to their new life, they began to travel around the country. "All that winter we explored the island in our Jeep. By 'we' I mean Margaret, Kenny, Donnie and me. I took all kinds of photos. It was a rough country, but Margaret was a real trooper; she liked the adventure as much as I did. We were very compatible that way—just not as man and wife."

They made many friends that first winter, including Sister Joan Margaret, an Episcopal nun from Boston who founded and ran the St. Vincent School for Handicapped Children in Port-au-Prince. "Margaret became friends with the sister and ended up helping out at the school; she had some training in physical therapy at the University of Wisconsin. We also took Sister Joan with us on some of our explorations.

"Occasionally we saw some people who came down on the boat with us, certainly Lionel, because we went looking for him at the fire station. We also met a woman on the boat, Carmita Perrault, who stopped by and visited us two or three times. We really liked her, but when we went back the next winter, we couldn't find her and never saw her again."

One friendship exposed Cave to a world that inspired fear and mystery back in the U.S., but it was a world that few people outside Haiti truly understood. Vodun (West African for "spirit") or as it is more commonly known, voodoo, is a religion that mixes Christianity, African tribal beliefs, and aspects of Haitian life. It was developed back in the 18th century by the original West African slaves brought to Haiti and today has strong appeal to the country's poorest inhabitants, providing meaning and escape from the hardships of everyday life.

"We made friends with a Haitian neighbor, Milo Rigaud and his French wife, Odette Mennesson-Rigaud. They were making a study of voodoo—Milo later wrote the book, *Secrets of Voodoo,* which is still in print—and through them I was introduced to some people with intimate firsthand knowledge of the practice."

One of those people was a voodoo mambo, or priestess, named Lorgina Delorge, or Maman Lorgina to her followers. She had a hounfor, the sanctuary where voodoo ceremonies are held. Her hounfor was located in a slum section of Port-au-Prince called LaSaline. Maman Lorgina was a very important mambo, known throughout Haiti by reputation. Milo Rigaud, who, it turned out, was a voodoo priest himself, arranged for the Caves to attend Maman Lorgina's services.

Cave's first meeting with the woman who would open this world to him is described in his widely read work, *Haiti: High Road to Adventure* (1952, Henry Holt & Company). Out of respect for Lorgina, he used a fictitious name in the book, Madame Julanie.

> Only one person was in evidence: a dignified-appearing black woman in a voluminous, multi-colored cotton dress, seated on a chair between the twin doors. I greeted her in Creole with "Good evening. I'm looking for Madame Julanie."
>
> She had unusual eyes, that woman. Many times later, at voodoo services, I noticed them and they always impressed me. She was neither friendly nor hostile, not even obviously curious, but when she had done looking at me I knew she would remember me.
>
> "I am Julanie," she said then. We shook hands.[13]

Maman Lorgina invited him to attend several ceremonies at her hounfor, and several days later he came with his camera, asking permission to take photographs. She allowed it, but became agitated with each flash from the camera. Her associates felt he was upsetting the hounfor's guiding spirit and asked him to step outside while Lorgina conferred with the spirit alone.

> . . . I recognized Julanie's voice and then quite distinctly heard another voice answering her—a much deeper, more resonant voice than hers. She was alone in the hounfor and it seemed to me, though I was admittedly nervous at the time and might have imagined it, that the mysterious voice spoke for several minutes without interruption. If so, it could not have been an echo.[13]

One of those visits to Maman Lorgina's hounfor later paid great dividends. "We went there for a service one night but she was bedridden in great pain with a badly swollen leg. Margaret decided that massage might help the old lady and asked Lorgina for some oil. She didn't have any, so in the middle of the night, I drove all over Port-au-Prince and found some. After an hour or so of massaging her leg, the swelling and the pain subsided. She thanked us and said we could have anything we wanted from her.

"We became friends after that, which gave me access to information and experiences I never would have had otherwise. By being her friend, and knowing enough about her to convince others that I actually did know her well, I was able to attend voodoo services all over the country.

"Lorgina was old even when we first met her. I once painted her portrait and it still hangs on a wall in my home. It was used recently for the cover of a small-press magazine called *The Tome*, edited by David Niall Wilson. When she died a few years after I got to know her, her funeral was one of the most memorable voodoo events ever."

He continued to gain the confidence of this key voodoo figure and she guaranteed him full access to their primitive, mystical ceremonies over the next few years. "Many tourists visiting Haiti in those days could witness 'voodoo ceremonies,' but these were simply performances to earn gratuities from them. The real voodoo rites occurred after the tourists returned to their hotels and cruise ships."

Cave's background as a pulp writer certainly helped him interpret these voodoo experiences to the reading public. His detailed accounts of the real ceremonies not only made for spellbinding reading—it established Cave as an expert on the subject where few existed, and helped to keep *Haiti: High Road to Adventure* in print for 16 years as an authoritative book on the subject.

I asked Hugh if he ever thought his son's strange illness that brought him to Haiti and his involvement with voodoo were related. He paused to reflect, smiled and shrugged his shoulders. Knowing the far reaches of his imagination by now, I took that to be a yes.

Cave and his family packed a lifetime of experiences in that first Haitian winter. They traveled over rough terrain in the most uncivilized of conditions to explore the countryside, places that few non-Haitians had ever visited. He often ventured out alone or with other friends he had made there, always for the purpose of taking photos. At this point, he did not plan to write a book about Haiti.

On one such occasion, he found himself at a river snapping photos of local women walking by with baskets of clothing balanced on their heads. They washed their clothes in the river, chatting with each other and watching their children. He spotted a very attractive young girl and asked to take her picture, offering her a gourde-note (20¢). Cave wanted her to stand in front of a picturesque cottage as background and she suddenly seemed reluctant to pose. He became frustrated because she spoke softly and he had difficulty understanding her Creole.

> By this time the usual crowd had gathered and I turned to an older woman standing at my elbow.
>
> "Ask her what's the trouble," I said. "Does she want more money?"
>
> Age and youth talked the situation over. "*Oui, msié*," the older woman said. "She wants a dollar."
>
> "A dollar for a photograph? Why, the girl's crazy!"
>
> For an instant there was complete silence. Then someone laughed, and in a moment they were all laughing. It was a huge joke—evidently on me. "Well?" I demanded when I could get a word in.
>
> "M*sié*," the woman gurgled, literally holding onto her sides, "the girl did not understand. A picture? Of course you can take her picture, and a gourde is ample. She thought you wanted her to go *in* the house with you, for pleasure!"[13]

The Caves stayed in Haiti for six months that first year before finally returning home. "Afterwards, we continued to correspond with Father Smith and Sister Joan, but no one else. Ken, after a winter in Haiti, never had any more problems with his mysterious illness. Our trip, the expense of it, taking Ken and Don out of school, was all justified. However, I had fallen in love with the country and its people, especially the country people."

Cave's love of photography approached his zeal for writing. He had been developing, printing and enlarging his own photos since his early teens and gained a newfound enthusiasm for picture taking in Haiti with "Kodak moments" popping up at every turn. He kept processing equipment and chemicals in the basement of his Gorton Road home. "When we got back from Haiti I immediately printed over 100 photos. I wasn't writing about Haiti that first winter, just taking pictures. I came back and started selling my work to the *Journal of Commerce.* I sent them photos ten to twenty at a time, including family adventures, exploration and later, voodoo. They picked what they wanted and return the unused ones with a check, about $25 per picture used."

Cave also took the photos to his agent, Lurton Blassingame, and suggested he try to find someone to publish a pictorial book on Haiti. "I kept a daily journal of all our experiences there, and I showed that to Lurton along with the photos. After reading my notes, he told me I ought to write a book about Haiti instead of just selling photographs. Lurton even thought he could get someone to give me a book contract on the strength of my photos alone."

In the meantime, Cave continued writing for his usual markets. In 1950, he saw two of his stories brought to life on radio and television. "The Woman Who Wouldn't Run" appeared on the CBS radio show, *Romance,* on September 22, 1951, and "The Ardent Woodsman" was produced as a teleplay on the *Ford Television Theater,* though the date is unclear. Of his 40 other published works, 19 were to foreign publications, an indication of how his postwar writing had universal appeal.

It did not take long for Cave's agent to find a publisher interested in his book on Haiti. "Lurton arranged lunch with the editor from Henry Holt—I've forgotten his name—who knew my writing and thought the pictures were great. However, he saw my book as more slanted to the tourist market. I told him no, that's not the way to do it. I said that if he insisted I write this as a standard travel book, it wouldn't be fun and I would not write the book at all. He went back and thought things over, then relented and told me to write it any way I want. He paid me a decent advance and guaranteed to publish the book."

Cave now had all the justification he needed to spend another winter in Haiti—not that he needed any encouragement. His advance could help cover their expenses while he gathered material to write the book. Cave looked forward eagerly to December when he and his family would head back to Haiti for the second time, full of purpose and enthusiasm.

Just before the trip though, he received some tragic news. "My mother had not been well for some time. She suffered from amoebic dysentery her entire life, contracting it first when she was a young girl in India. As she grew older, the attacks came more frequently. Mother had never remarried after Dad left, and she lived alone, working as a live-in nurse for other people. In later years she moved into a little cottage near my brother Geoff in East Sturbridge, near Worcester, Massachusetts. As the dysentery became more difficult to control, she moved in with Geoff and Alice.

"Mother finally died peacefully at age 80. She had asked to be cremated and have her ashes spread at Anesquam, Massachusetts, a place on the ocean that she loved to visit in the summertime. I took her ashes there, went out in a rowboat and put them over the side.

"Regardless of what happened in her life, through the troubles with my father, our tough financial straits, and her illnesses, Mother was always there for me. She was responsible for my love of writing and reading, always encouraging me. I loved her very much and I miss her to this day."

Chapter 23: Looking for Columbus

His experiences during that first winter in Haiti enabled Cave to write the first six chapters of his book, *Haiti: High Road to Adventure*. His experiences over the next few years would ultimately result in 52 short stories, seven non-fiction articles and ten books about Haiti, with more to come in the future.

He only needed that second winter in Haiti, though, to complete his book, and a new acquaintance would help provide much of the content. "Georges Leger, who had become a friend, called me at the house one day and asked me to come down and meet someone. His name was Dr. Charles Deichman, a pediatrician from Morristown, New Jersey visiting mutual friends—the Nowaks—in Haiti. Georges knew I wanted to visit the north coast of Haiti and thought I might want to meet Deichman, who was also interested in seeing that area."

> "What sort of trip does he have in mind?"
>
> "I don't know exactly (said Leger). But he and Al Nowak walked over the mountains from Furey to Jacmel last week. I think you'd like him."
>
> I thought so too. The desire to walk from Furey to Jacmel may be no guarantee that a man will be an interesting traveling companion, but it certainly indicates a soul with a lively spark of adventure. I called on the doctor and found him a rugged young man with an idea. The idea had to do with Christopher Columbus.[13]

Columbus discovered Haiti on his first voyage to the New World back in 1492. His records indicated that he sighted Môle St. Nicholas on the north coast and left 39 men to establish a colony before he sailed for home. The actual site for this colony, named Navidad, had been in dispute and never uncovered. That was all the excuse Cave needed to make the trip. "So Dr. Deichman and I rented a Jeep, leaving mine behind for Margaret to use, and set out to explore Haiti's north coast."

While they never found that first European settlement, they did run into an assortment of interesting characters, precarious situations and breathtaking natural beauty. They also forged a friendship that would continue for years.

Cave's experiences in the world of voodoo were also far from over. "When I was back in Rhode Island after our first winter, I received a letter from Milo Rigaud saying that Maman Lorgina would be pleased if Meg (Margaret) and I returned to Haiti to attend an important service called LaSouvenance. This takes place once a year around Easter at a 'secret village' in the foothills near the town of Gonaives. I put that in quotes because it really isn't secret—actually it's on the map as Souvenance. But the part of the village used for this service is fenced-in, containing only a few dozen small huts, and the area is used only for this particular service.

" 'La Souvenance' means 'remembrance.' To this service come all or nearly all the houngans (priests) and mambos (priestesses) who trace their roots back to Africa. The service lasts a week. Once you enter this fenced-in village for La Souvenance, you are not supposed to leave until it's over. It is said that if you try to leave without permission, you won't be able to. At the time of my visit, a very belligerent fellow shouted that no one was going to keep HIM there against his will. He stormed out through the gate and fell unconscious before he reached the dirt road. Later, I used this as a big scene in a novel called *The Lower Deep* (1990, Tor Books).

"I believe we are the only outsiders who have ever attended La Souvenance. If anyone else has, no one has written about it to my knowledge. I do try to keep up with everything written about voodoo because I have written so extensively about it myself. La Souvenance was by far the longest service I ever attended.

"It was indeed remarkable. I first saw someone play one of the rare, sacred Assotor drums; it was more than eight feet high, made from the entire trunk of a tree, and must be played by men on ladders! I also met a possessed old Haitian who claimed to be Moses and talked fluently for half an hour in what I think was Hebrew. Haitian peasants speak only Creole, so no matter WHAT other language he spoke so fluently, it was remarkable!"

Cave either witnessed or heard secondhand about numerous mystical experiences during voodoo ceremonies, many of which he reported in *Haiti: High Road to Adventure.* "There was an 18-year-old girl, possessed, who got on all fours and ate a raw egg off the floor, then slithered away like a snake.

"Another time, I was attending a ceremony and a young boy, about eight years old, sat down next to me. He was telling me in Creole where he came from, about his school and friends, when suddenly he became possessed. He jumped up and began to spin around, dancing, pinching ladies' bottoms, then went to the center post, kind of an altar where people placed offerings of food, drink or cigarettes for the spirits.

"He was being possessed by Papa Gèdé, a hard drinking, heavy smoking, fast-talking spirit. I saw the young boy pick up a pint of tafia, the first distilling of rum that is fiery and tastes like kerosene. Tafia is spiced with red hot peppers and steeped for weeks. The boy then donned a black top hat and lit two cigarettes, smoking them both at once, typical of Papa Gèdé. He drank the bottle dry and continued dancing around, then suddenly collapsed. Several of the other participants picked him up and carried him into the hounfor. Fifteen minutes later, he came out without the top hat, walked over and sat down next to me, picking up his conversation where he had left off as if nothing had happened. He didn't remember any of it. I poured some of the dregs from his empty bottle on the palm of my hand and tasted it. My tongue burned for hours afterwards. That boy should have been dead."

Cave always took notes through the ceremonies as well as his excursions and then went back to the rented house to write out a complete description. "I had a good memory for details. I carried a notepad in my hip pocket to make little notes to myself, then transcribed all the details later. For instance, one day I met a woman with a goiter. We talked and then I remembered how she came up the trail, how we stopped to talk, where she lived, how she lived, other questions I asked her, all remembered with one line on my notepad, 'woman with goiter.' "

The woman would later become a character in Cave's very first paperback novel, *Legion of the Dead* (copyright 1979, Avon Books):

> An emaciated young woman with a huge goiter on her neck and a small baby in her arms told them the stream was the Rio Malo now. She had a thatch-roofed hut, a garden, and a half-blind husband who could not speak . . . Like Julio Andar, the woman said she lived very simply. She had her house, she had the river for water, she had her garden for food. "We eat mostly yams. Sometimes we hunt for nuts and fruits in the forest. Now and then we catch a few crayfish in the stream."[4]

His experiences also included encounters with those well-known creatures of Haitian lore, zombies. One of them was used in *Legion of the Dead* word-for-word as told to him by a Catholic priest. Only the names were different:

> "He had an amazing experience while he was living back there in the mountains. A ten-year-old girl of his village died and he buried her. He was right there at the grave when she was put into the ground. He signed her death certificate . . . Two years later," Cary continued, "Father Lanier was transferred to another village some twenty miles distant in which there was a *bocor*, a witch doctor, who was giving the people a rough time. They asked him to get rid of the fellow for them. He went to the man's house to check up on him and found there a vacant-eyed, seemingly mindless girl the *bocor* was keeping in slavery, so to speak, to attend to his needs. The same girl the priest had buried two years before."
>
> "How could he be sure after two years?"
>
> "He couldn't be, of course, and knew it. So he took her away from the *bocor* and looked after her, and when she seemed to show some improvement he questioned her about her home village. It was no good. She didn't remember anything. But he couldn't let it rest with

> that, he told me, so he put her on his mule one day and took her back there. And when he rode into the village with her, the people looked at her in amazement and called her by name . . . She jumped down off the father's mule and ran straight to her own house."[14]

Cave never found himself far from danger during his years in Haiti, especially traveling over treacherous back roads and trails. "I didn't think of being in danger at the time because it was the only way to get around. The risks today are far different. I wouldn't go there with the family like I did in those days. Back then you worried about the car breaking down or getting stuck in a stream; today you worry about theft and bodily harm."

He may minimize the risks he took, but the risks were there, nonetheless. "The dirt road from Okeye over the mountains to Jérémie on the South Peninsula was often no more than one car wide. At one point along the way, we were on the edge of a steep decline next to a river that was hundreds of feet down. It was raining and a two-foot wide boulder fell off a cliff onto the mud-slick road. The only way to proceed was to drive over it because we couldn't wait for help. The Jeep had heavy treaded tires, so I figured if I kept the wheels on the boulder as they passed over it, I would be okay, but if the wheels slipped, our Jeep would go over the edge. I sent Margaret and the boys ahead, then drove over the boulder. At one point the Jeep slipped and almost fell off."

The Caves returned to Providence by the end of April 1951. He immediately plunged into finishing his book. As soon as it was complete, he sent his manuscript off to the publisher. Cave spent the rest of that year making up for lost time with his slick magazine markets. The competition for high paying stories was fierce and absence from the marketplace for any length of time could be costly. He published only 31 stories that year, 18 of them foreign reprints. One of his stories, "The Silent Horror," was broadcast on the CBS Radio show, *Escape,* August 2, 1951.

Haiti: High Road to Adventure came out in 1952. It wasn't a travel book, but a family adventure book. Cave did not recommend hotels to stay in or where to eat. He combined an interesting mixture of Haitian history, culture, lifestyle, exploration and personal family experiences. It sold well and Cave became an acknowledged expert. Reviews were quite positive:

> More than a guide book. An over-all writing job that is extremely competent, bright, and well organized.—*Christian Science Monitor*[1]

> Probably no white man has ever understood the complexities of voodoo, but Mr. Cave comes as close as professional anthropologists and vividly conveys his impressions to the reader. He gives an account of an exotic land that makes one long to catch the next plane or steamer for a first visit or a tenth.—*N.Y. Herald Tribune*[1]

> While invaluable for the Haiti-bound traveler, Mr. Cave's work is better yet—a sensible, undramatic insight to the strange African ways of the spectacular republic.—*Saturday Review of Literature*[2]

> An engaging story of family adventure, of life in one of the most picturesque Caribbean republics, presented against the background of the island's dramatic past. Supplemented by 47 magnificent photographs (taken by the author) it is a delightful book, the most up-to-date guide to this strange and exotic island that has yet been published.—*Travel Book Club*[1]

"I gave lectures about Haiti, appeared on television and radio. I might get $25 for giving a talk and I sent the money down to Sister Joan's school. I received a ton of publicity at the time.

Chapter 24: Mission to Massif du Sud

In January 1952, with *Haiti: High Road to Adventure* due to be released, the family returned for their third winter in Haiti. While *Haiti: High Road to Adventure* was the high point for Cave in 1952, it was not his only accomplishment. He sold the rights for his *Saturday Evening Post* story, "Murder Island," to CBS Radio. Of the 38 stories he sold that year, 18 went to foreign publications, including one to Malaysia in the South Pacific.

The following winter, in January of 1953, Cave made plans with Dr. Charles Deichman for a second tour of Haiti, this time across the country's mountainous Southern Peninsula, or Massif du Sud, and this time primarily on foot. The Massif du Sud featured vast tracts of unexplored rain forest.

"We flew to Les Cayes, rented riding mules and a pack mule, then proceeded along the coast to Tiburon. There at the end of the road we got rid of the riding mules because they couldn't navigate the wilderness, hired a 17-year-old lad to accompany us with the pack mule, and hiked up the Tiburon River to its source at the top of the Massif du Sud.

"After crossing the Massif, we followed the Grande Anse River from its source down to the town of Jérémie on the peninsula's north coast. Most of our travel was by raft, for which we paid 40¢. Standard pay for peasants on an inland plantation was $20 per year, which bought as much as $1,000 in the U.S. We met very few people in there. Some locals even thought Haiti was still a French colony. Most of the trip took us through heavy rain forest, which I'm told is now totally wiped out."

This trip served as the basis for his 1979 novel, *Legion of the Dead*, which takes place in the fictitious, but thinly-veiled country of San Marlo:

> La Cordillera del Sud, the mountains were called on the big, bamboo-framed map on the wall of the bungalow's sitting room. The map showed no roads, not even trails. That vast range of mountains separated the north and south coasts of San Marlo as effectively as a wall laid up to heaven.[14]

Cave enjoyed his excursions across the country, but gradually he did more and more of them alone. As Margaret's enthusiasm for the country cooled, Cave's grew. He even made several visits in between family trips to do research for stories or articles he was writing, or possibly for no reason other than his passion for Haiti. After the first few years, Margaret came more as the dutiful wife than explorer-partner. "She wasn't particularly happy about being left alone in a strange country, but filled her days working at the school with Sister Joan."

Eventually, with one exception, Margaret stopped coming altogether.

The next three years, 1953 through 1955, were productive for Cave. His Haiti book continued to sell and he published approximately 154 stories including reprints, 93 of them in foreign publications. The surge in foreign reprints since the late 1940's was because Cave now had an English agent, Innes Rose with the John Farquharson Ltd. Agency in London. "I would send him copies of all my published stories and he would sell what he could throughout the European market."

Cave did manage to break into some of the top slicks during this period, *Esquire* and *Cosmopolitan*. Pulps were not entirely out of the picture, still providing him a handful of opportunities each year to revisit his roots. Two more Cave stories made it to television in 1954—"The Woman At Fog Point" appeared on *Ford Television Theater* and "Danger By Night," a Haiti story that starred David Niven. One of his novelettes, "Drums of Revolt," was actually a 90,000-word novel published in the *Toronto Star Weekly.* They had published "The Midnight Horde" as a condensed novel back in 1938. *Drums of Revolt* would be published as a book too, but only in England (1957, Robert Hale, LTD).

Chapter 25: Cross on the Drum

Dr. Deichman wasn't Cave's only adventure-seeking partner during the Haiti years. In August 1956, he and Father Harry Smith, along with another priest, Father Leon Muller, trekked by Jeep to the Ile de la Tortue off Haiti's north coast. "It used to be known as Tortuga Island in the buccaneer days. A church mission was now on the island and Father Smith knew the priest running it. He was a former French Army officer, Father Pierre Riou, who decided to become a priest and go somewhere he would really be needed. He took some courses in medicine and dentistry, then got the church to send him there. He built a small house of worship on the island with help from the locals."

This trip formed the basis for what became Hugh Cave's best selling novel, *The Cross on the Drum.* The lead character in that novel, Barry Clinton, was fashioned after Father Pierre Riou (who later wrote a book himself, *Good-Bye To Turtle Island*).

> He had become infected with an obsession to do something about the poverty in these troubled countries. Quite deliberately he had chosen the church as his instrument, but what the church stood for was incidental, really. If his teachers at theological school had insisted he memorize the Bible backward to qualify for the mission field, Barry would have done so.[17]

This trip also served as the inspiration for his 1981 book, *The Evil,* as well as one of Cave's more recent short stories, "Mission to Margal."

"We explored every inch of the island, which was 15 miles long, one and a half mile wide, with steep cliffs that drop into the ocean on its north side. It faced the channel where Columbus lost his ship, the Santa Maria."

Cave also had an idea he wanted to explore. "Haiti had become a second home to me and I even thought of making it my first home. So Father Smith and I not only went to the Ile de la Tortue on that visit, we also looked around for plantations that might be for sale."

He returned home without finding a suitable property, but the idea of owning a plantation in Haiti had gripped his imagination as the next big adventure. Meanwhile, he began writing *The Cross on the Drum.* "I would sit on the living room sofa every evening with my portable typewriter while Margaret and the boys watched television."

While Cave spent evenings writing his novel in front of the TV set, his days were dedicated to writing stories which paid the bills. In 1956–1957, he sold 96 short stories and articles; incredibly, 60 of them foreign sales, not including the book, *Drums of Revolt,* published in England. He also adds more prestigious slicks to his dossier with *Redbook* (his first story, "Woman at the Shrine," was promoted on the February 1957 issue's cover) and *Woman's Day.* Eight stories during this period appeared in the *Saturday Evening Post.*

His greatest book writing success was yet to come, however. "One day I received a letter from Anne Einselen, fiction editor for *Ladies Home Journal,* asking me what I was doing lately. You didn't do everything by telephone in those days. I wrote back that I was just finishing a novel, but she probably wouldn't be interested in it because it had to do with Haiti and voodoo and the conflict between religions.

"She wrote to me again and said she wanted to see it. I telephoned to verify her interest, still sure I would be wasting my time sending it to her. I went ahead and mailed her the manuscript. I was surprised and delighted when she wrote back and said she wanted to do an excerpt in *Ladies Home Journal.*"

Einselen scheduled the excerpt to appear in November 1958. She was apparently so impressed with *The Cross on the Drum,* she contacted Cave again and asked his permission to show the manuscript to George Shively, editor at Doubleday.

"Shively called me after reading it and said he had read about voodoo before, but this was the first thing that was convincing. He told me they would like to publish it."

Cave was elated, but his good fortune did not end there. "Shively called me back one day and said I've got good news for you. Dollar Book Club is taking it and that will mean a printing of 500,000 copies. These are the days before Stephen King made half a million seem like piker's figures."

The book also ended up as a Literary Guild Bonus Selection. It was published in English and Dutch hardcover editions as well, then in paperback here in the U.S. and in England, all in 1959.

The book's main characters were Barry Clinton, the aforementioned white Catholic missionary patterned after Father Riou, and a black voodoo high priest, Catus Laroche. They are both friends and enemies, respectful of each other but competing for the allegiance—and souls—of the people they serve. In an interview with the *Providence Journal* on April 26, 1959, Cave says:

> In just over three years residence in Haiti I saw that both voodoo and Christianity were looking for the same answers, yet both have always been shown in conflict. I thought it might be useful to portray their similarities through a sensitive Christian and a wise voodoo leader. Implicit in the book's problems also are tangled relations of white and black.[1]

This story takes place on a small island called "Ile du Vent" (Ile de la Tortue), off the coast of the Caribbean island of "St. Joseph" (Haiti). The Reverend Barry Clinton is "banished" to Ile du Vent by an angry Bishop because of Barry's articles proclaiming the natives need medical and social help more than mere Sunday sermons. Barry is replacing an older missionary who has been defeated by the island's voodoo priest, Catus LaRoche. At once Barry finds himself in conflict with Catus, but, fighting back, proceeds to build a church.

Catus has a sister. She and Barry are the sole survivors when a small boat is caught in a storm between the island and the mainland. When the boat crashes against the island rocks, Micheline leads Barry to a secret cave where voodoo rites are held. There she offers herself to him, and when he explains that her desire for him could lead only to destruction, her love turns to hate. When she becomes pregnant with a white planter on the island, she blames Barry, causing a deadly war to erupt between Barry and her brother.

Attempts are made to kill Barry. He also has to fight Warner Lemke, the only other white man on the island and a contemptuous destroyer of everything Barry has achieved. But Alma Lemke, Warner's wife, is on Barry's side and ends up being Barry's wife after her husband is killed. Barry and Catus end up as friends.

As for the conflict between Christianity and voodoo, the novel ends with the following lines:

> *Mon frère*, Barry thought. *My brother.* A curious phrase for Catus to use, and the first time he had ever used it.

Brothers. A *vodun houngan* and a Christian missionary. A black man and a white.

This was the real beginning.[15]

The Cross on the Drum became Cave's best selling novel. The following reviews explained why:

> An exciting tale, told with chilling suspense. The characters will not easily be forgotten. Readers who haven't been to Haiti will be as close to that astonishing experience as a novel and an armchair will ever get them.—*New York Times*[1]

> The setting is exotic, the story line is twisted tight, the characters are recognizable, living types, and individual episodes and scenes scream with drama and suspense.—*Afro-American,* Baltimore, MD[1]

> Novels about Haiti, and specifically vodun (voodoo) in Haiti, are no longer a rarity; but "The Cross on the Drum" is the first to my knowledge that treats both the country and its African religious cult with profound sympathy. It is a sympathy born of understanding. Even were one not familiar with the author's delightful account of living among the Haitians ("Haiti: Highroad to Adventure") one would be certain from the novel that he had entered into native life with much more than a tourist's curiosity or a novelist's determination to mine a rich vein.—*Haiti Sun*[1]

The last review held particular significance because it came from local Haitians, not the foreign press. Albest Bertrand founded the *Haitian Sun* in 1950, and came to know Cave over his years in the country. He now lives in Miami, Florida. "We knew the same Haiti," says Bertrand. "I am glad someone is writing about Hugh; he is a wonderful subject."

The Cross on the Drum became movie material as well. "Doubleday thought they would get a movie from the book. Harry Belafonte was considered for the role of Catus Larouche and James Mason as priest Barry Clinton. However, Belafonte had just finished making *Island in the Sun,* and it hadn't done well. So the movie based on my book was never made."

Chapter 26: The Unwelcome Tourist

After the first three years, Cave continued visiting Haiti, but Margaret rarely joined him and the boys never came at all. His love for the country had diminished little, but he was anxious for a new adventure.

"One day in 1957, I visited with *Saturday Evening Post* editor, Stuart Rose, telling him I was thinking about what to do next, when he said, 'We've published a lot of your West Indies stories, Hugh; why not take a trip to Mexico and write some fiction based on it.' "

That was all he needed to hear. "It was summertime, the kids were out of school and I didn't want to just stay home and work around the yard."

So they jumped into the family Packard and drove to Mexico. "We left in June and came back in time for school to start in the fall, traveling all over Mexico, staying in tiny pensions, exploring caverns and then continuing up to Niagara Falls.

"It was a great trip except for car troubles. About halfway to Mexico, the roof began to drip black sealant and something in the door rattled. The Packard four-door sedan was an expensive car in those days. In San Antonio, the window glass fell out and we couldn't get it back in to lock the car, so we had a new window installed. Just outside Mexico City, the rear end was acting up, so I pulled into a garage. They sent me to the Packard garage in Mexico City. Many wealthy Mexicans were driving Packards. The garage was almost a block long with sections for engine, body, rear end, etc. It turns out the manufacturer had neglected to put any grease in the rear end."

In spite of his car troubles, Cave spent most of the summer driving around Mexico. That trip resulted in a number of stories. Cave relates how these stories came about. "In the town of Pachuca, where we stopped at a small hotel, a boy about ten years old named Miguel volunteered to wash our Packard and we became friendly. He took us to visit his family nearby.

"The boy was a big baseball fan and his two heroes were Ted Williams and Yogi Berra. Upon returning home, I wrote to both players asking them for autographed photos I could send to the lad. Ted Williams signed his name; Yogi Berra wrote something like, 'To my friend Miguel with all good wishes, from your friend Yogi Berra.' The youngster was ecstatic and wrote me a long thank you letter in Spanish. We continued a correspondence for more than a year. He would take my letters to his school where they were used as lessons in his English class. I translated his letters to me with the help of a Spanish dictionary and what I remembered of my high school Spanish course.

"Several story ideas grew out of remarks he made in those letters. 'The Unwelcome Tourist,' 'Terror in the Town,' and the novelette, 'Bannigan's War' come to mind. After a while our correspondence just faded away. I often wonder what kind of life that little Mexican boy had."

"Bannigan's War," probably the best known of the three, was optioned for a movie at one point. Cave describes it as "one of the best adventure yarns I ever wrote."

It concerns a Texan in the fictional Central American country of San Nicolas, trying to reclaim water and land so local peasants can grow bananas. He runs afoul of some politicians and a revolution sweeps the country. Bannigan ends up saving the country, getting rid of the evil politicians and saves a young nurse.

Meanwhile, back in Haiti, Papa Doc Duvalier came to power. The country was losing its innocence, the mood darker. "On our visit to Haiti the prior year, we saw a great deal of political unrest. It was just before Papa Doc Duvalier became president. Margaret and I were both in Port-au-Prince at the time.

One morning I went to call on a friend, Joel Kenter, a Swiss man who owned a little pension (hotel) across the Champ de Mars from the National Palace. This is the pension I called The Etoile in my book, *The Witching Lands*; it's real name was Mon Reve (My Dream). Margaret meanwhile, had gone to the School for Handicapped Children to spend some time with her friend Sister Joan Margaret.

"Well, Sister Joan had an errand to run, so Meg went with her and they got caught in one of the worst riots. As they headed back to the school through the erupting city, with cars being overturned and store windows being smashed all around them, Sister Joan said something like, 'Keep looking straight ahead. Don't say anything. They know who I am—I'm the Sister who helps their children.' It was a frightening experience, especially with the rioters pounding with rocks and sticks on metal street poles all over Port-au-Prince."

This incident, along with the general unrest surrounding Duvalier's ascent to power, ended up in Cave's 1960 novel, *Black Sun* (Doubleday and Company), set again in a fictitous country—St. Joseph (Haiti) and city—St. Joe City (Port-au-Prince).

> They were striking the steel utility poles along the streets with sticks or stones. The wires were carrying the vibration, setting the air in motion.

> Down a line of shops they went, smashing windows.
>
> Hour after hour the rioting continued. Rifles could not stop it. Machine guns could not stop it.[16]

"Meanwhile, I was at the Mon Reve. I went up to the top floor and looked out. As I've said, this little pension was directly across the Champ de Mars from the Presidential palace. The Champ was a sea of people marching, yelling, threatening to take the city apart. Joel and I fully expected them to storm the pension, and at one point it seemed they were going to, but soldiers appeared and broke up the mob. All that rioting in *Black Sun* is basically true, along with the business of the general strikes, the shopkeepers being forced to keep their shops open, etc."

The book's main character is David Middleton, an American writer who returns to the fictitious island republic of St. Joseph to live permanently. His return during a presidential campaign mirrors Cave's own circumstances around the political upheaval that brought Papa Doc Duvalier to power. Middleton and the book's other main characters are swept up in a carefully staged revolution that shatters their lives and forces them to leave the island.

One of the characters, Philip Grant, worked for the island's newspaper, called *The Banner.* It is based on the actual newspaper, the *Haiti Sun,* and the Danny character, on a real newspaper man named Bernard Diederich, an Australian by birth. According to Diederich, who lives today in Miami, Florida, "Cave used to visit me when he was in Port-au-Prince and I once made him 'Personality of the Week.' His book was modeled on my own trials and tribulations during the 1957 election period. We knew the same Haiti."

Diederich went on to author three books on Caribbean dictators and wrote for *Time,* the *New York Times,* Associated Press and *Life.*

In January 1958, Cave returned for another trek across the northern half of Haiti with Father Smith. He sensed immediately that the country had changed. However, he still kept alive his dream of owning a plantation. On his north trip with Father Smith, he finally found a property that intrigued him.

"I was interested in becoming a coffee planter and found a place up in Port Margot on the north coast. It was in a lovely valley and a river ran through the property. I could have bought 500 acres. Father Smith had called the property owner and said he wanted to come up and look at this land we were going to buy together. Georges Leger was my attorney, which helped give us credibility. I made an offer and a friend even designed a house I could build. I purchased the materials and shipped them to the valley. I also bought a secondhand yellow Jeep pick-up truck that Father Smith called 'The Beast.' We loaded it up with supplies we would need to build the house and drove it to the valley.

"But then Georges Leger advised me not to buy the property. He said there was an old man who lived in the valley named Mitredot; I had actually met him. Georges said he had loaned money to many peasants in the valley, then foreclosed on them when they couldn't pay him back. Bits and pieces of the valley property I wanted to buy actually belonged to him. To get them, there was no telling what might happen down the road if I became successful growing coffee. Georges told me the old man would find a way to get the property back, so don't buy it."

Cave did not go through with the purchase, which was probably fortunate because he had never discussed it with Margaret. He and Father Smith continued on their north coast trip. They returned to Ile de la Tortue and visited the missionary priest, Father Riou, whom they met two years earlier. "We had a great time and forgot about the plantation, giving Father Riou all the materials on our truck. We drove back to Port-au-Prince and donated our truck to the Boy Scouts."

Cave knew his relationship with this country he had grown to love was nearing its end. He booked a return flight to the U.S. and spent a nostalgic last night at Mon Reve pension with his friend, Joel Kenter.

"I met two girls at the Mon Reve's outdoor café, Mary Evans and Lela Dutt. They were English, but lived in Jamaica. Lela was a school teacher; she taught botany and had written a book on botany of the West Indies. Mary was the ex-wife of Peter Evans, who had been the attorney for Jomo Kenyatta, Kenya's founding father, and had written a book called *Law and Disorder,* about the Kenyatta trials.

"We had a nice talk; they became characters in *The Witching Lands* along with Joel—Max Hahn in the book. As the evening drew to a close, they said they were headed back to Jamaica and suggested I fly back with them to see the island and meet Peter."

Of course, Cave the adventurer could not resist, and accepted their offer without hesitation.

The next day, he left his beloved Haiti, but he was less concerned with that than the prospect of starting his newest adventure.

"When we arrived in Kingston, Peter Evans met us at the airport. In fact, I ended up staying at his house. Mary and Lela lived together."

Cave only spent a few days in Kingston, but it was enough to convince him that he wanted to spend some quality time there. He never imagined how much time.

PART SIX: FOUR PATHS TO PARADISE

Chapter 27: Welcome to Kingston

THOUGH HE DIDN'T KNOW IT AT THE TIME, CAVE would never return to Haiti. "The country lost its innocence under him (Duvalier). Today it is a dangerous place; you couldn't go there to live anymore like I did. Much of the beauty is gone too. I look at the photos I took, even the ones in my book. Today, those forests are gone. The country was deforested under Papa Doc and his cronies. They gave the peasants permission to burn trees on government land and make charcoal to sell, but half the money had to go to them. The peasants didn't know how to make charcoal efficiently and wasted so much of the wood."

However, he had not seen the last of his friends, Father Harry Smith and Dr. Charles Deichman. Nor was he finished with Haiti as subject matter for his story mill. Sister Joan Margaret of the School for Handicapped children in Port-au-Prince had introduced Cave to children at her school. Some of them inspired several of his stories, "Little Girl in Black Stockings," which appeared first in the *Saturday Evening Post,* "The Child Who Didn't Exist," published in *The Toronto Star Weekly* and his most famous slick story, "The Mission."

"The Mission" appeared in the March 14, 1959 issue of *Saturday Evening Post.* Based on a true story, "The Mission" is about a six-year-old Haitian girl named Yolande St. Juste. In the story, her mother dies and she walks alone to Port-au-Prince, 90 miles away to find a father who may or may not exist outside her mother's imagination. Yolande touches many people's lives along her way. One encounter involved two women washing their clothes in the river and having an argument:

> Yolande halted and looked down at them. "Hello," she said. Her voice was a song—a sad one, true, but still a song.
>
> One of the women sullenly looked up, flipping soap from long black fingers. "Hello, yourself. What do you want?"
>
> "I don't want anything, thank you. Just—would you tell me if this is the road to Port-au-Prince, please?"
>
> "The road to where?"
>
> "Port-au-Prince. You know, the capital."
>
> "*Mes amis!*" the woman exclaimed in wonder, and thrust out a bare foot to nudge her companion. "Did you hear that? The child wants to know if this is the road to the capital!"
>
> Her companion stopped work and frowned at Yolande. "You are thinking of going to the capital, *ti-fi*?"
>
> "I have to. My papa lives there and I have to find him. *Maman* died yesterday."
>
> "Oh-oh. Where do you live?"
>
> "Nowhere now. I did live in Aquin. *Maman* kept house for some people there."
>
> "Well, little one, you have come sixteen miles and have seventy-five more to go."
>
> "That far?"
>
> "That far, yes."
>
> "I'd better hurry then," Yolande said, and put her dusty feet in motion again. Then, remembering her manners, she turned her head. "Thank you very much."
>
> The women watched her go down the road, then looked at each other in silence and returned to their washing. As the paddles flew, a gob of soap sailed through the air and splashed against a dress spread out to dry.
>
> "Oh-oh, that was clumsy of me," the culprit said. "I shouldn't have let that happen, no. I'll wash it over for you."
>
> "A little soap won't break a friendship," the other replied. "Get on with your work so we can walk home together."[17]

The story was accompanied by a full-page portrait of the heroine by painter Peter Stevens. "The *Post*'s art department reported no other illustration had rivaled it for amount, duration and enthusiasm of reader reaction. I was in Haiti when the story came out and showed the picture to Sister Joan Margaret, who had told me about the girl on which I based my story. She said the artist's painting looked just like the actual girl and then introduced me to her. Peter Stevens only had my story on which to base his concept, yet you would think she actually sat for a portrait."

The story became so popular, Doubleday did a hardcover gift book the following year. Reviews were highly complimentary:

> Into 31 handsomely printed pages, Hugh B. Cave has managed to compress the clear-eyed innocence of childhood, a quality universal in the very young but so evanescent that it is seldom successfully transferred to paper.—*Milwaukee Journal*[1]

> A beautifully told tale, warm and moving, tugging at the heart. A short and simple story, but a story powerful in its emotional impact. —*Times News,* Kingsport, Tennessee[1]

It ended up being reprinted 16 times in seven countries, including what is now Malaysia. Cave also sold film rights, but, just as with "Murgunstrumm" and *The Cross on the Drum,* no movie was ever made.

In addition to "The Mission," Cave published 46 short stories and reprints in 1959, 34 of them in foreign publications, as well as his book, *The Cross on the Drum.* Though the book did very well overall, thanks to the book clubs, it didn't make any bestseller lists. "Bookstores generally didn't handle book club selections and mine was in two book clubs."

However, the time had come for Cave to stoke the fires of his imagination with a new adventure and his sights were set on Jamaica. Based on the strength of his success with *Haiti: High Road to Adventure,* he had no problem finding a publisher to finance his first trip to Jamaica so he could write a similar book about that country.

His newfound friends, Mary Evans and Lela Dutt, helped him arrange a rental house in Kingston. He looked forward to exploring the country and reliving the excitement of his family's first days in Haiti.

Unfortunately, his family didn't feel the same way. "Ken had graduated from high school and found a job, so it was just Margaret, Donnie and me. We enrolled Donnie in a private school called The Priory, on Hope Road. It had a very good reputation, English system. Donnie played soccer there and enjoyed it.

"Margaret wasn't very enthused though. I had purchased a car, a little English Prefect, navy blue. We were going to drive around to visit some of the old great houses, and her first time behind the wheel she almost ran into someone because they drive on the left side of the road. From that point on, she refused to drive anywhere. Eventually, we bought a home that was 17 miles from the nearest town and she became a prisoner in her own house. We lived there 15 years and she never drove. Margaret had a streak where once she made up her mind about something, nothing could change it."

About a month after they arrived, their 20-year-old son, Ken, paid them a visit to discuss something very urgent and important in his life. "He wanted to marry his high school sweetheart and came down to talk with us about it. We went out to the veranda of our rented house. I had a dart game, so we played a while. Then I said we have to talk.

"I told him he was much too young for marriage now, that everything seemed wrong about it—she didn't have the same personality, they belonged to different religions and he really didn't know her. She probably didn't even know herself since she was younger than Ken. She had thrown herself at him and it appeared that her family was pressuring her to get married. I was fairly well known at the time and speculated that if Ken had a different Dad, her family might not be as anxious for them to get married.

"We had a good relationship with our boys and they always felt they could discuss personal problems with us. So Ken took our advice and broke off the relationship. Several years later, we were back home and he called us one night to say, 'I've met the girl I'm going to marry. Will you come up and meet her?' We did, met her folks too, went out to dinner and had a great time. Her name was Betsy and they had a lot in common—they were both teachers and musicians, he on the trombone, she on the flute. They've been married over 30 years."

That brought up a point. I asked Cave if people treated him differently, being known as a writer. "There was a small sense of that, living in Warwick and having pieces about me and my trips to Haiti in the local paper. I guess people knew that I wrote, but no one ever asked about what kind of work I really did."

His comment was tongue-in-cheek. Most people do not see writing as a career nine-to-five job, but more as a hobby that can make you rich and famous if you are lucky. Movies and books about writers leave the impression that they don't have to work too hard and lead glamorous lives. Ironically, the people who write those movies and books know best how difficult a job it is.

Cave plunged into his new Jamaican adventure with childlike enthusiasm, dragging Margaret along for the ride. "We drove around investigating great houses and ended up in the Blue Mountains. The beauty of the area was stunning and not well-known to vacationers who tended to limit their visits to the outlying beaches. I decided to find a rental house up there where I could finish writing my Jamaica book in the cool mountains away from Kingston's heat and noise.

"We found one abandoned coffee plantation called Arntully, with a 17-room, 200-year-old house. It was the nearest place to Blue Mountain peak, at 7,400 feet, the highest point in Jamaica. The house sat at the end of a road, the last parish (district) dirt road above Morant Bay. Eric Foote was the chap who showed us the house and he suggested we rent it. The place was partially furnished and cheap."

He describes the great house in his book on Jamaica, *Four Paths to Paradise: A Book About Jamaica* (1961, Doubleday & Company, Inc., Garden City, New York):

> First, the house. You get lost in it. You start for somewhere and meet yourself coming back. . . . At Arntully, nothing is functional. You don't get from Point A to Point B in the fewest possible steps; you are lucky to get there at all.[18]

In spite of his criticisms, Arntully Great House found its way into a number of Hugh Cave stories and books, including *Run, Shadow, Run, Disciples of Dread, Lucifer's Eye* and *Conquering Kilmarnie.* Among the short stories woven around the house would be "The Island of Eve," in *Good Housekeeping,* "Jamaica Storm," in the *Saturday Evening Post,* and "The Wild One" in *Ladies Home Journal.*

Arntully Great House was located three miles from the nearest post office and telephone. He hadn't settled in for long when Cave found out he could buy the property. His fantasy about owning a coffee plantation was alive and kicking again, except this time in Jamaica, not Haiti. As was so often the case for Hugh Cave, the line between fantasy and reality became blurred.

"Margaret must have thought I was a Don Quixote at some point, always going off on some adventure. I think she really didn't want to go to Haiti, but became interested once she got involved with the school for handicapped children. Every day she would drive the two boys to school, then go on to Sister Joan's school and work with the little black kids."

Jamaica didn't spark that same level of interest for Margaret though, as he soon found out.

Chapter 28: Hugh Cave, Farmer-Author

The following winter, Hugh and Margaret Cave returned to their 17-room rental home, but this time neither of the boys joined them. Ken was now attending college and they had placed Donnie in the Moses Brown private school in Providence before leaving. Cave had also made a major decision. "I bought all the land north of the dirt road, 541 acres, everything except the Great House we were living in, which we rented while building a new home for ourselves."

The new Cave home, designed by architect Hugh Cave, and built by general contractor Hugh Cave, featured a 40-foot living room, two bedrooms, a master bath and a second bath near the back for a maid. "The Great House had electricity provided by a turbine at the coffee co-op. I put in my own turbine for the new house. Fresh water came down from the mountain peak in open gutters. We were at 3,000 feet and the peak was over 7,000 feet. Water was gravity fed right from the river without any filtration; there were no humans above us to pollute it. We used the same water to drive our turbine, as well as the turbine down at the co-op. Our only problem occurred when the gutter would block up with leaves, so we had to clean it out regularly, but the water was fresh and natural."

The home cost him about $20,000 to build, the same price he paid for the 541 acres of "ruinate" plantation. "When the English settled Jamaica, the Scots came to farm coffee. Arntully was built by a Scot named Shepherd back in 1779. I still have the survey information going back to then. No one had worked the plantation for more than 100 years.

"The co-op owned the plantation and sold it to me when I told them I would farm it. They knew the land was capable of producing prize coffee but they didn't have the capital to plant it. I had just come off *The Cross on the Drum,* which made me good money, so I put that money into the plantation."

He was ecstatic about owning a plantation with a storied past. However, the co-op wouldn't allow him to name his new plantation "Arntully," since it did not include the original great house, so Cave decided to call it "Arntully Highlands."

His wife was less than ecstatic. "Margaret went along with everything but I don't think she liked the idea of becoming coffee farmers."

So Cave tried to make living conditions as comfortable as possible for her. "We didn't have a live-in maid like in Haiti, but the maid we did have came every day at seven in the morning and went home after dark. She was the only help we hired, unlike Haiti where we had a cook, gardener and a maid."

Cave then set about learning how to grow coffee. "I went to the Jamaica Institute in Kingston and researched the archives to learn the history of this plantation. In its heyday, the coffee grown there won all kinds of prizes and Blue Mountain coffee was the most expensive in the world."

He acquired his knowledge about coffee growing the same way he learned about everything in his life—by reading books and asking questions. His interest in the subject began, of course, in Haiti. Now he actually owned a plantation—a real one and no longer a book-inspired fantasy.

"The local co-op was most interested in my success, especially its manager, Eric Foote, who happened to be the same man who first rented Arntully Great House to me. He owned the plantation next door to us and we became friends.

"Foote was an almost white Jamaican, handsome and rugged; he looked a little like early movie actor William S. Hart. His wife, Nelly, was very nice and we got to know them well. He had shown us around the area when we first visited the prior year, before we even considered buying a plantation."

Foote convinced Cave to buy the plantation—not that he needed a great deal of coaxing. "The co-op was nearby and they agreed to buy all my coffee. They also processed and shipped our coffee beans. Maybe 50 peasant farmers sold to this co-op, called the Moy Hall Cooperative, which also grew its own coffee.

"Eric helped me get a head man and workers, then showed me how to plant trees. We had to remove all the existing trees first and it was backbreaking work. Anytime I had a question though, I just walked one-third of a mile to Eric's place for an answer."

Cave quickly adapted to the farmer's life. He was up at the first light of dawn to meet with his workers in their yard. Then he would get something to eat, and go work in the fields all day, inspecting, managing, and transporting crews.

His plantation workers came from the little town of Ness Castle. He had no permanent employees; they just showed up every day. "This part of Jamaica was originally settled by Scots—Arntully was the name of a clan seat in Scotland. Shepherd was the original owner of the great house, so the black slaves took the name of their master. Many of the locals were still named Shepherd."

"Some days, Margaret would go in to town with me, or occasionally we drove to Kingston, which took half a day, but that was the only time she got away from the house.

"It was an awful life for her. I think she would have liked the plantation, except she made herself a prisoner from the first day. She was very stubborn—'no' meant forever. She could have had a good life there on her own, particularly since she wasn't fond of me anyway."

While Cave worked most of his days on the plantation, he spent his evenings writing the books and stories that paid their bills. In 1960, which reflected his writing efforts before the plantation purchase, he was published 53 times. One of his short stories, "Spell of a Stranger," made it to *General Electric Television Theater.* Though published 53 times, he accomplished it with only 14 different stories. That included 11 reprints and other rights to "The Mission." Not surprisingly, 36 of those 53 published works were foreign sales.

He also published his previously mentioned novel, *Black Sun,* in the U.S. and England. Reviews of the book were generally positive:

> Riot, rebellion, issues of race, grim political chicanery, dictatorship, police brutality and assassination. The action occurs in a convincingly three-dimensional world, especially when the native characters have the stage.—*New York Times* [1]

> Cave writes with a narrative power and skill which lift this novel beyond the ordinary run of political West-Indies-set books.—*The Gleaner,* Jamaica, W.I.[1]

> The reader's interest is sustained from the start and develops later into an engrossed fascination by the passionate and fast-moving denouement. This novel is of interest and excitement to the reader who has tired of the superficial.—*Kirkus Reviews* [1]

> Hugh Cave has written about a people he knows well and he

keeps his story as taut as a bowstring from first to last.—*Personality*, South Africa[1]

> As exciting as a best-seller thriller. The English author, H.B. Cave, is a natural story teller, with a fine sense of situation and character.—*Belfast Ireland News-Letter*[1]

The book once again demonstrated Cave's breadth as a writer. While *The Cross on the Drum* dealt with conflicts in belief, *Black Sun* was a mainstream political thriller. Its thinly veiled portrayal of actual Haitian political events provides tremendous insight about the island nation's character, insights that are as sound today as they were back then. The book did fairly well, but quickly sank into obscurity, which begs the question: given Cave's talent for writing what people want to read and his formidable resume, why weren't his first two major novels more of a lasting success? Some answers will emerge later.

Cave's publishing credits in 1961 reflected a sharp drop in his creative output and preoccupation with coffee farming—he sold one book and 24 stories, 16 of them reprints.

The one book, *Four Paths to Paradise: A Book About Jamaica,* did for Jamaica what *Haiti: High Road to Adventure* did for that country. A review in the *Newark News* best describes it:

> Hugh Cave, his wife and two sons established a home on the island of Jamaica. Then the author looked, explored, read, talked, felt, listened, smelled and tasted, and his impressions are skillfully woven with the history of the island into a book named for two of the island's villages, "Four Paths" and "Paradise." The author has a real talent for imparting the flavor of people and places, his book is "must" reading for anyone who plans to visit Jamaica and an exciting visit armchair travelers won't want to miss.[1]

Once again, reviews overall were quite positive:

> Hugh Cave moved his family to Jamaica, burrowed into the life of the country, and wrote the most thorough, and most interesting book ever about the island.—*Miami News*[1]

> Those of you who have read Mr. Cave's book about Haiti and know his insatiable curiosity about people, places and things, will be delighted to learn that he has now explored Jamaica. "Explored" is a weak description; actually he probes and digs. No archeologist sifts the sand of an excavation more carefully or more eagerly—the difference being that Mr. Cave's report is no dry case history; it is as colorful as a travel folder. Though far more accurate.—*Tulsa World*[1]

> A vivid story . . . An almost irresistible narrative that dodges in and out of history as it ties the past and present together.—*Yorkshire England Evening News*[1]

Cave's energy was now consumed with running a plantation. "I had found an old map of Arntully, done when it was bearing coffee and winning gold medals. I saw where the trees had been planted on the plantation and then reopened those fields first."

He goes on to give a brief overview of coffee growing: "Coffee trees should only be six feet tall so the women pickers can reach them with both hands. However, coffee trees will keep growing if you let them. When I started, there were trees already there that had grown to 20 feet tall. Coffee beans only grow on new wood, so we had to cut them down and start over. That meant four years before any of the trees would bear a crop, four years of putting money into the trees without getting anything back.

"First you plant a seedling and let it grow so high, then bend it over with a forked stick. Three or four new branches grow vertically like trunks. Weeding was done with machetes. I tried to introduce new tools, but the crew wouldn't keep them up and they rusted out. They kept going back to their machetes, so I finally went along with it.

"We didn't have to spray for anything in the Blue Mountains; the combination of altitude, rainfall, cooler weather, climate and serpentine soil were perfect. Most West Indies coffee grows in limestone base soil, but coffee with the unique Blue Mountain flavor won't grow in limestone. If you take a lower altitude tree grown in limestone and transplant it at Arntully, it will produce Blue Mountain flavor coffee.

"There was serpentine rock all over the plantation; people collected it and polished it up like gemstones with rich, dark green and black coloring. In the mountains, that rock was pulverized into a consistency like mincemeat and coffee trees loved it.

"We planted the trees on slopes with good drainage. Coffee doesn't like to get its feet wet; plant it in a flat and it will die. Coffee beans grow in berries and when the berries are red, you pick them. We didn't strip-branch like in Mexico where they picked red and green berries, because it gives an inconsistent flavor. Instead, we picked each tree four or five times as the berries turned red. I designed a special apron for the pickers with a large pouch for them to use instead of buckets, making it easier for them during the harvest.

"The trees don't like too much sun, either. We had an eight-acre flat called 'Tennis' because during colonial times they had tennis courts there. It was constantly in the sun, and when we tried to plant trees there, they wouldn't grow."

Cave fed his trees using only natural fertilizers, a strategy that would be very consumer-friendly and marketable today. However, he made that decision because the more effective artificial fertilizers had their risks. "We started out using store bought, but found an ounce of carelessness cost you a tree. I used a can that held the exact right amount, but then decided that chicken manure would do better. That meant less risk and less cost. The largest chicken farm in the West Indies was ten miles away and you had to ford a river at Hadley Gap to get there, but a big truck could bring me 18 tons at a time. We had mountains of it on the property and sprayed constantly to prevent the flies from laying eggs and to keep the odor down. We loaded the manure on donkeys for women to carry up to the trees."

Many of his ideas were original, at least to Jamaicans. "I probably read books on how they grew coffee in Africa. I read everything I could get my hands on about the subject and ended up with quite a library."

Cave found much of the land on his plantation unsuitable for coffee trees, however, because it was on the side of a mountain and inaccessible due to steep ravines, or out in the flats like the area called Tennis. It was in Tennis that the seed of a new idea took hold.

"The government provided free coffee tree seedlings in an attempt to encourage growth in this industry that brought hard currency to the island. So this was one expense I didn't have to worry about. The government also did the same thing with pine tree seedlings, but with much less success.

"A local forester, who was a good friend, came to me and said the Jamaican government was experimenting with pine trees, trying to determine which ones would grow on the island. He suggested planting Caribbean pines on those inaccessible slopes. I agreed and started planting pines everywhere on the plantation where I couldn't plant coffee trees.

"I read out of a book how to grow pines and got the free seedlings from the government. I left the house at three in the morning and brought along a few helpers. They took the seedlings out of pots and wrapped them in burlap by the hundreds. Each worker would take a bundle of 100, still wet, and carry them up to the mountain to plant using a machete. I paid them after they did the 100 trees.

"I started planting pines around 1963, about a year before we started producing a regular coffee crop. I gave the government that eight-acre Tennis flat in front of our house which they used to try and grow pine trees from all over the world."

He didn't plan it this way, but Cave essentially started the Jamaican lumber industry. "Caribbean pines grow to maturity in nine or ten years for lumber and they re-seed themselves, so the trees are low maintenance. They don't mind the sun either, so in accessible areas when the pines grew tall enough, I planted coffee trees in the shade under them. That was actually Margaret's idea."

Hugh B. Cave, pulp master, novelist, travel writer, war correspondent and slick story writer extraordinaire, was now a farmer, growing coffee and pine trees on his 200-year-old plantation in Jamaica. Could life get any better?

Not for him, perhaps, but for his wife, life was getting worse. "I was so busy on the plantation every day, then writing in the evening, I didn't have much time for Margaret. She stayed home most of the time and she didn't have many friends. One of them was a white Jamaican named Dorothy Watson and her husband Jimmy. They bought a great house nearby and Margaret would walk over there."

The Caves had little contact with the outside world. They were three miles from the closest telephone, located at the post office in Cedar Valley. "It could only be used in an emergency; there were no public phones. That phone was at the post office because in Jamaica, telegrams are sent post office to post office by telephone. We corresponded with our sons by mail. I got telegrams from editors and a boy from town would walk up to the house with the telegram, handwritten on pink paper."

That's how Cave received the unexpected news about his father. "It was 1964; I remember because that was the first year I sold my coffee. As I mentioned before, the telegram indicated that my father had died and the medical center wanted permission to do an autopsy. I had always believed that my father died during the London Blitz in 1941. I told Meg about it and we discussed what I should do. A few years earlier I had received a letter from the Salvation Army in Boston, saying a man claiming to be my father had been working for them and was ill. At the time, I figured anyone could have said that, and the letter to me wasn't signed, either.

"So I answered the telegram saying I couldn't give or withhold permission since I thought my father had been dead for years. I never heard anything again and regretted not following up on it."

That incident still weighs on Cave's mind. So far, attempts to verify either version of his death have not produced results.

Other, more positive memories from past lives turned up at his doorstep in Jamaica. "After writing my *Four Paths to Paradise* book, there was an item about me in *The Gleaner,* Jamaica's daily newspaper. It caught the eye of someone who had a key role in helping to launch my career as a writer."

W. Adolph Roberts, editor of *Brief Stories* magazine back when Cave's very first pulp stories were published, had retired and moved back to Kingston—back because he was Jamaican by birth. "He now worked at *The Gleaner,* trying to help Jamaican novelists get published. I was quite surprised when he called me one day. I invited him up for a visit.

"He came to our house and brought some things he had collected on voodoo. He thought I might be interested, knowing of my books on the subject. He had read them all and brought along a book written by a Haitian friend of his. We had a very pleasant visit, but that was the only time we ever got together."

He also had a visit from Gwen Cowley, his first editor at *The Toronto Star Weekly,* who was down from Canada on vacation. "I had met her once before, when Margaret and I were vacationing in Canada."

Other visitors came from his more recent past. "I had learned that Father Harry Smith left Haiti very suddenly, leaving behind all his photographic equipment. Something happened, possibly to do with politics or the church. Anyway, he showed up one day at the plantation. We were in the midst of a drought and he pitched in to help dig a trench from a stream on the property to irrigate one of our coffee fields. He stayed several weeks, then returned to the States.

"We kept in touch afterwards. The church reassigned him to Louisiana bayou country so he could make use of his French and Creole. Then he had a heart attack and moved to Texas, into a retirement home for priests.

"I saw him again a few years later. He was in Fort Lauderdale to visit a friend. I went with him and while there, he introduced me to a Father Kennedy from New Jersey. I said, 'Not *the* Father Kennedy who used to be editor of *The Sign*?' He answered, 'Yes.' So Father Harry Smith had a reunion with his old buddy and I reminisced with Father Kennedy. I last heard from Harry about five or six years ago."

Another guest at his plantation was Dr. Charles Deichman. "He came down for a visit, fell in love with the place and bought an adjoining piece of coffee property called Sherwood Forest."

Then there is the story of an invited guest who never showed up. "I received word through my publisher—this was in 1960 or '61—that Hollywood was interested in adapting my novel, *Black Sun,* into a feature film. I had been down this road before, most recently with *The Cross on the Drum,* but I wanted it to happen. A well-known movie producer, Lester Cowan, wanted to come down and talk about scripting the novel and changing its focus a bit. He would plan to spend several weeks with me.

"A few days before he was due to arrive, I received a telegram from Doubleday saying the trip was off. Cowan was flying to Europe to make another movie. My deal fell through the cracks. *Boy on a Dolphin* is the movie he did make."

Once again, Cave just missed an opportunity that might have thrust him into the public consciousness. Could he have fared better with an agent, one familiar with the Hollywood culture? How famous would he have become with an aggressive agent throughout his career?

Cave did not waste much time or energy fretting about what could have been. He was now thoroughly engrossed in the coffee business. His plantation eventually thrived, with 80,000 coffee trees and 70,000 pine trees. Ever the creative soul, he came up with another idea. "The co-op processed and shipped our coffee beans. I approached them and suggested they could make a lot more money for all of us if they roasted the coffee themselves and sold it as a gourmet brand. They agreed and we created Mountain Gold coffee. I wrote the brochures and helped with marketing. It was —and I believe, still is—the highest priced coffee in the world. I don't think they can it anymore; the Japanese buy most of what they roast. In the U.S. today, it sells for \$30–\$50 a pound."

Cave's ability to fit in anywhere provided unique opportunities for him in both Haiti and Jamaica. At the heart of this ability was his attitude towards people of color. He made friends easily with the locals because he sincerely respected them. Inter-racial tension always runs just beneath the surface in any part of the world where whites have traditionally dominated or enslaved blacks. This tension just did not exist for Hugh Cave though, and the people he lived with in Haiti and Jamaica could tell.

His experiences must also be considered in the context of U.S. race relations at that time. While only 40 years ago, segregation still ruled the South and blacks endured second class status throughout much of the country. Cave was politically correct long before anyone invented the term. He could not have behaved otherwise. For him, it wasn't a conscious act—he just did the right thing because they were fellow humans and he treated everyone as such.

Cave was also a pacifist by nature, although he fully supported the war effort he wrote about. His attitude towards guns provides some insight. "Although I always enjoyed fishing, especially fresh water fly fishing, I never liked the idea of hunting. I don't think I ever went hunting as a teen or an adult.

"In the mountains of Jamaica, most of my neighbors had shotguns and hunted wild pigeon for sport and food. They advised me to buy a gun if only to discourage mongooses from raiding my garbage pit. One day a mongoose got into my pit and I shot it. When I went down to look at it, the animal was dying but not yet dead. A short time later, the government declared that all guns had to be registered. I walked into the local police station, handed my nice new shotgun to the Red Stripe in charge, and said, 'Here, this is a nice gun, a Beretta. You keep it. I don't want it.' "

By 1965, Cave's coffee plantation was making money. The previous four years, he had supported the plantation with his writing. It is surprising he had time to write even one story considering the hours he worked as a farmer. His professionalism, work ethic and most of all, his love of writing, kept him churning out copy and adding to an already impressive resume of writing credits.

In 1962, his book of short stories about Haiti, *The Witching Lands,* had came out and sold well, offered by two book clubs. He based most of the 13 stories in that book on real life experiences. "The storyteller in my book was the proprietor of a small pension, or hotel, named The Etoile, which was actually the Mon Reve in real life. Some of the stories, such as 'The Brats'—which originally appeared in the *Saturday Evening Post* as 'Hard of Heart'—and 'The Impossible Thief,' involve the pension itself. 'The Prowler,' (also known as 'Danger By Night'), was later done on television starring David Niven, came out of an incident where our home in Haiti was burglarized. 'The Mountains of Fear' is about the problems of a superstitious Haitian youth who accompanies two white Americans on a walking trip across the Massif du Sud. The two Americans were actually Dr. Deichman and me.

Reviews were again very positive:

> A lively, colorful volume which translates the customs and emotions of a bewitching people into a language that runs the gamut from low comedy to high tragedy.—*Sacramento Bee*[1]

> Such imaginative writing that each story is, in itself, a gem.—*Natal Daily News,* South Africa[1]

> Only a man with deep feeling for the lands of which he writes and the people who inhabit them could clothe his characters with such an aura of reality. This is no mean feat within the narrow scope of the short story, but Cave does it time and again.—*Journal Star,* Peoria, Illinois[1]

Between 1962 and 1966, he had 249 publishing credits. His short stories appeared in *Boy's Life, Good Housekeeping, Ladies Home Journal,* and *Reader's Digest,* to name the most widely read.

Cave tells how one *Good Housekeeping* story, "In Your Own Backyard," came about. "The story is about a boy who has an after school job in a neighborhood hardware store. He gets fired for trying to organize the hopelessly disorganized store so customers can find what they want. There was such a store in my Warwick, Rhode Island neighborhood. My son Ken went there one day to buy something and didn't see it on the shelves. The owner knew he had the item but couldn't find it either. Ken remarked to me that if he owned the store he would reorganize it, and described how he would do it. The story grew out of that."

In 1965 alone, he was published approximately 82 times. That year mystery stories were again in vogue as he appeared in *Alfred Hitchcock's Mystery Magazine, Ellery Queen's Mystery Magazine,* and *Mike Shayne Mystery Magazine.* Even though many of these credits were reprints, they were reprints of stories written within that year—and the U.S. sales were all made directly by Cave, not through an agent (foreign sales were handled by Innes Rose).

One of his stories, "The Perfect Gift" (*Good Housekeeping,* December 1962), came right out of the family album. "My son Ken and his wife had taken a year off to teach at an impoverished Mexican community down in Albuquerque, New Mexico. For Christmas 1961, he took one poor kid to Sears and bought him clothing, shoes, toys and candy, then took him home to his parents, who had nothing. He did that as a Christmas present to his mother that year."

Chapter 29: Good-bye Providence, Hello Florida

One day in the spring of 1967, while still in Jamaica, Cave received a disturbing letter. "It was from our bank in Providence, telling us that someone was using our checks and forging my signature."

Since they would soon be returning home anyway, they decided to close up the Jamaica house and fly back to Providence. The Caves were shocked at what they found upon their arrival.

"Some teenagers had broken into our house during the winter and were apparently living there. We found cigarette burns all over the carpet and condoms on the floor. There were things missing, too. I found my portable typewriter in the pond by our pier. Apparently, they had come across the lake in a boat. My checkbook was in the desk along with a carbon and my signature, so they wrote and cashed checks, $25, $50 each."

He soon discovered a much greater loss though, one that Cave found heartbreaking. "We had a shed behind the house where I kept the lawnmower and garden supplies. It had caught on fire, or a fire was set, while we were down in Jamaica. The shed was far enough away from the house so there was no danger from that standpoint."

The shed contained more than garden supplies, though. "I kept everything from the pulp days out there, including magazines, hundreds of them, most with stories I had written, going back to my very first days as a pulp writer. There used to be a company that bound them for you with a hard cover for about $10. I would tear out my story, the cover and the contents page. I had at least four thick-bound volumes of pulps that were lost in the fire along with records of all my pulp sales."

For the most part, those were the only existing copies of the stories in his possession. "This was before computers. Once a story was published, I destroyed the carbon and just kept the magazine it appeared in. Many of those publications had gone out of business, too, along with the companies that published them."

The only tangible evidence of his long and storied career as a pulp writer seemed lost forever. He was now a slick magazine and book author though, and a Jamaican coffee farmer.

It was time to sell the house.

"The effort to prep the house for winter—draining water out of the heating system, putting the car on blocks—was getting to be too much trouble. The kids were both adults, out on their own, and now my entire past as a Providence-based pulp writer was also gone. We had no reason to keep the house. My life centered around Arntully Highlands now and it didn't make sense to run a coffee plantation in Jamaica from Rhode Island. So we decided to move closer."

The most logical place to move was Florida. They had wintered there often over the years and it already felt to them like a second home. "Margaret had two girlfriends who lived in Pompano Beach, so that's how we decided where to look for a house. We actually stayed with them while we were house hunting. Before long we found a nice condominium near the ocean and bought it."

Another reason for settling in Pompano Beach is that they would be close to their son, Donald. He taught English to special education students in Coconut Grove, outside Miami.

"Donald graduated from the College of William & Mary in Virginia, where he broke school records on the swim team and won a writing award. It was a literary prize for some short stories. One story he wrote was about how you felt when swimming in a race. He wrote from the perspective inside a man who was racing. Don broke a Southeastern record and his name is still on the William & Mary swimming pool.

"He continued writing out of college, even when he went to England as an exchange student to study law. He loved England and drove all over the country, even going to Chester to see my birthplace, Ways Green House.

"About two months before he was to get his law degree, he came to me and said he didn't want to become a lawyer. He said, 'I know you put a lot of money into it, Dad'—but of course, he put a lot of money into it himself, all through school he worked as a motel lifeguard to help pay his expenses. He said he wanted to drop out because what they were teaching him in law school is how to tell lies and be a crook, teaching tricks to win cases, and he didn't want to live that way. He asked would I mind if he went into teaching?

"I told him that it was fine with me, so he earned a degree in education. His first job was working with special education students in Coconut Grove."

While there, Don became ill. He was diagnosed with hepatitis, and after a long stay in the hospital, he moved in with Hugh and Margaret at their Pompano Beach condominium. "Don did a lot of writing while he was bedridden, and painting, just like his father. He adored my paintings. Before we left Providence, he took one of my works, a floral yard in Jamaica, and had it framed. I believe it is hanging to this day in one of the schools where he taught in Miami.

"Don spent a month with us before he was well enough to go back to work. Soon afterwards though, he decided to move out to California and landed a teaching job in Torrance, outside Los Angeles. That's when he decided to write a book to help teach these special kids English. Don and I corresponded frequently while he was writing it. Ultimately, he wrote two books put out by a California publisher. Unfortunately, I don't know what they are and neither Ken nor I have copies of them."

While Don was in the LA area, he became involved with movies. "On the movie, *Grease,* Don was a teenage dialogue coach to be sure it was authentic. When I tried to write young adult novels, they were good stories but didn't do well because I didn't know how kids talked those days and had no contact with any of them. This is what Donnie did. He went with a crew to the Mediterranean once—I have the letter—and they put him in a luxury villa because his hepatitis came back and he was very sick. At the premier of *Grease,* he escorted Olivia Newton-John's sister. John Travolta escorted Olivia."

Ken Cave followed a different path. "I taught Ken photography, taking pictures, developing and enlarging. We had a darkroom in the basement of our Providence home and three or four times a week I printed photos, often with him.

"He went to college at the University of New Mexico in Albuquerque and earned quite a bit of money taking all the school sports pictures for the local newspaper. Ken planned to major in foreign affairs; he wanted to work for the State Department after our experiences of living in Haiti and Jamaica. Thought it would be great to put that knowledge of foreign countries to use and make a career out of it. He backed off though, because there was much he didn't like in the State Department.

"So he went into psychology. After graduation, he went to

Boston University for his Master's and didn't quite make it to the doctorate degree. He met his future wife, Betsy, one summer in a music camp in Maine, where they were both teaching and playing.

"He accepted a job as school psychologist back in Albuquerque. Margaret and I visited them there. We came from Jamaica, flew to Meridan in the Yucatan Peninsula, and then took a train to Mexico City. It was during the Christmas season and the train was filled with people carrying pinãtas. I bribed the conductor into giving us our own compartment, which was the size of a telephone booth. We then caught another train from Mexico City to a town across the border from New Mexico, then flew to Albuquerque from there.

"A flu epidemic was around then, so by the time I arrived in Albuquerque, I had the flu. Ken took me to his doctor, a man in his 70's. He looked at me through a fluoroscope and asked if I was a heavy smoker. I told him I had been, but quit 15 years ago, and asked how he knew. 'From the scar tissue on your lungs,' he answered."

Aside from the illness and the upsetting condition of his lungs, the Cave family enjoyed themselves on that trip. They always seemed to enjoy each other whenever they got together, either as a family or individually.

Meanwhile, Cave's writing markets were in a steep decline. His first fiction piece about Jamaica, a 25,000-word novelette entitled, "Island of Eve," was published by *Good Housekeeping* in 1967 and picked up in six foreign publications, primarily in Europe. Aside from that, only six of his stories were published that year, two of them original, his lowest output of any year since he became a writer in 1929. The same would be true in 1968, with two new stories and a novel, *Run, Shadow, Run,* based on "Island of Eve" and published only in England.

In 1969, he published four new stories in *Good Housekeeping,* and another novel, *Larks Will Sing* (Robert Hale & Company, 1969), again put out only in England. This novel was somewhat of a departure from his others. It had nothing to do with the West Indies, World War II, or a fishing trip. *Larks Will Sing* does, however, draw on Cave's personal life.

The story revolves around a large condominium complex in Fort Lauderdale, Florida, named Lark City, the lives of its residents, most of whom are retirees. This book was written soon after Cave sold his home in Providence and moved to the Ocean

Monarch Condominium in Pompano Beach, not far from where the story takes place.

The main characters are the condo manager, Sam Kendall, a widower whose college-age daughter has come to stay with him for the summer. She attends William & Mary, where Cave's son went to school. Another key character is Arthur Crane, a retired music professor trapped in a loveless second marriage and looking for affection among the widows living at Lark City. Kendall's daughter, Lee, makes friends quickly with Mike Gallo, son of another resident, Vincent Gallo, who is a good friend of Kendall's.

The plot tracks a number of residents, their meaningless retired lives, and constant gossip about each other. A subplot involves the rioting that was going on in Miami at the time this book was written. The son of one retired couple, Jimmy Shore, competed for Lee's attention, but she doesn't like him because of his drug use. He tries to rape her one evening and she is rescued by Mike, who she does care for. The rape attempt is not reported, but Jimmy decides to exact revenge with a few dozen of his druggie friends, who come to the condo and ransack it, steal from each of the units, beat up, rape residents, and end up killing two them, Arthur Crane's wife and Sam Kendall's friend, Vincent Gallo.

The residents rise up against the rioting young men and end up chasing them off. They have now all found meaning in their lives and greater respect for each other.

Larks Will Sing is actually one of Cave's better efforts, although it only had one printing in England and never appeared in the U.S.

During these years, the slick magazine market paid better than ever, up to $3,500 for a story, but the short fiction market itself was declining with the popularity and low cost of paperbacks as well as the American public's preoccupation with television. After *The Cross on the Drum* did so well, Cave thought he would now break into the big money book market like many of his better known contemporaries, and as he had done previously in the slicks.

But Margaret saw things differently. "She wasn't keen about books, didn't think the future was there. I could write a slick story in about a week and get around $1,000, up to $3,500 if I sold it to the *Post* or other majors. She said, 'Why are you wasting your time writing books. What do you make, maybe $2,000, and you work six months on it?' Margaret didn't appreciate the fact that I had a career at stake. She thought more in terms of immediate income. My books, the early ones certainly, were written in my spare time anyway. So, I agreed with her."

Regardless of the direction he chose, however, he faced a limited selection of writing markets for the first time in his career. The only bright spot was Arntully Highlands, where he spent more and more of his time. "The Jamaica Agricultural Society had an annual fair at Denbeigh, where they held a coffee competition judged by an industry board. My coffee won a prize year after year."

Cave produced award-winning, world-renowned coffee, the plantation was profitable and he saw the day when this might replace writing as his primary source of income. He even considered moving permanently to the island nation he had come to love.

"The first seven years we closed up the house in Providence and spent every winter in Jamaica. After we moved to Florida, I spent three months in Jamaica and one month in the U.S. I couldn't wait to get back down there—I used to have a limo take me to the airport in Miami and I hopped on a plane. Then Eric Foote's truck driver picked up my car at the plantation, drove down to meet me at the airport in Kingston, and we drove back. I would get the key from our housekeeper, who looked after the house while we were gone."

Soon he questioned whether it was necessary to spend any time in Florida at all.

Cave belonged to the Moy Hall Cooperative, the organization that helped him get started as a coffee grower. His best friend and neighbor, Eric Foote, ran the cooperative. "I told Eric that I had concerns about the prices Moy Hall paid its growers. Another co-op, run by Keble Munn, offered much better money to me and the other growers, so I planned to go with him."

Keble Munn was, and is today, a name internationally associated with Jamaican Blue Mountain coffee. The Munn family had been growing and processing coffee for four generations, and owned the coffee-based liqueur, Tia Maria. Munn served two terms as Jamaica's Minister of Agriculture in the '70's and still owns the Mavis Bank Central Factory, which produces Blue Mountain coffee under the Mavis Bank and Jablum labels.

"Keble Munn lived nearby and I had known him for some time. Besides offering more money, Munn offered to come by and pick up our coffee by truck, saving us the trouble of delivering it to Moy Hall. I turned around and offered to let the other smaller growers bring their coffee to my place, then I would collect payment from Munn and distribute it back to the growers."

Cave handled the situation in his usual diplomatic manner. He had always been a peacemaker, probably from the time he stepped between his mother and father during that heated argument back in 1925. People found it difficult to become angry with him because he always seemed more concerned about the welfare of others rather than his own.

While admirable and a civilized way to act, he now lived in the rough and tumble world of Jamaican politics. His decision to leave Moy Hall, no matter how graciously handled, would create some ill feelings.

Chapter 30: Trouble in Paradise

There were other developments on the horizon though, which would have a much greater impact on Cave's plantation—they had to do with the Jamaican government itself.

American businesses and investors have learned that doing business in a foreign country can be risky, especially a developing nation (or Third World countries as they were previously known). Cave learned that lesson firsthand when he attempted to buy a plantation in Haiti. Fortunately, he had a good local attorney who steered him away from the deal which would have probably turned out bad.

Cave saw Jamaica as a much more developed country than Haiti, with stronger political institutions. Jamaica was a democracy, with an elected government headed by a prime minister. Elections were often testy and sometimes violent, but the government generally received high marks, especially in the United States.

The 1972 election had some disturbing implications. One of the candidates, Michael Manley, called himself a socialist, but the U.S. government, deeply mired in Cold War paranoia, considered Manley too much of a Fidel Castro fan. The people had elected him prime minister in a relatively fair contest, violence notwithstanding. However, the public mood began to turn darker almost immediately after he took office.

"He had written a book subsequently published in *The Gleaner* that contended no foreigner should be allowed to own land in Jamaica, and no Jamaican should own more land than needed to build a house. After that book came out, foreigners began to scurry like rats on a sinking ship."

Cave would have to face this new crisis alone, however. The other change which occurred in 1972 had to do with Margaret. "She came down with me every winter, even after we moved from Providence to Pompano Beach. Then we went to Jamaica three months or so and spent a month in Florida, primarily because Margaret wanted to. Finally, she stopped coming with me to Jamaica altogether."

The boys, Don and Ken, now both adults, only visited Jamaica once, while their parents were still renting the Arntully Great House. Margaret refused to drive when in Jamaica, so she stayed on the plantation. Eventually she stayed in Florida. The family adventure years were over—Jamaica was Hugh Cave's show.

"Michael Manley had a place of his own in the Blue Mountains; you could see it from the top of my property. He came and went by helicopter, which flew directly over my house. One day, there were a number of flights and a great deal of commotion. I saw quite a few military personnel at Manley's place—Cuban military.

"Castro would come over on weekends from Cuba in a small plane and land at the outer edge of the airport, away from the public. Then a Jamaican Defense Force helicopter carried him to Manley's place. Everyone said that Castro was teaching Manley how to run a Communist country. At one point, a huge group of Cubans came over, ostensibly to build schools. I don't know why, since Jamaican schools were far superior to Cuban schools at that time.

"They picked a site and erected a ten-foot high wooden fence around it. Nobody could see inside. Presumably, they were building a school, but they were really building barracks. These were Cuban military men, ready to take charge if Manley was in danger of losing the next election.

"Manley had so devastated the Jamaican economy as prime minister though, that he lost the election in a landslide to Edward Seaga. Then the Cubans didn't dare follow through on their apparent plan. The first thing Seaga did when he assumed office was tell the Cubans to get out."

It turns out that Washington's Cold War concerns about Jamaica had been justified after all, which may have pleased the pundits, but it did little for Hugh Cave. Economic conditions had deteriorated so much after Manley took office, especially for foreigners, that Cave was forced to make a gut-wrenching decision—he would sell his beloved plantation.

He had no problem finding a willing buyer—coffee grower and government insider, Keble Munn. "Munn was still buying all my coffee. He came by to see me as soon as he saw my 'for sale' ad in *The Gleaner.* He asked what I wanted for the plantation and how did I justify the price. I told him I have 70–80,000 coffee trees here and almost that many pines. I told him I wanted $200,000 in U.S. currency. He said 'okay, I'll buy it, but there's a problem here. Even as Minister of Agriculture, I can't guarantee to get you payment in U.S. dollars. I can get some of it though. I can almost promise you $100,000 U.S., the rest for so much a year over ten years, again in U.S. dollars. At that time, the Jamaican dollar equaled about $1.15 U.S. dollars.

"So we went ahead with the deal. The government took $30,000 off the top from my $100,000 down payment as capital gains tax. That left me with $70,000 and the promise of $10,000 a year for the next ten years. I bought the property and built a home 15 years earlier, all for less than $45,000. Of course, I spent quite a bit before the plantation started making any money and continued to pour my profits back into it, but this was a handsome profit. Remember, these were the days before hyperinflation in real estate."

His delight did not last long when he faced the harsh realities of doing business in a developing nation. "Manley passed a new law that forbid foreigners from taking money out of the country. There had been a tremendous flight of capital after he took office."

Manley's mismanagement of the country, especially his announced desire to institute Communist-style reforms, sent the economy into a tailspin. Cave's hoard of cash from the sale lost most of its value, leaving him with less than he paid for the plantation back in 1960.

The news wasn't entirely bad, because the money kept its face value as long as he used it in Jamaica (not accounting for the hyperinflation that inevitably followed). He could use the funds to invest in some new venture or simply leave the cash in his bank account and return to writing full time.

Whichever course he chose to pursue, Cave once again faced a new chapter in his life—except this time he didn't know what it would be. He decided to fly back to Florida and discuss his options with Margaret.

She had another option waiting for him which he had not considered.

"I walked into our condo and Margaret stood at the door waiting with six packed suitcases. She announced that she was moving to California. The condo was almost completely empty, just a cot for me to sleep on and my books. We had this expensive Haitian mahogany furniture, but she had already shipped it out to California along with all our silver and crystal. She didn't take any of my books though; she didn't want any of them."

Her decision did not come as a total shock to him. " Margaret was never happy in Jamaica, right from that first day when she decided never to drive there again. She could have had many friends. We lived near Morant Bay where there were many sugar plantations. The owners liked us and often invited us to parties. Eric Foote and his wife had us over often. I ran the plantation and tried to keep up with my writing, but whenever she wanted to go to Kingston to shop, I had to drive her, which ended up taking all day. We had a housekeeper who cooked for us, so she didn't have that much to do around the house.

Now Margaret was leaving him as well. "She said she wanted to move out to Los Angeles and be near our son Don, who taught school there. She didn't like Florida that much and I was gone most of the time."

Cave, ever the gentleman, offered to fly out to California with Margaret and help get her settled. "Don met us at the airport. He had been living in an apartment, but found another place, so Margaret moved into the first one for the remainder of Don's lease. The place needed fixing up, so I put up a new screen door for her, fixed the lights and so forth. Then I helped Don move into his new place. This was around Christmas time.

"My other son, Ken, lived at the time in Northern California, a town named Atascadero. Ken and Betsy had moved there from Albuquerque after getting a better offer from the school system. They put Betsy's prize possession, her piano, on a U-Haul trailer, threw everything in a car, and moved to California.

"I didn't go up there, but we agreed to meet halfway one day, in Santa Barbara, and spent the day together. Then, the day after New Year's, 1976, Don and Margaret drove me to the airport. I said good-bye and never saw her again after that."

The marriage had last 40 years. Few couples break up after that many years together, but it had been a long 40 years. "Margaret should never have married. She had no men friends and discouraged all my friends from coming around. I lost practically all my friends except for my fishing buddies, who never came to the house. We never really had other couples as friends, either. She had girlfriends though, and would go off two or three days at a time to New York or Bermuda."

"We never had a happy marriage, but neither was it dramatically unhappy. We talked at times about separating, but never did, I suspect, because we both loved our two sons, Kenneth and Donald.

"There was very little affection in our marriage. On the other hand, Margaret seemed willing enough to spend the best part of five years in Haiti with me, and then to live part of the year on my Jamaican Blue Mountain coffee plantation for more than a dozen years."

He felt frustrated by her lack of interest in a physical relationship that prevailed throughout their 40 year marriage. "She used to sew in the evenings, often well into the night. I would ask her to come to bed and she would say just a little while longer, until I eventually feel asleep. I wrote a story about it once, in "The Sign." I don't have a copy, but I remember that writing it was a catharsis of sorts to me."

In retrospect, he accepts much of the blame for the way their relationship turned out. "We both came from families that would never consider divorce, even if they no longer lived together. When you married and things didn't work out, that was too damn bad. You stuck it out.

"We never discussed our relationship much. She would be alone in the condo and I popped in for a month from Jamaica, then be gone. People asked her what goes on, Meg? Where's your husband? Why isn't he ever around? She probably grew tired of answering questions and decided to go where nobody knew her. I have no idea how she occupied her time when I was gone. She did love to sew, but didn't have any close friends in Florida. She probably never wanted to leave Rhode Island where she had many friends. She let me know she wasn't keen about moving to Florida, but went along with it anyway. Once she left for California, we didn't try to patch things up. We both knew the marriage had ended. We were just two incompatible souls.

"Yet, in other ways we were compatible. What woman would go to a place like Haiti, didn't speak the language, rent a house, ride in a Jeep over dirty, dusty roads? Once, we went to Cap

Haitien and stayed at a pension where the bedroom was about the size of a closet and the food terrible. We were eating dinner one night by a trough where water runs from the public toilets and watched human waste float by. It was a big joke and she never complained. She had a good side; the only thing bad was our relationship.

"My son, Ken, said it best once. He was schooled and trained as a psychologist, but eventually went into real estate and became a builder. He once pointed out to me that while my marriage to his mother was not a happy one, I have her to thank for a number of things that have been important in my life. Finding so little joy in the marriage, I sought it in other things. I would strive to become a better writer, seek adventure in Haiti and Jamaica, paint, surround myself with music, go to the South Pacific as a book-writing war correspondent, and so on. Psychologist Ken said, 'Had yours been the usual kind of marriage, you might never have done those things.' "

Ken was probably correct in his assessment, but now Hugh Cave found himself alone. With nothing to keep him in Florida, he immediately headed back to Jamaica.

Chapter 31: Life in Limbo

Cave had no idea what he would do next with his life, but he had a comfortable bank account in Jamaica once he decided. The only catch was he must spend the money there in Jamaica.

After selling his plantation, he rented a house in nearby Devon. Devon was not a tourist stop, although it lay near a popular town named Mandeville. "Outside of Mandeville is Shooter's Hill, where world famous Pickapeppa sauce is made."

He moved to Devon for one simple reason. "If I stayed near Arntully, it would look like I had to sell the coffee plantation and then I would lose face."

He didn't stay in Devon for long. "The place I rented had no electricity or running water and I didn't like it. A few days later I heard about a place in Christiana. I asked our housekeeper from the plantation, Beryl Williams, and her daughter, Edith, to join me. I was fond of her, a very attractive woman and a nice person. Beryl didn't care where she went, otherwise she would be living in a shack with no running water and no job. Christiana had a good school for her daughter, who was about ten years old."

He, Beryl and Edith Williams, drove to the small mountain town of Christiana where he took two rooms in a local hotel, the Villa La Bella. Then he proceeded to look for a more permanent residence. "I found a cottage, which I rented for $75 a month. It had a view of the entire valley and space for a garden. The town market was a short walk away. The owner lived in the house above it.

"The house had no running water, so rather than have Beryl carry water from a standpipe to the washtub, I ran a pipe to the house, installed a tap and water heater. Then I bought a bed large enough for her and Edith to sleep together.

"I placed Edith in a good school. I had to spend the money, so why throw it away while it just continued to lose value?"

All the years he lived among the locals in Haiti and Jamaica, Cave became quite knowledgeable about their mystical, primitive beliefs, including Obeah, the Jamaican equivalent of voodoo in Haiti. While he never practiced those beliefs, he witnessed the very real effect they had on those who did. His tolerant and non-judgmental approach may have created the impression he believed as they did. Occasionally, he may have thought so himself.

"We lived within walking distance of Mother Jackson's Church. She was a faith healer, in her 50's or 60's, who incidentally, ended up as a character in my novel, *Lucifer's Eye.*"

> Mother Jarrett . . . possess(ed) certain powers, including an ability to heal the sick when doctors could not. . . . She was easily seventy, yet taller than he and straight as a eucalyptus tree. All in white, even to a white headcloth, she looked as though she ought to be striding down some hospital corridor on an urgent errand. . . . (Her) eyes . . . glittered like black opals set in as dark a face as he had ever seen. Not brown as were most of those in the Armadale area. Not even dark brown. This face was as black as though carved out of coal, and by an artist with a message.[19]

"Beryl, Edith and I went to her church regularly. I was the only white person in attendance. After Mother Jackson saw me there three or four times and got to know me, she would say, 'So glad to see Mr. Hugh and his family,' whenever I came to church. After a few months, I asked her if I could tape a service. She agreed and I still have that tape in my collection.

"Anyway, Beryl's daughter, Edith, started having bad dreams about this young boy she knew who had been killed by a bus. She would wake up at night crying. Edith never liked the boy and didn't know him that well. I suggested going to Mother Jackson for help.

"We went there and she prepared a bath outdoors in a big washtub. Edith undressed and sat in the tub. Mother Jackson didn't say any chants or spells, just talked softly to the child as she gently washed her entire body. I don't know what she said or did, but Edith never again dreamt about the boy after that."

Cave had his own experience with island mysticism. "My house lay at the bottom of a steep hill. Since the road to my house was difficult to maneuver, I kept my car at the top of the hill next to a local bar.

"One day I went to the bar for a few beers and to talk with the locals as I often did. I was walking home down the hill when I suddenly fell and sprawled forward, hurting myself enough to yell for someone's help. Beryl heard me and ran to my aid, then said we have to get Mother Jackson.

"They helped me back to the house and into bed. The pains in my chest and legs were bad enough I could hardly walk. I got undressed and lay there as she ran her hands over me, speaking soft incantations as she did with Edith. The next morning I felt fine, like nothing had happened."

> But Mother Jarrett's hands were cool and whisper soft. And in a moment, though they did nothing but remain motionless against his face, the soreness that had been deep enough to make even his bones ache seemed to melt away.[19]

Over the next several months, Cave and his "family" spent time exploring the island, almost playing tourist. "I considered Christiana one of the most beautiful little towns in Jamaica, or on earth for that matter. The entire area had fascinating caves and I had been through there on my island explorations in the past. It was near Mandeville, a fairly large city and favorite of Canadian and English tourists. The weather was pleasantly cool in the Blue Mountains, yet, we could go to the beach just an hour away and to Montego Bay just an hour or so further. We went to Mo Bay, the three of us, and stayed at a small hotel two or three days at a time. Or we went shopping in Kingston. We had a good old time."

His relationship with Beryl and Edith may have fueled the local gossip mill, but he doesn't recall any direct conversation with anyone about it, one way or the other.

Cave lived the life of a bachelor—and a writer. He went back to Florida every few months because he found it convenient for staying in touch with his writing markets. The condo also provided a different writing environment. "I had a few acquaintances in the condo, but pretty much kept to myself. I would go for a swim in the ocean every morning, or go to the pool, then shower and get to work. I commuted to Jamaica through Montego Bay, which was only a one and a half hour flight away."

When Cave stayed at his condo in Florida, he occasionally corresponded with Margaret or talked with her on the telephone. "One day she said to me, 'Don't you want a divorce so you can get on with your life?' I assumed that she had met someone and that's why she asked, but I figured 'why not.' She asked me to have a lawyer draw up an agreement, so I went to one in Pompano Beach. He set everything up in writing and sent her the papers. I proposed giving her half of everything we owned and the promise of half the condo when it was sold. She already had all our personal belongings of value.

"At the very last minute though, I get a letter from this lady Hollywood lawyer, telling me that Margaret intended to sue me for divorce. She demanded one half of everything I would earn for the rest of my life. I called my son Ken and asked him what I should do. He said to let his lawyer handle it. So his attorney drove down to LA and got the case thrown out of court. California had no jurisdiction over me—I didn't live there, never did, never paid taxes, never owned anything there."

Cave stopped corresponding with Margaret after that, leaving the divorce in limbo where it is to this day. "I sold the condo and sent her half the proceeds. When the deal was completed, I moved to Lake Placid in central Florida and bought a small condo with my half."

This is a good place to catch up on Cave's two sons. While Cave remembers their time together as typical of a loving family, an underlying current of conflict would eventually affect the boys' relationship with each other.

"They had been raised by a mother who treated her sons like the good seed and the bad seed. Donnie could never do wrong in his mother's eyes and she clearly favored him. On the other hand, she was sometimes unmercifully strict with Ken. I often tried to talk with her about it and even her friends counseled her on it, but she wouldn't change. For my part, I was just an easygoing guy and enjoyed my time equally with the boys. I can't say how her treatment of them ultimately affected their lives, but those kids dubbed "The Worry Wart" and "The Character" turned out as two entirely different people."

At some point, after Margaret moved to California, the relationship between Cave's two boys suffered as well. "They were close as kids. I have this published photo of them standing at the edge of our backyard pond in silhouette, Ken looking out, Don looking at Ken. Ken felt very protective of Don, in spite of the way Margaret treated the two of them.

"I wasn't strict with either of them—I'm not strict with anyone, just an easygoing slob. I will push myself but not other people. My relationship with both boys was always good, as I remember it. I taught both kids how to fish and we went fishing often. We swam together, went skating, and of course, took many trips together. Don wanted to become a writer and showed interest in writing at a young age, like me. Of course, I wanted to read everything he wrote. Ken tended to be more mechanically inclined. He was also a musician; he played trombone in the high school and college bands as well as the Rhode Island Youth Symphony.

"Both boys became teachers. Donnie taught school in the Miami area until he moved to Los Angeles in 1974. Ken lived in Northern California. I'm not sure how much of a relationship they had once they were both in California, but whatever it was, their relationship was to end sometime after Margaret moved to Los Angeles.

"I got along with both of them fine after she left me, but I think Don played down his feelings for me in the presence of his mother. The incident that seemed to pit the boys against each other occurred when Don dropped Margaret off at Ken's house on one of his visits to San Francisco. He often did that and then picked her up on his way back to Los Angeles, but he would never stay overnight.

"As Ken tells me, he received a box of secondhand books from a dealer. He opened it and they were all books by me that he purchased from a list. He was all enthused and said to Margaret, 'Look what I got!' According to him, Margaret says, 'Well, you lied to me! I'm leaving now and taking the train back.' She didn't wait for Don. She apparently thought Ken had nothing to do with me.

"Anyway, they haven't been in touch since then. She still lives in L.A. and Betsy stays in touch with her occasionally; but Don, who had been in declining health at the time of their blow-up, never spoke to his brother again."

* * *

Cave's creative output during this time reflected all the changes in his life. He had gone from plantation owner to retired local, from married man to bachelor, and the short story market that he mastered as he once mastered the pulps, was about to go the way of the pulps.

The year 1975 would be his last as a slick magazine writer, with the exception of a reprint in the resurrected *Saturday Evening Post*. Slicks were no longer interested in publishing fiction because the public had fallen out of love with the short story. This brought an end to Hugh B. Cave's long-time career as short story writer extraordinaire. He had written and published more than 1,000 of them, an incredible feat.

Cave's life, starting in that year, offered few victories to offset his many defeats. Maybe his fantasy-driven life of adventure, often pursued impulsively, had now caught up and reminded him that he was a mere mortal. Fortunately, he didn't engage in self-pity, always looking ahead, confident that his next big adventure was waiting for him right around the corner.

Little did he realize that it would come up from behind.

"Karl Edward Wagner had written me in 1974 about putting together a collection of my old weird menace pulp tales. He had founded a new publishing company, Carcosa, with David Drake and Jim Groce. Their expressed purpose was to preserve the best works of writers they felt had been overlooked in the past."

Cave wrote to Carl Jacobi about this proposed new volume in a letter dated March 19, 1974:

> You mentioned Carcosa. Yes, I guess they're going to bring out a collection of my old horror tales and fantasies. Karl Wagner has been collecting my stories and has found some that I had completely forgotten . . . *Murgunstrumm and Others* will probably be the book's title if it becomes a reality.[1]

Of course, the book did become a reality. *Murgunstrumm and Others* (Carcosa) came out in 1977 to rave reviews, and excellent sales, earning Cave recognition anew for his early work. *Murgy*, as Cave refers to the book, included 26 of his most memorable pulp tales, including, among others, "Stragella," "The Prophecy," "Dead Man's Belt," "The Brotherhood of Blood," and, of course, his signature weird menace tale, "Murgunstrumm." Renowned pulp artist, Lee Brown Coye, did artwork for the book. It was to be the first of many collections, with new ones still being published to this day.

In October 1978, Cave attended the fourth World Fantasy Convention in Ft. Worth, Texas. "I had been invited to attend because *Murgy* had been nominated for one of the convention awards."

Upon arriving in Ft. Worth, he was somewhat taken aback by the reception he received, and not only from familiar names in the industry. He saw many younger faces, people born long after his pulp heyday, who seemed to know his work better than he did.

Cave was especially pleased to renew his friendship with someone from the distant past. "I first met Manly Wade Wellman back in 1932, during my brief stay in New York City. He was at Arthur J. Burks' apartment that night we played cards and Burks came up with that glass doorknob thing. Now, here it is 1978 and I'm meeting him the second time.

"Physically, Manly was a big, jovial guy who loved to talk and have a good time. When he talked only a fool wouldn't listen. He took me under his wing and introduced me to editors and other writers. He helped me quite a bit because I had just started back into fantasy fiction, novels this time, and the people I needed to know were right there in attendance. My *Murgy* collection had been nominated for an award, too, so some of the folks there at least knew who I was."

Cave and Wellman reminisced about the bygone pulp days, becoming fast friends in the process and continuing that friendship long afterwards. That's what happens with Hugh Cave—he makes friends easily, H.P. Lovecraft notwithstanding.

He also hit it off with Karl Edward Wagner. "We had only met through our correspondence during the time we put together *Murgy* and afterwards."

Cave forged another new friendship in the person of David Drake. "I had been corresponding with him about his writing and mine. Dave was part of Carcosa, which Wagner founded, and assistant editor of Stuart David Schiff's *Whispers* magazine, one of the finest horror magazines ever published. Many of today's best-known writers of horror appeared in *Whispers*. Stuart Schiff eventually published 11 stories of mine altogether."

These new friendships included Wagner's wife, Barbara, Wellman's wife, Frances, and Drake's wife, Jo. "Later, after Peggie and I got together, we spent a week in Chapel Hill, North Carolina with the above-named 'Chapel Hill Gang,' because all three of them lived in that area. When Manly faced his last surgery a few years ago, an amputation of both legs after a fall, Peg went up to help Frances out.

Cave's presence at the convention was well-rewarded, not only by making new friends, but by winning the "Best Collection" award for which he had been nominated. Ironically, he received the "Howard," an award trophy named after H.P. Lovecraft.

He wrote about the award in his October 29, 1978 letter to Jacobi:

> I guess you know that Murgunstrumm won the award for best collection. To say that I was surprised would be the year's biggest understatement. Considering the quality of the competition, I didn't think Murgy stood a chance. Anyway, I now have a Howard on my desk and am damned proud of it.[1]

In that same letter, he informed Jacobi of his intention to move from Pompano Beach.

> And I must tell you that I am moving. The humidity and heat and worsening tourist traffic of Florida's Gold Coast finally got me down and I put this condo up for sale. Sold it in four days, which just goes to show that some people like all that tourist stuff. Anyhow, I have found an apartment in a small condo on a three-mile-long lake in central Florida and will be moving there November 8, unless someone throws a monkey wrench into my finely tuned schedule.[1]

Nothing happened to change his moving plans. However, once he arrived at his new home, something would happen to change his life.

Chapter 32: Peg O' My Heart

"I had gone to Lake Placid with a friend whose brother lived in this condominium. I looked through a unit and met some of the people who lived there. It had a nice, small town atmosphere. I sold my condo in Pompano Beach for $65,000. I had paid $20,000 for it. I sent half the proceeds to Margaret, and with the other half, I bought the condo in Lake Placid for $35,000.

"I occupied myself by writing. There was a golf course across the street from my condo and I would go to the clubhouse for lunch. Then in the evening I walked to the eighth hole with my adjustable club and play a few holes after the course closed, just before dark."

For Cave, typically shy around people, he felt most comfortable being alone. The writer's life is a lonely one anyway, so his personality certainly fit his occupation.

Cave's condo was on the eighth floor. He knew many of his neighbors in the building just from seeing them around, though he kept to himself most of the time. One person he met was a woman named Nellie Thompson, "Peg" to her friends. Peg tells how they first met:

"Hugh had a condo on the top floor. I saw him in the elevator, the hallway and the laundry room. He was such a shy man and seemed quite sad. I didn't know anything about him other than he had separated from his wife. Lake Placid was a small town and everyone was friendly in the condo.

"I invited him down to dinner on occasion. I felt sorry for him; he seemed like a little lost boy. Sometimes I also saw him at the local bookstore and we would stop for coffee."

Peg was married at the time, unhappily, to a man named Art Thompson. "I had been single a long time and my job involved a great deal of travel. My kids worried that I had worked too many years and needed to settle down again. I knew Art and he had been after me to marry him for some time. I finally gave in and said okay, we'll get married."

His behavior changed almost immediately and the relationship soured. That had occurred ten years earlier, but she stayed married to him. His health had been declining in recent years and kept him close to home. In spite of all this, Peg retained a positive outlook on life. She made friends easily and exhibited a vitality that belied her years.

At the time she and Cave met, neither of them had thoughts of getting involved. However, Cave felt drawn to her outgoing, yet caring, personality. She was totally unlike Margaret, and at this point in his life—living alone with not much more than a typewriter and a bottle of scotch to keep him company—she provided welcome relief.

Something about Hugh Cave kept her interested in him. "I felt from the moment I met him that I had known him. There was something there, a familiarity. I just couldn't put my finger on it."

Then, one day the "it" came out over coffee in the bookstore. According to Cave, "We were talking about our respective family backgrounds. I told her how my grandfather helped build the Great Indian Peninsular Railway, and then she tells me her grandfather, who also lived in India, built the bridges on that railway. They were probably friends and drank together!"

Hugh Cave and Nellie "Peg" Thompson made a connection at that moment. For a long time afterward though, their relationship didn't advance beyond occasional coffee in the bookstore, dinners, and brief encounters in the hallway. All the while, their connection was evolving into a bond.

Her daughter Jacky Leggitt, recalls meeting Hugh the first time.

"She wanted me to meet Hugh Cave, a writer who lived in the same building where she lived. I noticed when she answered the door she was smiling for a change, and seemed excited about an invite to dinner with this new friend. The doorbell rang and Mom moved very quickly to the door and let in a fine-looking gentleman. We had a before dinner drink, if I remember correctly, and then we took off for a local restaurant. Mom and Hugh sat across from each other and I noticed how kind and gentle Hugh was with Mom. I found her laughing over what Hugh was saying, which was a first in a longtime. Their eyes never left each other, even if they were talking to me. I finally reached out with my hand and waved it between them, to let them know I was there."

Peggie Thompson's life, like Cave's, had taken many twists and turns. "I was born Nellie Gwendolyn Chester in San Francisco, an hour off the ship from Australia. My mother was only 15 years old and my father just 20. His name was Frank Reginald Chester, born in India. A good-looking, bright man, full of fun, he is best known as the man who invented the pinball machine.

"My mother was very striking, half English and half Maori. We were in San Francisco because of my grandmother, Nellie Pollard, my father's mother, who ran a touring Australian opera company of about 100 young girls. It was known as 'Pollard's Lilliputian Opera Coy' or 'Pollard's Australian Juveniles.' They did Gilbert and Sullivan, things like that. She was very strict and domineering, English, and played God with a lot of people's lives.

"My mother had tuberculosis, a death sentence back in those days. When I was born, my grandmother didn't want any part of me, so she placed us both in a convent, then went back on the road. If my grandmother didn't like the wives of her children, she got rid of them. My mother's friends eventually got her out of the convent and kept her alive by taking her every other year to a sanitarium when they had enough money. She finally died when I was 18.

"I spent most of my childhood in a foster home with Grace Lee, a wonderful woman who raised me until I was almost 14. Her husband knew the man who wrote *Peg O' My Heart,* and he would come over and sing it to me as a child. That's how I acquired the name 'Peg.' When I lived with Grace, people knew me as Peggy Lee. I used to go visit my mother in San Francisco, but I couldn't live with her because of the TB. I went to the family doctor after each of those visits.

"Mrs. Lee was like a real mother to me. We lived in Redwood Canyon country and had a country store with our living quarters in the back. Her husband managed a codfish company and was away all week. Grace had a son named Harold, a beautiful boy, who died of what they called brain fever back then.

"Grace loved children and animals. She would take on other young people and had many animals around the house, including raccoons and skunks, all tame. Everyone brought strays to her. We lived on a hillside, with big trees down below. You could see the fog coming in through the trees. Every evening the animals came in and sat around our wood stove. One day a trapper brought us a mountain lion cub with a missing front left leg. He said he should have killed it, but felt bad, so he thought of Grace. I was about three at the time and the lion grew up with me.

"My family never paid a thing to the Lees for raising me; Grace did it all on her own. She was 'Mom' to me."

Hugh Cave adds, "In the 15 years I have known Peg, there hasn't been a week go by that she doesn't mention Mrs. Lee."

When Peg was almost 15, she found papers that indicated where her real father lived. She decided the time had come for her to go back and live with him. "I wrote to my Dad and found out he and his second wife, Daisy, were just getting ready to adopt another child. I told him I wanted to come home. He knew Daisy before my mother. They were supposed to get married years before, but it didn't happen because he fell in love with my mother and married her instead. She was 14 years old at the time. He met her in Australia and they married when she became pregnant with me. Now that my parents were divorced, Dad finally went ahead and married Daisy. She was insanely jealous of me, which I could understand. Fortunately, I looked just like my Dad and nothing like my mother.

"You can imagine how Daisy reacted when she learned that I was coming to live with them. They were well off financially and lived in New York City. I ended up staying with them about six months before they put me in a boarding school, Bernard School for Girls. I guess they thought I had become a problem, although, of course, I didn't understand why.

"I graduated from school at age 16 and my father thought I had the talent to become an artist, so he sent me away to an art school for about a year. The family moved to Canada about the time of the stock market crash, taking me with them. They got their money out in time and brought it with them. My Dad enrolled me in another art school, this one in Vancouver, British Columbia."

Peg is a very attractive woman who must have broken many hearts in her youth. She enjoys telling this story from her teenage years: "While I attended art school, the girls would get together and walk down to an isolated beach where we sketched each other in the nude. I had very long hair down to my knees, and I hung once from a tree branch with my long hair draped over me. Two professional photographers happened to be in the area and they took my picture without my knowing it.

"They sold the life size picture to an innkeeper, who hung it in his bar. My father happened to be in Vancouver two months later and went to the bar with an Australian ship captain. There was my picture, big as life, and my father recognized me immediately. He pulled me out of school and sent me to business school instead.

"I eventually went to college and graduated from the University of Washington. After completing school, I took a job in banking, and then during World War II, I moved back east and worked for the War Department in New York. From there, I ended up in Greenwich, Connecticut.

"During these years I also got married and had children. I met my first husband when I was 21 and went with my father to a restaurant one day. He was a tall, good-looking pilot. We had two children together, 13 months apart, Jackie and Meg. I even had another pregnancy between those two. His mother came to live with us and he wasn't making much money then, about $75 a week, so I went to work.

"Neither of us were very happy. I wouldn't let him touch me because I seemed to get pregnant every time he walked by me. Then he became involved with a teenager. She called me one day to say she was pregnant. I did love my husband and wanted to save our marriage, but help wasn't available in those days, so you just had to grin and bear it.

"We finally broke up after five years. That's when I went back to New York, at age 27, to work for the War Department. "I had no money and my daughter Meg was sickly, so I had to leave Jackie out west with my ex-husband until I could afford to have her live with me. I went back east to live with my daughter, Meg. I remember being so short of money, I played bridge on the train and used my winnings to buy meals for us. I had a photographic memory for cards. My ex-husband and his new wife then disappeared with Jackie and I didn't see her again until she was 12 years old.

"I met Walter Anderson when I lived in Greenwich. We married and had one child, Joanie. My marriage to Walter also turned out bad, though at times we lived the good life. But Walter was a playboy, gambler and alcoholic. One night he came home drunk, picked Joanie up and threw her against the wall. I took the kids and locked myself in the bathroom. By the time I finally left him, we had no money and I had to start over again. He had a wonderful family though and we are still in touch.

"I tried to improve myself and started going to night school in New York City, commuting from Greenwich, and taking a course in public relations. At one point I received an attractive job offer from the president of a bank in Ft. Lauderdale, so I moved down with my girls.

"I loved public relations work and traveled quite a bit over the next 20 years. Then, in 1964, anxious to get back in touch with my original family, I went to Australia. I had cousins there and stayed with them for six months. I even thought about moving there permanently, but I didn't want to be away from my kids and grandkids. So I came back to the states. I went back to Australia for one more visit back in 1971.

"I met a salesman named Art Thompson while working a trade show. After that, wherever I went to do a show, he seemed to follow. My kids were concerned about my hectic schedule—I would hit ten cities in ten days—and said I couldn't keep up this pace. They wanted me to start thinking about settling down and getting married again.

"I tried to decide where I wanted to live and considered Costa Rica. I had friends in San Jose and they let me use their house whenever I wanted. However, I couldn't see myself living there permanently.

"Then Art Thompson asked me to visit him in Lake Placid to see his new condo. I did and fell into a relationship. He asked me to marry him and I agreed, even though I didn't really love him.

Then he changed almost overnight. While charming and friendly on the surface, he was a nasty character underneath. He had diabetes and that may have affected his personality."

Peg reached a point that she could no longer tolerate her husband's abusive treatment. That was when she met Hugh Cave, who, on impulse, had recently purchased the last available condo in her building.

Chapter 33: Last Call to Jamaica

As Hugh and Peg were getting to know each other, he still spent most of his time at the typewriter. He worked on his novels and wrote a few short stories for minor publications, but his largest market now seemed to be in reprints of stories he had written many years before.

Cave still maintained his longstanding correspondence with Carl Jacobi. They had been writing back and forth almost 50 years. While that fact alone is remarkable, another aspect of their correspondence deserves note.

They had exchanged hundreds of letters over 50 years, discussing every aspect of their professional and personal lives. Yet, in all those years they never once had any form of personal contact with each other, in person or on the telephone.

That was about to change.

Christmas Eve, 1979, Hugh Cave sat alone in his Lake Placid apartment. Peg lived in the same building, but she, like everyone else, had family to keep her busy for the holidays. As he sat there, isolated from the joy and sharing of the holidays, he suddenly thought of his nearly lifelong friend and fellow pulp writer, Carl Jacobi. Almost as quickly, an impulse grabbed him.

"After all these years and so many letters, I decided to call him. I picked up the telephone and nervously dialed his number. My heart pounded as the phone rang. Then this strange, almost feminine voice came on the line. It was Carl. He certainly seemed surprised to hear from me, but I could tell he felt uncomfortable."

They carried on an awkward conversation for a few minutes. Then, just as quickly as it had begun, the conversation ended.

"He mentioned soon afterwards in a letter that he hated to talk on the phone because his voice always came over like a feminine squeak. He had been that way all his adult life. Carl was a loner and never married. He lived at home until his father died, and then he lived alone in their big old house in Minneapolis. He sold the home after being mugged in front of it. Then he took an apartment where he was mugged by two black men and two white women, who beat the hell out of him and left him half dead in the bathroom."

Those few moments would be the only personal contact between the two writers from that day forward. Their correspondence continued for another 12 years, until 1992 when he received the following postcard, from Jacobi, but handwritten by someone other than him:

> Somewhere I have lost the ability to type by touch. I have any number of plots in my head, some in detail, but am unable to put them down on paper. I can type a little by the old hunt and peck system, but it's slow going.[1]

Cave continued writing to Jacobi and occasionally received postcards on Jacobi's behalf for several more years. Jacobi finally died on August 25, 1997, after spending his last years in a suburban Minneapolis nursing home.

He left behind an extensive body of work in a pulp career that paralleled Cave's. One of his better known stories, "The Satanic Piano," was produced for the television show, *Tales from the Darkside.* In addition to his sixty-seven year relationship with Cave, Jacobi also left behind forty years of correspondence with August Derleth, editor of Arkham House.

Another long-standing relationship of Cave's finally came to an end.

The curse of growing old is losing the friends, relatives and loved ones who shared your journey through life. Sometimes the people who survive those losses cannot overcome them. Conversely, studies on aging suggest that people who live into their 90's and beyond have the emotional resilience to withstand such losses. Hugh Cave certainly experienced his share of personal loss, but he seems to possess an uncanny ability to deal with his losses and look forward to that next great adventure.

It was on the verge of one such adventure that his world seemed to come crashing down around him.

One morning in 1980, Cave heard a knock at his door. He opened it to see Peggie. "The night before she had a real problem with her husband, Art, and Peggie came to tell me she had decided to move to Sebastian, where her daughter lived. I was shocked. I said, 'You're what? You're leaving?' She had packed her bags and come to say good-bye. I said, 'Before you go, let's have breakfast.'

"So we went to breakfast, and I looked at her and said, 'You know I love you.' Just like that, she went to pieces.

"I wanted her phone number and told her to go over and look for a little place. She said she was in no position to look for anything; she just wanted to stay with her daughter a while, maybe see her other daughter in Ft. Lauderdale. She just wanted to try and get her life together and decide what to do next."

Peggie explains her feelings that morning. "I felt I had finally met a man, a wonderful, kind man, who cared for me and could not possibly do anything to mistreat me. Hugh was the man I should have met years earlier. But, still being married and having suffered from the effects of rebound relationships in the past, I needed to get away and sort out my feelings. Whatever decision I made now, I would probably have to live with it for the rest of my life."

Just like that, Peggie Thompson was gone. However, they both sensed that it would not be for long. They were destined to be together—their grandfathers had ensured it.

Cave still maintained his house in Jamaica, but he found less and less reason to go there. In his July 14, 1978 letter to Carl Jacobi, Cave wrote:

> Incidentally, I won't be here in Jamaica long this time. It's not a happy country any more, and I don't have a chance of persuading them to keep their financial commitment to me, I now realize. Guess my long Jamaican adventure is slowly fading to a finish, and not a happy one.[1]

That unkept financial commitment was reminiscent of his early pulp years during the Depression, when he often went hungry because publications folded owing him money for stories they had run. This situation differed from the past because it represented payment for 15 years of effort. After receiving his initial down payment of $100,000 and giving back $30,000 in taxes, he had little to show for his time. "I spent about $50,000 in Jamaica and I think I still had around $80–90,000 left in the bank, but with the devalued dollar, it was only worth $6,000. I couldn't take even that out of the country until finally, about ten years after the sale,

I needed the money to cover medical expenses and they let me have it."

His relationship with Jamaica came to a rather ignominious end in 1980. "A hurricane had hit and washed out the road to my house as well as the plumbing, but I had no interest in starting over again. I now lived in Lake Placid and knew Peggie. On top of that, I found out that my housekeeper, Beryl, had pilfered my checking account for her son. So I gave her what I had left in the account, about $3,000 Jamaican and more money than she had ever seen. Then I left Jamaica for good without looking back."

After his generous gift and all that he had done for Beryl and her daughter through the years, she only wrote to him a few times after his final trip. Then he never heard from her again. "I did get a letter from her son though, asking me for more money. I don't think I answered it."

Author's note: Several years ago while vacationing in Ocho Rios, Jamaica, I went into a grocery store to purchase some Blue Mountain coffee to take home with me. Imagine my surprise when I saw a burlap bag of coffee beans with "Arntully Highlands" printed on it. I bought several bags, one of which I gave to Hugh and Peggie as a gift. He beamed from ear to ear, after having recently relived his Jamaican plantation life with me in our interview sessions. That bag is still in Hugh's freezer to this day.

Hugh and Peg were not apart for long. After saying good-bye to him, she drove to Sebastian and stayed with her daughter, Joanie. "I had driven over from Lake Placid on a dismal, rainy Sunday, and I felt really discouraged. My marriage was awful, I wanted to be with Hugh, and I knew I couldn't look for a home because I had no money.

"That evening, Hugh called to make sure I had arrived okay. Then he called the next night to ask if I had looked for a house yet. My daughter, Joanie, overheard the conversation. She said she had a friend building small houses, so why not take a look. I found the cutest little place. Hugh called again and I told him. He said he would come right over."

Cave arrived at nine the next morning. Joanie and her husband had just gotten out of bed. Cave describes the scene: "Peg came running out of the house, as did Joanie and her husband. Joanie then pulled me aside and said, 'If you hurt my mama, you're going to have to deal with me.'

"Joanie drove us to look at the house. It was still under construction. I asked Peg, 'Do you like it?' She said, 'Yes, but there's nothing I can do about it.' I said, 'Well, I can,' and pulled out my checkbook."

Peggie was astonished. "I couldn't believe he just wrote out that check for $50,000. He didn't bargain then and never does. He is a shy, sensitive man, who doesn't like to put anyone out and tries to go along with everything. At times, people really take advantage of him. With my business background, I have tried to bring him out of it, to get him to ask questions and bargain. He's never been in the business world; he's an artist. He hides behind his writing and painting, escapes in his work."

Cave put his condo up for sale and moved in permanently with Peg. A few weeks later, Joanie and her husband, John, took them out to dinner. After a few drinks, Joanie leaned over to her mother and said, "Mom, if you blow this one, we're going to keep Hugh and let you go."

Soon after Peg left Lake Placid for Sebastian, her husband, Art, finally succumbed to his diabetes and other ailments resulting from a life of hard drinking. He died alone, having chased off the people who had cared most about him.

PART SEVEN: A NEW START

Chapter 34: Good Times, Bad Times

> Cave to Jacobi, May 20, 1981: I've moved again. Was tired of living in a condo where everyone minded everyone else's business all the time. Looked around and discovered this lovely little village of Sebastian—a fishing village on the east coast of Florida between Vero Beach and Melbourne. Have bought a small but pretty two-bed, two-bath in the pine woods about three miles from the beach, with room in the back yard for a garden, and we—Peggie and I—have been working our butts off ever since, having the garage made over into a study, screening in the back porch, getting a garden house erected, etc. It's like being born again to move into a real home, with privacy, and a yard to tinker around in.[1]

CAVE'S PERSONAL LIFE HAD TAKEN A DRAMATIC turn for the better, but so did his writing career. He felt the same enthusiasm and anticipation—the same joy of writing—that he felt when he first became a writer more than 50 years earlier. "A Summer Romance," originally published by *Good Housekeeping* in 1973, was reprinted in a nine story Cave collection, *A Summer Romance and Other Short Stories* (Longman Group Ltd., 1980). It was also published in Japan, as part of a series for Japanese students learning to speak English. *Romance* is now in its 12th printing as such.

"The Mission" was reprinted in a re-introduced *Saturday Evening Post* (date unclear). The Zenger Company reprinted Cave's wartime books, *The Fightin'est Ship, I Took the Sky Road,* and *Long Were the Nights.*

Clearly though, the primary thrust of his career rebirth, had a darker edge to it.

During the last years in Jamaica, his focus had shifted to novels: *Legion of the Dead* (Avon, 1979), *The Nebulon Horror* (Dell, 1980), *The Evil* (Ace Charter, 1981) and *Shades of Evil* (Ace Charter, 1982). He based all these paperbacks on his experiences in Haiti and Jamaica, each inspired by actual places or events, then embellished by Cave's tireless imagination. The supernatural element in all the books came from the voodoo rituals, which were prominent, and, of course, authentic.

Legion of the Dead, his first horror novel, sold only 15,302 copies. Its main character was a writer who returned to a fictitious island named San Marcos (Haiti) to search for a cult of zombies. "I based the book on my trip to the South Peninsula of Haiti with Dr. Deichman, and the hero was a man just divorced from his sexless wife."

This novel was his first with new agent, Eleanor Wood, whose firm worked with Kirby McCauley. "Kirby was too tied up with others at the time, one of those others being Stephen King."

The Evil became his best seller of the group, shipping almost a quarter million copies when it came out as an "Ace Charter" book, the publisher's top-of-the-line imprint.

It concerns an anthropologist, Dr. Bell, who, while investigating voodoo in the remote mountains of northern Haiti, falls under the power of Margal, a legless *bocor* who is capable of controlling people's minds. Margal sends Bell in a zombie-like trance to the capital, to murder the President responsible for Margal's being a cripple.

Arriving in Haiti at this time are Dr. Bell's daughter and Sam Norman, who is helping her search for her missing father. Sam previously worked in Haiti as an agricultural expert. While there, he loved a nurse, Kay Gilbert, but lost her when he went "crazy" one night and abused her. He doesn't know that Margal, the sorcerer, is responsible for what happened to him.

Nurse Kay Gilbert at this moment is en route to Margal's village with a little peasant girl who was brought to her hospital months before by a mission priest, as a zombie. The priest himself had pronounced her dead, officiated at her burial, then discovered her alive in a distant village months later. (The same incident that appeared in *Legion of the Dead.*) At the hospital the child recovered and remembered her past. Kay is now taking her home, first by jeep to the end of the last driving road, then on horseback over difficult mountain trails.

These story lines intertwine throughout the novel. As Margal becomes aware of the two "expeditions" approaching his village, he throws all kinds of mental obstacles in their way. At one point they think the trail is engulfed in flames as they are crossing a dangerous cliffside. At another, a harmless lizard becomes a devouring dragon. Rivers they think safe are actually in full flood, nearly drowning them. Meanwhile, each "expedition" learns of the other's existence and our separated lovers, Kay and Sam, begin thinking about each other anew. In Sam's case this is significant because Dr. Bell's daughter is in love with him.

The child is delivered safe; the lovers are reunited. But Margal, to be present at the death of the President, is himself transported to the capital.

This brings all our people together in Port-au-Prince for the climax. Kay and Sam learn that it was Margal who caused the rift between them. The prof's daughter sacrifices herself to save them from a new assault. Margal is trapped in a house fire that he himself "thinks" into existence while trying to escape capture by the President's bodyguards.

The story naturally contains a good deal of voodoo and zombie lore along with its authentic Haitian background.

While they printed 240,000 first run copies of *The Evil,* only 80,000 were sold because of the returns policy in force at the time. Publishers shipped books on a 60–90 days net basis. Books that didn't sell were returned stripped, or with the covers removed. The publisher would then issue a credit and destroy the stripped books. This policy came back to haunt them later. Major booksellers like Barnes & Noble ordered huge quantities of a title and ended up shipping back more books than a publisher could absorb without a very bad case of indigestion.

"Michael Seidman was editor of Ace at the time, and I would still be writing the "Evil" series today if Putnam hadn't bought out the company and let Seidman go."

The Evil was followed up the next year by a sequel, *Shades of Evil,* also an Ace Charter imprint. Although it borrows some background and one of its main characters from *The Evil,* the story line is new. It also weaves more of Hugh Cave's personal real life experiences into the novel than most of his work to date.

The main character is Will Platt, a writer of supernatural thrillers. His best selling books are based on his experiences living in Haiti and Jamaica. He now lives in a small, Central Florida community, alone because his wife, Vicky, has apparently left him. His home is on the top floor of a condominium, which overlooks a large lake.

Strange happenings begin to occur when two dogs are found dead by the lake and some residents report sighting a large alligator as well as a strange shape-shifting mist which rises from the lake at night and moves ashore. When one of the residents turns up dead for no apparent reason, the residents become scared. In the meantime, a youthful widow, Lynne Kimball, moves in and immediately becomes friends with Will Platt. They soon become lovers. Though Platt's wife disappeared under mysterious circumstances, we learn they had been husband and wife in name only because she was a lesbian.

After several more residents die mysteriously and sightings of this strange mist that becomes human-like occur more frequently, many residents leave. Will and his new lover, Lynne, however, stay there with a few other brave souls. We learn that when Platt and his wife, Vicky, lived in Haiti, she had come under the spell of Margal, the legless *bocor* in *The Evil.* He begins to suspect that she has something to do with this murderous mist that happens to take human—specifically, female—shape before it kills.

After the apparition begins to stalk Will, he becomes convinced that it is the result of something that happened in Jamaica just before Will moved to the Florida condo. We flash back to that time. Will is in Jamaica at the request of a friend of his from Haiti, Sam Norman, a key character in *The Evil.* It seems an associate of Sam's, Juan Cerrado, has mysteriously disappeared. His disappearance seems related to an evil obeah woman, Sister Merle, with powers similar to Margal. Sam himself now fears he is a target of her wrath and that is the reason why he has summoned Will.

They begin their search for Juan and confront this Sister Merle, who says she knows nothing. Soon afterwards, Sam himself disappears. Now Will's wife, Vicky, decides to fly down and meet him in Jamaica, even though Will would prefer she stay back in the states. He is concerned that she had changed after her involvement with Margal and now wants to become involved with obeah.

Will is relieved when he finds Sam alive, although someone had tried to murder him. They continue their quest to find Juan Cerrado, following leads through primitive Jamaican mountain terrain, only to find his murdered body in a cave. All evil points to Sister Merle, who has befriended Vicky and now controls her. Sam's housekeeper, Ima Williams, had been Juan's lover, and now seeks vengeance for his death. She is actually from Haiti and something of a voodoo priestess. Ima battles for mind control with Vicky and Sister Merle. She avenges Juan's death by going to Sister Merle's home and killing her.

Sam leaves for Boston, while Will and Vicky decide to move to Central Florida and buy a condo where this story began. They had agreed to divorce in Jamaica upon returning to the States, but after a few days in their condo, Vicky begins to act strangely, and in a trance one night, tries to murder Will. He ends up killing her though and disposes of her body in the lake.

We find all this out after Will calls Sam Norman and asks him to come down and help. Will had been under suspicion because of Vicky's sudden disappearance after they moved in to the condo. Clearly, this lake apparition is Vicky, bent on killing Will. Sam and Lynne go to Jamaica and bring back Ima Williams so she can use her voodoo skills to defeat Vicky's demon spirit. It turns out the spirit is actually that of Sister Merle, but she is defeated.

This is not one of Cave's finer works. Although the background, with its description of Jamaica, the people and their language is authentic, and his masterful grasp of voodoo and obeah are evident, the story itself includes too many contrived plot devices. When I recently asked Hugh about this book, he only chuckled and said he couldn't even remember writing it.

It was published within a year after his successful Ace Charter debut with *The Evil* and he agrees it must have been written in haste to fulfill a request for a follow-up sequel. The true sequel is *The Evil Returns,* which came out just recently in the summer of 2001 from Leisure Books. More on that later.

"I also wrote a novel called *The Human Inclusion* around 1976. The story was originally based in Florida and I didn't sell it until about four years later, after changing the setting from Florida to Haiti. I had become known as the man who knew so much about voodoo, so had no problem selling it to Tor Books as *The Lower Deep* (1981). They bought it at first look."

The story is set on the north coast of the Caribbean island of St. Joseph, Cave's fictional name for Haiti. Warned that he will encounter mysterious problems probably related to voodoo, Dr. Steve Spence arrives to take charge of a hospital retreat for alcoholics. The man he is replacing is an old friend, Dr. Tom Driscoll.

On the staff are a young Cuban medic, Juan Mendoza, who worked with Steve in the States, and a nurse, Nadine Palmer, with whom Steve was in love during a former sojourn in St. Joe. Steve and Nadine parted company, violently, after he attended La Souvenance, a secret voodoo service at which he offended an evil loa and was "possessed."

The story line is centered in deep water off the coast, where an undersea cave is occupied by creatures who stayed behind in the sea when the forerunners of mankind emerged to become land dwellers. They now realize their mistake and want to mate with land dwellers so their offspring can escape from the sea prison. They have the power to control human minds and lure land dwellers into their domain.

A number of patients at the hospital are already under the influence of these creatures. Also a number of people in the nearby village of Dame Marie, where a respected St. Joseph doctor, Louis Clermont, is struggling to find out what's wrong with his people. One of the latter is an American, George Benson, a U.N. fishing expert, in St. Joseph to teach the peasants how to fish more efficiently. He and his wife Alice are on the outs, and he has a local girlfriend, Danielle.

Dr. Clermont and Steve Spence become buddies and work together at solving the mystery. The two principal villains, already trained by the undersea creatures and now doing the "recruiting" for them, are the Cuban, Mendoza, and Benson's wife, Alice.

There is an undercurrent of voodoo throughout this novel, but in the end voodoo is on the side of the angels. There are several other subplots. A Dame Marie teenager, the daughter of a respected family, disappears. When found (after she has escaped from the undersea cave) she is pregnant, and with Steve and Dr. Clermont at her bedside she produces a monstrous infant.

In the climax, George Benson and his girlfriend are forced by his wife to swim with her to the cave. They have been mentally and physically prepped for the journey and can remain under water for long periods of time. But after an undersea battle with the monsters they manage to escape to a pursuing boat manned by

Steve and Clermont. The monsters and the cave they live in are destroyed.

In his April 13, 1976 letter to Jacobi, Cave mentioned another novel he wrote about the same time:

> I wrote a new novel when I was over there this time (in Jamaica). Was there better than 3 months. It started out to be a *Weird Tales* type of science fiction at the end, so I may end up with a big fat nothing.[1]

Years would go by before he published this book as well, 12 to be exact. The "big fat nothing" became *Disciples of Dread* (Tor Books, 1988).

The "Disciples of Dread" is an international terrorist organization of mind control experts led by their master, Khargi. Vin Donner, an American secret agent on the trail of the Disciples, captures Khargi, but he escapes and nearly destroys Vin by controlling his mind.

Vin's twin brother Mark arrives in Jamaica to hide from the Disciples. The secret U.S. agency of which Vin is a member has convinced Mark, an innocent school teacher, that he is in danger because of his brother's assignment. Actually, though Vin doesn't know it, Mark is being used as bait.

It has been arranged for Mark Donner to hide out in the Great House of an old Blue Mountain coffee plantation (Cave's, of course) pretending to be a writer. There he will be taken care of by Eve, a young deaf, mute Englishwoman. Mark falls in love with Eve, and they learn to communicate through a kind of ESP, at which he and his brother have always been adept and Eve has acquired through a nanny who was an obeah woman.

The Disciples track Mark down and he has to hide out deep in the mountains, Eve remaining behind to get information to him. But her link with him is discovered by the Disciples, and through mind control they force her to reveal his whereabouts.

At this point Vin arrives in Jamaica realizing that his brother has been set up as bait to trap the Disciples. After some dramatic twists and turns of the plot, the brothers eventually destroy Khargi himself in the mountains of Jamaica. Mark marries Eve and good conquers evil.

All the above-mentioned books were considered supernatural horror thrillers, although by today's standards they were quite tame. While Cave once again felt excited about the future, this venture into horror novels and the revival of his weird menace stories might have hurt him long-term. "I hadn't written a book in about ten years because I was selling to the slicks. Then I wrote a string of horror novels. While horror seemed the right way to go with all my experiences and background, and I did enjoy writing in the genre, it ended up pigeonholing me. Who knows, if I had continued with mainstream fiction novels, I might have become another John Updike."

An interesting footnote to Cave's creative output should be noted here. *Disciples of Dread* actually started out as a love story, namely the relationship between Mark and Eve. It ran in a 1967 issue of *Good Housekeeping* as the previously mentioned 25,000-word novelette entitled, "The Island of Eve." *Good Housekeeping* promoted it the month before as "A romantic novelette with adventure—the tenderest love story ever!"

"The Island of Eve" proved immensely popular, and Cave was asked to write a sequel. "The Search for Little Mary," another 25,000-word novelette, ran in June, 1969. In it, Mark and Eve get married and have a child who is kidnapped. Of this, *Good Housekeeping* wrote:

> "Those of you who remember the same author's "Island of Eve" know the sense of romance and adventure you'll find in this dramatic sequel. And anyone just being introduced to the Donners—Mark and his lovely Eve and their little daughter—will discover fresh, rewarding reading in this suspenseful novelette."[1]

Prior to writing the sequel, however, Cave also expanded "The Island of Eve" into a novel entitled *Run, Shadow, Run* (copyright 1968, Robert Hale Ltd) that was published only in England. In 1976, as indicated in Cave's letter to Jacobi, he further expanded *Run, Shadow, Run* into what he called "a big fat nothing," which became *Disciples of Dread.*

Cave was pleasantly surprised at the market for his newer short stories as well as his older works. *Whispers* began publishing mostly new Cave stories in 1975, about one per year over the next ten years. Later, Doubleday did a series of *Whispers* anthologies, and one of his stories appeared in *The Best of Whispers* (Borderlands, 1994). "It was a handsome hardcover edition that sold for $65.00, and was signed by all the writers therein with a striking dust jacket by award-winning artist, Lee Brown Coye."

From his pulp days, 26 stories appeared in *Murgunstrumm and Others* in 1977, and he would find more Cave tales published in multi-author anthologies over the next eight years. Then, beginning in 1988, other Cave-exclusive collections started hitting the market.

The revival of his pulp works meant attending pulp conventions and conferences, like the World Fantasy Convention in Fort Worth where he became good friends with Wellman and Wagner. He soon became friends with another pulp icon.

"Peg and I were invited to attend the 1983 Pulpcon in Dayton, Ohio. I was particularly excited because Robert Bloch of *Psycho* fame would also be a guest. I had admired his writing most of my life, and in my opinion, he was—and has been for years—a master storyteller. Although we wrote for some of the same magazines in our pulp days, we had never met. Now I would shake hands with him for the very first time.

"As it happened, our planes arrived in Dayton fifteen minutes apart, We were being picked up by the convention's Mark Tatman, so Bob and I met at the airport. Fate operates in funny ways. United Airlines had lost part of my ticket when Peg and I changed planes in Columbus. While Peg, who's had experience in public relations, was trying to straighten this out, Bob and I sat on a bench and got acquainted. By the time we arrived at Dayton University where the convention was being held, we were friends."

He clearly has a great deal of respect for Bloch and humbly gives him all the credit for their fast friendship. However, Cave's record in that arena, from World War II heroes to voodoo priestesses, shows that he has no problem making friends either.

Robert Bloch's version of their first meeting, as captured in his introduction for the Audrey Parente book, *Pulp Man's Odyssey*, also demonstrates that the respect went both ways:

> The first time I shook hands with Hugh B. Cave was fifty-one years after we first met. Our hands clasped in 1983, at a convention in Dayton, Ohio. But our first meeting took place in Milwaukee, Wisconsin, in 1932. It was then that I, a budding teenager, encountered Mr. Cave, already in full flower as a writer. He appeared to me via the pages of the June issue of *Weird Tales* magazine, and my introduction came in the form of his story, 'The Ghoul Gallery.'[20]

"Bob and I served on a panel together—Rusty Hevelin was the moderator—and we talked about the old days of the pulps. I felt as though I had known him all my life."

Cave and Bloch both received Lifetime Achievement Awards at the event. Bloch spoke of Cave by saying:

> In one person incarnate we have a virtual living history of the pulps. He embodies and personifies that era, and you're not going to get a chance to meet a gentleman of this stature again.[21]

They continued to talk, correspond and see each other at conventions right up to Robert Bloch's death in 1994. Cave paid tribute to his friend at the 1995 Pulpcon, reflecting on their last correspondence:

> Then one day in August of 1994 I received a letter from him, handwritten in red ink, informing me that he had inoperable cancer and would soon be gone. I had to answer it, of course, and after half a dozen false starts, I finally got some words on paper. (Bob, if writing this, would surely have said 'I finally got unBloched.') Among other remarks, I repeated something I had heard years before and never forgotten: "Death is the greatest adventure of all. That's why they save it till last."
>
> I don't know who wrote that, but as I get closer to my own time of departure, I find it comforting. I hope it comforted him. He was a great writer, a good, gentle man, and a warm, wonderful friend. I have a hunch I'll meet him again sometime and be just as glad as I was that first time in Dayton.[1]

Cave's time of departure was still a long way off, but that didn't prevent him from coming face-to-face with this greatest adventure of all.

His typical day with Peggie meant getting up around seven in the morning and going right for the computer, where he would spend most of his morning. By now, Hugh Cave had gone digital. "I purchased my first computer in 1980 and now have a scanner, laser and inkjet printer and use America Online for e-mail and Internet research."

He spent his afternoons with Peggie. At night, he read to her before turning out the light. His life had changed dramatically from his days with Margaret. Financially, he did not have the income he once enjoyed, nor did he have as much money in the bank as he had hoped. Yet, he felt perfectly happy with his shorter work hours, often just answering fan mail and publisher offers for his older work, then spending time with Peggie.

Cave led a truly satisfying life, but never far from reminders of how delicate that life can be.

"I was going to the drug store one day and Peg told me to pick up two stool specimen kits she had seen advertised in a magazine. The kit contained a bottle and package for shipping your specimen to a lab where they tested it for the presence of cancer cells.

"I went to the drug store, then almost forgot to buy the kits, remembering as I walked out the door. I went back, but only found one kit on the shelf. So I paid for it and started out the door again, when a clerk stopped me. She had gone in the back and found another kit. I'm telling you all this because at any point I could have walked out of that drug store with no kit to test myself.

"The next day we mailed out our specimens. Several days after that, I received notification from the lab to see my doctor immediately. So I called the doctor and he fit me in right away. He examined me and said I have a tumor, that I should check-in to the hospital immediately, and he would be available for surgery the moment I got there.

He went in the next day for surgery. They removed a section of his colon and the operation was a success, but his doctor debated whether to give Cave chemotherapy because of his age. "I asked him what he would do if I was his father. He said he wouldn't recommend it. So I had no chemo. I made a complete recovery and have been cancer-free since 1985."

To help pay the medical bills, Cave contacted his attorney in Jamaica and asked if he could somehow transfer the money he still had in his account. The attorney went to a politician he knew and had the money converted to U.S. dollars. Cave finally received his last payment of $6,000, ten years after he sold the plantation and far less an amount than the buyer had promised him at the time of sale.

Cave was relieved to close the books on his Jamaican adventure. Like his experience in Haiti, he had gone in to it somewhat naively and full of enthusiasm, then left on a sour note. But also like Haiti, he held no regrets. In both cases, he acquired a lifetime of memories resulting in many books and short stories, and he found a new, more exciting adventure to pursue in its place.

Cave's relationship with Peg now became the focus of his life. She gave him the love and affection he had never experienced. She also encouraged him to stay in touch with his family, particularly his brothers.

After Cave moved to Florida in 1967, he made several visits to brother, Tom, and wife, Gladys. They lived on an island near Tampa and when Hugh visited, Tom would take him out in their boat. Cave enjoyed spending time with his brother, finally out from the shroud of secrecy that had always seemed to govern his life. Now they were just like brothers, enjoying time together they rarely shared as children, Tom being eight years older.

Unfortunately, Tom's health began to deteriorate after 1980. "Then one day in 1985, a policeman came to our door and said, 'You're Mr. Cave? Hugh Cave? We received a telephone call from your brother's wife and she hasn't been able to get you on the phone for some reason. She wanted me to report to you—he took a deep breath—that your older brother, Tom, has died. Please get in touch with her.'

"She had apparently lost my number and was too upset to find it. She has since died, too."

Tom's death and Cave's cancer surgery did not make 1985 a year he wished to remember. But the bad news was about to get worse.

Cave's son, Don, had contracted hepatitis while he lived in Miami and continued to battle it off and on for more than ten years afterwards. "It returned once again in California, this time, Don thought, from something he ate in a restaurant. He was in bed for weeks, then he suddenly contracted pneumonia and died soon afterwards.

"Don was only 41 years old and never married, but he was a talented, caring boy who enjoyed life. I couldn't bring myself to go to his funeral. I don't like funerals in the first place; you end up with that image of someone lying in a coffin and that's not the person you knew. That's not the way I wanted to honor his memory."

If Cave, as any parent, looked to see which of his children would take after him, Don was certainly the one, being both a writer and a painter. His death was a loss that Cave could never replace. He rarely talks about it, but when he does, the pain is still there.

Back when Cave first told his son, Ken, that he was in love with Peg, Ken was happy for his Dad. "Ken was enthusiastic and said it's about time that I had a little happiness. 'God knows you haven't had any yet,' he said. I wanted a divorce so I could marry Peg, and of course, I wasn't speaking to Margaret at all by then. Ken's attitude was, 'What's the difference whether you get married; it's just a piece of paper.' At that point, he had had his fight with Margaret and wasn't speaking to her either."

Of all his family members, Cave was closest to his brother

Geoff. They had always been the best of friends growing up, and stayed in touch with each other as adults. Geoff never left New England, and lived close to their dear mother, Edith, who moved into Geoff's house for her last years.

Geoff had always felt uncomfortable around Margaret, but he quickly fell for Peg's warm nature. "Geoff and Alice started visiting us on a regular basis, for two or three weeks every winter. They had three kids. David was a Navy pilot and captain, who lived two years in Thailand and flew the early hurricane hunter planes. He lives in East Douglas, Massachusetts with his wife, the former Susan Shuster of Shuster Mills. The other kids are Judith, who married an Army man, and Marge, who is a librarian.

"They sold their home to their son David, who later bought a larger home with an in-law apartment so Geoff and Alice could move in with them."

Hugh Cave's son, Ken, eventually moved to Washington state, near Puget Sound. Hugh and Peg were tiring of the hot Florida summers and Ken's description of the area's beauty and cool weather, became a temptation they couldn't pass up. Peg was also familiar with the area having lived there years back. "Ken found a house for us on Whidbey Island, a great spot for a writer. So Peg and I put our house up for sale and started packing."

Chapter 35: Coast to Coast and Back

The house was perfect and the area just as beautiful as Ken had described. Ken and Betsy were delighted to have his Dad close by.

> Cave to Jacobi, April 14, 1988: Well, old boy, Peg and I are getting settled in our new home, and are we glad we made the move. She grew up in the Northwest here, so feels she has "come home." As for me, I'm glad to get away from Florida's ever-hotter summers, and this little island town of Oak Harbor is just my cup of tea.[1]

Brother Geoff expressed disappointment that he wouldn't be seeing Hugh in warm, sunny Florida anymore, but became enthusiastic about coming out to Washington for a visit. "We decided on a date and I wrote him a letter with directions on how to get here."

However, the trip never happened. Soon after Hugh and Peg settled in to their new home, they received word that Geoff Cave had died unexpectedly.

Hugh Cave had lost his brother, his boyhood chum and lifelong confidante. He had lost the last connection to his childhood and the family that came to America back in 1914. Cave grieved, as he had grieved for his son and brother Tom in recent years. But something about his outlook on life, always looking forward to his next adventure—even if it was only the next day—sheltered him from the terrific sense of loss he must have felt.

In 1988, Cave saw the release of his novel, *Disciples of Dread* (Tor Books). He also published two new young adult novels. *The Voyage* (Macmillan and Co., 1988) concerned the adventures of youngsters growing up on Cape Cod. He drew from his own experiences as a boy at Camp Ascension and other childhood memories. *Conquering Kilmarnie* (Macmillan, 1989), told the story of a black boy and white boy living on a Jamaican plantation. The aforementioned Hugh Cave biography written by Audrey Parente also came out in 1988, *Pulp Man's Odyssey* (Starmont House). A second anthology of his pulp work, *The Corpse Maker* (Starmont House, 1988), fed an increasingly hungry pulp enthusiast market. *The Lower Deep* (Tor Books) hit bookstore and supermarket shelves in 1990, and *Lucifer's Eye* (Tor Books), his first novel about Jamaica, was published in 1991. After that, he would not have another novel published for eight more years.

He continued to write short stories though, and still does. Between 1990 and 1994, Cave wrote and published 20 brand new tales. In 1994 alone, he was published 39 times, rivaling his most productive pulp years! One of those original stories, "Genesis II," was later expanded into book length form as his 2000 novel, *The Dawning* (Leisure Books, 2000). Another, "Vanishing Point," (copyright 1993, *Northern Frights II,* Mosaic Press, Canada) was based on a drive Hugh and Peg took one day in Washington. "We were exploring the state and discovered a little mountain village that intrigued us. It became the setting for this story."

Pulp enthusiasts had by now become interested in anything "Hugh Cave," as is evidenced by the publication of his personal letters to Carl Jacobi in *Magazines I Remember.* Yet his other writing accomplishments had not gone unnoticed, even to the general public. "One day Peg and I were at a yard sale—it had become a real passion for both of us, especially when I started finding copies of some of my older works. I handed my card to a man so he could phone me about something he was selling. He looked at the card and then said, 'Hey! You're not the Hugh B. Cave who wrote all those great stories in the *Saturday Evening Post,* are you?' It turned out that he had purchased several of my books just because he liked the *Post* yarns."

Cave's earlier work had also been discovered by a most unlikely new fan, Jonathan Demme, Academy Award-winning director of *Silence of the Lambs* (1991) and *Philadelphia* (1993).

"He is also an expert on Haiti, having gone there to do a documentary on their search for democracy. He fell in love with the country, just as I did, and while there, he heard about and then saw some of my Haiti books. He returned to New York and started hunting them down. He found everything I had written except for two or three books including my novel, *Black Sun.* He contacted my agent and asked for my address. One day I received a package in the mail including a CD of Haitian music and a letter from Jonathan Demme asking where he might find a copy of these missing books."

In typical Hugh Cave fashion, he sent Demme the requested books from his own personal collection. "Since then he has kept in touch, sending letters with pictures of his kids, Christmas cards, even calling once in a while. He also sends me videotape copies of his new movies. He has since gone back to Haiti and done several more documentaries. He also reintroduced Haiti liberation music and keeps in touch with other people concerned about the future of Haiti, like Harry Belafonte. I have a copy of a letter from Jean Bertrand Aristide to Jonathan Demme thanking him for his help in bringing democracy back to Haiti. Of course, that never really happened and the country is still in turmoil. It's funny, I never even knew what Demme looked like until I happened to see him on the Academy Awards telecast one year."

After receiving his 1978 award for *Murgunstrumm and Others* and the 1983 Lifetime Achievement Award at Pulpcon, Cave's next recognition came in 1987. He received the Phoenix Award at the Deep South Convention for "Outstanding Contributions to the Arts by a Southern Writer."

In June, 1991, Cave received yet another honor, for his lifetime achievements, this time from the Horror Writers of America at their annual meeting in Redondo Beach, California. It would show him the strength and devotion of his fan base—which included other writers, agents and publishers. He also discovered, finally, what it meant to have the love of a woman who supported his career.

"This was strictly a convention of writers, no fans. I was only the sixth writer ever granted this recognition, others being such greats as Robert Bloch and Ray Bradbury. I went up to the podium for my award, then everyone stood clapping for four or five minutes. I looked at Peg and she sat at our table, crying her eyes out.

"I remember giving my acceptance speech, telling the audience, 'You are looking at a very lucky man. I've been able to eke out a pretty fair living doing what I most enjoy most—putting words on paper and seeing them in print. I want you to know that with the encouragement and support of my fair lady, I'm still doing it—57 years after some nut editor bought and published my first manuscript. That's a long time to be writing. This is just the frosting on that big, wonderful cake.'

"I went back to the table with my trophy, put it down and Peggie stood up so I could put my arms around her. Everyone rose a second time for two or three minutes, applauding. It was one of my most thrilling experiences."

While in Los Angeles, a local bookstore set up a signing for him. "I went to this famous bookstore for fantasy, horror and sci-fi in Sherman Oaks, called Dangerous Visions. They had advertised that I would be there. People came from all over with grips and boxes of my books to be signed. Next door was an empty building the size of the bookstore. They had put tables down the sides and the middle. People were lined up all around the block for me to sign books. I spent the next two solid hours writing my signature before the line finally went down. By then, I had serious writer's cramp."

Interestingly, twenty-seven of Cave's books had been published by that time, including a new one, *Lucifer's Eye;* yet, he signed more copies of *Murgunstrumm and Others,* published 14 years earlier, than any other single volume.

I asked Hugh why he felt he had not become as widely known as some of his contemporaries.

"I think not having any of my books made into movies had a lot to do with it. When Stephen King published his first novel, *Carrie,* it was not hugely successful. Then they made a movie of it, which became a big hit. Afterwards, when *Carrie* came out in paperback, it sold millions and King was on his way. He used to come to the World Fantasy Convention—in fact, we once served on a panel together—but after he became so popular he couldn't attend anymore because he would be mobbed by fans."

The Cross on the Drum and *Black Sun* were both excellent books and sold well. Why didn't he continue writing mainstream fiction like that?

"Don't forget, I was routinely making $3,000 or more for a short story and upwards of $12,000 for a novelette. That was excellent money and more than I made on novels. I had a family to support, so I wasn't about to walk away from that kind of money."

He had also become a coffee grower, which took up most of his time. While that no doubt enriched his life's experiences, a strong agent might have tried to talk him out of it and use that time to write more novels.

While Cave enjoyed a career renaissance, he was not enjoying life on the West coast. "Ken and Betsy were involved with their own lives and we didn't see that much of them. I went fishing quite a bit with Peg's cousin who lived in the area, but other than that, we kept pretty much to ourselves. The weather was also getting to us. The country is beautiful out there, but it stays so green because of all the rain. We had gloomy weather much of the time, which means it was also cold and damp. We were used to having plenty of warm sunshine and began to really miss it."

There were also several unpleasant incidents involving his son, Ken. "He can get very angry, like Margaret used to, and stay that way for a long time. We were watching TV once and disagreed over something minor. He didn't speak to me for six months. He snapped at Peg once and she said, "Don't you ever speak to me like that again." Other people were stunned because they said no one ever talks to Ken like that. He's a big guy, about 6'3" tall and husky. He could be just like Margaret was that time in Jamaica, having a bad day driving and then not getting behind the wheel for the next 15 years.

"He gradually got over it though and things returned to normal—until the day we told him we wanted to move back to Florida. That was in 1994 and the last time we spoke."

As of this writing, Cave has still not heard from his only surviving son, although Ken's wife Betsy stays in touch, primarily by letter and e-mail.

Neither Cave's son, Ken, nor his wife, Margaret, was interviewed for this book, so we can only speculate on how they might interpret the events he described on these pages. The evidence suggests that Cave dealt with emotional situations by simply accepting them "as is" and moving on to the shelter of his work or his next adventure. By walking away from problems and not confronting them, he may have left a great deal of frustration and anger in his path.

The intent of this book, though, is to tell Hugh Cave's story from his point of view. Whether or not he could have handled his relationships—or his career—better is a judgement left to you, the reader. We all face these kinds of decisions in our lives and rarely do we make our decisions with the unanimous approval of those around us.

Whatever decisions Hugh Cave made along the way, the fact remains that he has left us with a body of work we admire and led a life that most of us could only dream of leading.

Chapter 36: Plenty of Tales Left in This Cave

Hugh and Peg returned to Sebastian in August 1994. Their good friends from before, Cricket and Jere Pechstein, helped them find a new home. They were glad to be back in Florida; however, he discovered another literary loss upon his return. "Somewhere in the moves between Florida and Washington, I lost copies of all my stories that had appeared in *The Sign*. Worse than that though, I also lost all my Carl Jacobi letters."

Cave continued to accumulate new publishing credits after returning from Washington. Collections of his work have been brought out on a regular basis. They include *Death Stalks the Night* (Fedogan & Bremer, 1995), *The Dagger of Tsiang* (Tattered Pages Press, 1996), *The Door Below* (Fedogan & Bremer, 1997), *Escapades of the Eel* (Tattered Pages Press, 1997), two chapbooks of Officer Coffey stories, a collection of cat tales called *The Lady Wore Black* (Ash Tree Press, 2000), *Bottled In Blond* (Fedogan & Bremer, 2000), a collection of his Peter Kane detective stories, and *Long Live the Dead* (Crippen & Landru, 2000), a collection of all Cave's *Black Mask* Magazine stories.

Death Stalks the Night held particular significance to Cave. "After his success with *Murgy,* Karl Wagner decided to do a second anthology of my stories, again illustrated by Lee Brown Coye. The project didn't go forward for a number of years, and when it finally did, Karl died unexpectedly just before publication. Fortunately, the folks at Fedogan & Bremer put the book out, complete with Karl's introduction and Coye's wonderful artwork."

Between 1995 and 2001, he wrote and published three novels *Isle of the Whisperers* (Pumpkin Books, 1999, *The Dawning* and *The Evil Returns*) and 43 *new* short stories. That would be a respectable output for any fiction writer today, but this is from a man between his 85th and 91st years!

One of his short stories, "Nights In the Mountains of Haiti," reminded him of his pulp days. "Marty Greenberg sent me a letter telling me he was about to publish a book of werewolf tales and asked me to write a new story for it. So, I sat down and wrote a 6,500-word story, just like old times."

The anthology, *Werewolves* (DAW Books), came out in 1995. It joined a number of multi-author anthologies for which Cave has written new material over the past several years. He even used one of his pen names, Judy Case, for a story in *The Liguorian* magazine ("Planned Encounter," February 1995).

Cave thought little about recognition for his accomplishments through the years. To him, he was simply doing his job, albeit a job he thoroughly enjoyed. Once the recognition started coming, however, he humbly accepted it and looked forward to more.

One day in early 1996 he received a letter from Jo Fletcher, chairman of the upcoming World Fantasy Convention in London, scheduled for October 31, 1997. In the letter, she invited Hugh and Peg to the convention as guests, all expenses paid. "Peggie and I were both delighted. I sent Jo a response telling her so, and asked what was expected of me in return. She wrote back, saying I would participate on a couple of panels and give a short speech at the awards ceremony. Based on all the good things happening to me in recent years, I thought they were going to give me some type of award, possibly lifetime achievement."

Cave couldn't stop talking about his upcoming trip, returning triumphant to his native England where he would be honored by his peers and fans.

In early July 1996, I called Peggie to discuss plans for Hugh's upcoming 86th birthday. She told me she wanted to call me back about something important. Then Peg called a few days later. "Milt dear," she said, "I don't think I'll be able to go with Hugh to London this fall."

Why not? I asked.

"My cancer is back."

She had two cancer operations several years earlier and they had planned a third, but decided against it because the trauma might be too much at her age. Now the cancer had returned.

In her typical fashion though, she only showed concern for Hugh. "He doesn't know about it yet; he's been depressed because he doesn't have a U.S. agent and nothing much is happening in Europe. He's also experienced some periods of forgetfulness. But ever since he found out about going to London, he's been so happy and excited. I don't want him worrying about this."

I asked her what I could do to help.

"Take Hugh to London in my place. He would love it and I wouldn't have to worry about him knowing that you were there to watch over him."

I told her I would be honored.

One day I paid them a visit and found Hugh quite excited. He couldn't wait to tell me that yesterday he received a telephone call from popular English author and friend, Brian Lumley. They talked for an hour about a possible new U.S. literary agent out in California who was very familiar with the film industry.

Peg added, "He tossed and turned all night before getting up early this morning and writing a letter to this agent with a copy of *Murgunstrumm and Others,* as Brian had recommended. He was like a kid in his enthusiasm; that 86-year-old body seemed like a costume on a teenager."

Peg implored me not to say anything to Hugh about her problems and I agreed. I was also worried because Peg looked more frail than I had ever seen her.

It turned out the cancer had spread to her lungs and kidneys. Her doctor advised chemotherapy because her constitution was strong for an 82-year old woman.

Peg began her treatments, but the chemo took its toll. After two rounds it had left her thin, emaciated, hairless and weak. She didn't look like she could pull through. A third series of treatments was scheduled, but again, as before, her doctor decided against proceeding because of her frail condition.

Then on February 2, 1997, Hugh called me full of excitement to say that Peg was in total remission. "There isn't a trace of cancer anywhere in her system. We both danced around the living room when she received the news."

Peg recovered completely and was back to her old self again. However, she still felt the London trip would be too much for her.

So arrangements were finalized and I accompanied Hugh as a guest of the convention. I had also written a tribute to him for the convention program.

The convention was a tremendous experience for Hugh Cave. He spent every waking moment visiting with old friends, attending functions or signing books, and at the final banquet received a special recognition award. While not the lifetime achievement award he originally thought (that would come a few years later), he felt no less enthusiastic about it. I had never seen him so animated and full of energy. Our days were long and action-packed, but he just didn't want them to end.

By the time we left for home, he was visibly exhausted. We flew back to Miami and then drove more than three hours to Sebastian. I left him at 10:00 that night, after we recounted to Peg and her daughter Joanie, every wonderful detail.

Two days later, Peg called me to say Hugh was in the hospital. He had become ill in the middle of the night, vomiting blood until he passed out in the bathroom. The ambulance came and rushed him to the hospital at 4:30 a.m., where he received six pints of blood before they found the problem—a perforated duodenal ulcer.

His prognosis was guarded the next two days as he continued to lose blood; compounding his condition, he suffered a stroke. When I first saw him, he looked weak and pale, but alert. His face sagged from the stroke, but he didn't realize it. His enthusiasm had not been daunted, though. He couldn't wait to show me the problem he had writing his name. He never sounded like a critically ill senior citizen—he talked with his same youthful enthusiasm, curious and fascinated by his inability to write, but unfettered by it.

Peg pulled me aside and said the trip was just too much for an 87-year-old man. She was worried because the doctors still didn't know if he would pull through this ordeal. She cried and said she could never go on without him, she loved him so much.

But she was talking about Hugh B. Cave, adventurer, spinner of tales, and survivor. He had faced death many times in those 87 years and he was not ready to leave this world just yet.

Hugh recovered fully, but not before doctors discovered another ticking health bomb. In a routine examination, they found that both his carotid arteries were almost completely blocked. The doctors said it was a miracle he did not suffer a massive stroke. He went back to the hospital for two operations after recovering from the ulcer, each to remove plaque from a carotid artery. One piece of plaque was the shape of a pencil.

I have often thought that if he had been stricken by this perforated ulcer just hours earlier on the flight home from England, he would not have survived. Yet, if he hadn't been rushed to the hospital for that ulcer, he might never have known about his blocked arteries, which surely would have been fatal. Isn't it interesting how life turns out sometimes—especially Hugh Cave's life?

Chapter 37: All Good Things . . .

From the moment Hugh Cave and Peggie Thompson began their lives together, they found the relationship they had each longed for all their adult lives. According to Peg, "My years with Hugh have been the happiest time of my life. We probably never would have met unless we both had the kind of life experiences that taught us to appreciate each other. We have lived together 21 years without an argument."

Although Peggie had gone into remission, that was nothing more than a clock ticking away. Her overall physical condition began to deteriorate in 2000, until back surgery made her practically an invalid. Hugh became her caregiver—cooking, cleaning, shopping, driving her to physical therapy, helping her in and out of bed. He rarely complained, although the effort clearly took a physical toll on the 90-year old man.

Peggie's cancer returned and she finally died in February 2001. Hugh's grief was mitigated somewhat by finally getting some rest and, as he had done all through his life—writing. He received all kinds of mail from friends, fans and acquaintances around the world. I was fortunate to have a last visit with Peg in the hospital. She was in a great deal of pain, but we laughed and she was beaming from ear to ear when I left. Hugh told me she went into a coma after that visit, never to recover.

Fortunately, Peggie's three daughters took turns staying with him in the weeks after her death. Her youngest daughter, Joanie, lives nearby in Sebastian, while Meg is a few hours away in South Florida and Jackie lives in West Virginia. They care about him as if he were their natural father, and in so doing, keep their mother's spirit alive.

At the time they met, Hugh and Peg hoped to have five years

together. They decided then to make every minute count and were rarely apart over the next 21 years. Peggie's daughter, Jacky Leggitt, wrote a fitting tribute to her mother for this book:

> In looking back on my mother's life I found her to be a survivor, street wise, tough, shrewd, loving, giving, & kind. Her sport in the early days was diving & she loved to swim. Dancing was another activity she enjoyed. Bridge she excelled at, as well as entertaining. She took advantage of the good & sometimes the bad to make ends meet. There were times in her life that she was unable to fulfill her obligation as a mother to her children, that I heard her say she regretted, but at the time it was all she was able to do to keep her head above water. Her life story to me is a sad one, but never dull or mundane. The one highlight in her life that is filled with sunshine & love is meeting up with Hugh. She was finally rewarded before the end of her journey here on earth.[1]

Hugh Cave has shown remarkable resiliency since Peggie died. He has placed photos and other mementos of her in every room of the house. "I talk to her all the time and I truly believe she is here in the house with me."

For the year after her death, he did not have the time nor the strength to do any new creative writing. Since then, Hugh has once again plunged himself into his work. In the two and a half years since Peggie's death, he has written and published six short stories with two more (one of them a novella) scheduled for publication in the coming months. His second Leisure Books paperback novel, *The Evil Returns* came out in July 2001, and a third from the publisher, *The Restless Dead,* was published in January 2003. *Isle of the Whisperers,* originally published in England only, is currently scheduled by Leisure for 2004 release.

He still travels, too. I have accompanied him to five book signings in the last two years around Florida. Hugh also attended Pulpcon in 2001 and the Windy City Pulp & Paperback Show in 2003, both times as Guest of Honor.

For Hugh, the consummate writer, life goes on. "My sleeping patterns have changed a bit since Peggie died. I sometimes wake up at one or three in the morning and go to the computer for a few hours. Then I go back to bed and get up at my usual time, around 6:30, and back at the computer again."

Every morning he answers his endless e-mail (and it is all from friends, fans and industry folks—no "spam!"), corresponds with publishers on reprints of his work, and yes—writes stories.

He still shops his stories around, just like the old days. He insists on retaining foreign rights in every contract. "Most editors don't ask for all rights, only the beginners."

Cave has a number of unpublished stories sitting under his desk, too. He also has a manuscript for the largest book he has ever written. "It's an epic novel about Haiti, along the lines of *The Thorn Birds.*"

Oh, and in case you forgot, *he is 93 years old!* That's body years though—his mind is still his most vital organ, still seeking new adventures to put down on paper.

Hugh Cave summed up his own life in a letter to Carl Jacobi dated May 23, 1974:

> Anyway, Carl, I don't expect to be remembered for ten minutes after I'm gone—for anything I've written, that is—but at the same time I don't regret the course my life has taken. Being a writer has kept me from slaving away in an office all my life. I've been able to go where I wished and do what I wanted, within the limits of a reasonably good income, and as I look back on it all, I feel I've had a lot of fun.[1]

Thanks to the tender loving care of pulp anthologists, his afterlife will surely last more than the ten minutes he predicted. However, what really counts—how he lived his life—is his true legacy. He developed a dream in childhood and followed it throughout the course of his adult life. He lived every minute of his life with the enthusiasm of a child, always seeking, always learning. He dealt with problems, obstacles and even his own mortality, not by feeling oppressed or sorry for himself, but by keeping himself focused on the horizon beyond those obstacles. That was where he would find his next adventure. Those adventures, whether in Borneo, Haiti, Jamaica or simply in his prolific imagination, guided his journey through life and made it what life should be for all of us—a gift to be cherished every minute of every day.

Thanks, Hugh, for teaching me how to live.

AFTERWORD

Over the past few years I have had a number of in-depth conversations with Hugh Cave about his work, his life, and life in general. Here are a few of those conversations, like most of the Hugh Cave quotes in this book, recorded and transcribed or annotated.

What are your thoughts on being a writer?

"I always wrote for the love of it. I do it today for the love of it. I would rather be writing than doing anything else."

"I never read someone else's fiction in the middle of writing a book because there is a tendency to subconsciously imitate the style and other nuances of that writer."

"Characters must be three-dimensional in a story. The good guy must have some fault, defect or flaw of character to be believable, and the bad guy must have something good in him. Ice cream is sweet because there is salt in it. Certain parts of a book are in slow motion, others move along quickly and you have to get it down as it is happening because you are excited yourself. Toward the end of a book, I would work 10–12 hours a day because I was anxious to see the results as everything comes together."

"I used to write non-fiction in my voice and it sounded just like me talking. My war books were in the voice of the real life hero, with a fiction voice wherever necessary. Many editors and readers don't like first person and new writers are advised not to do it. It used to be popular with horror because it helps the reader feel the suspense and horror. You can't write an entire novel in the first person, because it would only be one point of view. You can only say what you know, what you've seen through one pair of eyes. To drag that on for 3–400 pages would be pretty boring."

"You can't go to a creative writing class and learn how to write. You have it in you, the desire that makes you read and you learn to write."

"Here's a lesson that taught me to keep copies of things. I had written a long adventure story, a serial, and mailed it to *Argosy* without making a carbon copy. The editor at *Argosy* wrote back and said that if I made certain changes in it, they'd buy the story. This would have meant a sale of about a thousand dollars, which was big money in those days. The manuscript never got to me, it got lost in the mail. To this day, I don't remember that story."

"Robert Bloch sold his first story at age 17 to *Weird Tales* for one cent a word. In those days, people were familiar with only a few writers; they didn't have interviews on radio, no TV. Today, writers are media personalities, lecture in colleges, on the lunch circuit. A writer today sells based on public persona. You have got to start out being bad in order to get better, so opportunities are less today. Many great ideas came to Bob, but they came too soon in his career. The young writer today doesn't have any of the markets I had as a young writer. He only has small publications that print 500 copies, not enough exposure to build a name for himself."

"I find book writing more enjoyable because of the freedom. You have room for digression in a novel that you don't have in a short story. Characters can be more complete, hence more meaningful. Their conversations can probe into things with a relaxation not possible in a short story. In a short story, every word must serve four purposes, at least figuratively. But the problem and its resolution are all that can concern the writer. He has a space limit of so many thousand words which he cannot exceed by much. Also, he must be aware of the market, of what will sell and what won't."

"I have been with Peg since 1980. My creativity during that

time has been less because my relationship was richer. I wouldn't have been as prolific if my relationship with Margaret had been satisfactory. So I owe her a lot for making my career possible."

"Carl Jacobi could never write a novel because he was so damned self-critical."

"I have never experienced writer's block."

Some thoughts on writing today

"I wrote back in the days when there was a clean story line with characters you could care about. Writers looked to Stevenson, Poe, and others for inspiration; nobody consulted Sigmund Freud. Today's stories are not stories—they are rambling, incomprehensible, slices of life, things that wouldn't have been published 50 years ago."

"It is legitimate to have one character mislead another in a story. It adds to the suspense, the drive, the 'Oh boy, he got his comeuppance!' at the end. It is not legit for the author to use his word-tricks to fool the reader. Many of today's writers bend the rules to give themselves an advantage. There is a word that needs to be applied here. It is INTEGRITY. I don't read a book to have its author play games with me. I am not entering into a contest with him. I demand he be honest with me as a reader. It simply isn't good enough for a writer to claim he is 'creating atmosphere' when he indulges in such games with the reader. He is not. What he is creating is confusion, and when you confuse a reader, you very soon lose him. He says to hell with you and turns to some writer he doesn't have to play games with."

On writing letters

"Try not to write too many and don't answer them too quickly, because then the next one will come right back and you'll do nothing but answer letters instead of writing. I deliberately wait a month. Look at the great H.P. Lovecraft; he wrote letters, volumes of them in longhand and tiny script, to his admirers. Yet he only wrote much fewer than 100 short stories. He starved and died at 47. Think of how many more stories he would have written if he didn't get involved in this letter writing."

"I am appalled at some of what gets published today. You can't find a book without the "F" word and expect the public to buy it. I will use swear words—not that one—to shock the reader at a certain point, but not every second line. When you do see it, you jump, because it means something is happening."

"There's too much sensational gore in horror novels these days. It used to be about the supernatural. You can't outdo the real life horror you read today. We are desensitized. Classic horror novels had an element of the supernatural that lifted them above the level of daily, dirty crime. Editors don't want supernatural today, they love serial killers."

About agents

"I have had four agents in my career, Lurton Blassingame, whose brother Wyatt was a big name in the pulps, Innes Rose in England, Eleanor Wood, Kirby McCauley and most recently, Dorothy Lumley in England. From 1941 to when I quit writing for the slicks in 1977, I handled all my own stuff without an agent, except for the first books. Eleanor Wood handled me from 1977 to 1984. Then in 1986, my good friend Karl Edward Wagner learned that I was working without an agent and put me in contact again with Kirby McCauley. I had gone to him in 1977, but he referred me to Eleanor in his office because he didn't have time to take on someone new. This time though, he took me on. He was handling Stephen King at that same time. In 1991, I met Dorothy Lumley, then Brian Lumley's wife, who ran the Dorian Agency in England and she became my agent for England. These days, I'm working again without an agent."

Examples of payment

"I kept a log of how I was paid over the years for different publications. Here are some examples:

AMERICAN MAGAZINE. My first sale, in 1942, brought $400. My last sale, 1955, brought $1,150.

BOYS' LIFE. First sale, in 1944, brought $125. Last sale, in 1965, brought $700.

COLLIER'S. First, 1945, $500. Last, 1954, $1,250.

COSMOPOLITAN. First, 1953, $850. Last, 1960, $2,000.

COUNTRY GENTLEMAN. First, 1948, $750. Last, 1954, $2,000 (for a 1950 serial they paid $7,000).

GOOD HOUSEKEEPING. First, 1962, $2,500. Last, 1975, $3,000 (for 'complete novelettes' they paid $12,500).

REDBOOK. First, 1957, $1,000. Last, 1960, $1,250.

SATURDAY EVENING POST. First, 1944, $600. Last, 1961, $3,000 (after I had sold them 43 stories).

TORONTO STAR WEEKLY. First, 1942, $75. Last, 1965, $375. (I have no record of what they paid for the complete novel, 'The Midnight Horde', but I believe it was about $1,000.)"

What would you change if you had it to do over again?

"I would have started writing books a lot sooner. I take the blame for that because of my weakness for making money and Margaret's determination for me to continue making money. I wrote two book-length pulp serials, but they didn't have the potential to be books. *Murgunstrumm* was about 35,000 words, half a normal book in those days.

"When I was writing for the slicks, I turned out a story in a week or two and made $1,500–$2,000. I was making $25–$30,000 a year when you could buy a good car for $4,000, like an Oldsmobile. On the other hand, it took two or three months to write one book and I had a family to support.

"The second thing I would have changed, was going back to mainstream novels like *The Cross on the Drum* and *Black Sun* instead of pigeonholing myself in the horror genre. Actually, my first paperbacks, *Legion of the Dead* and *The Evil,* were sold as mainstream fiction. Then publishers started calling my work horror and marketing it that way because of the demand for horror created by Stephen King."

Do you have any vices?

"Smoking and drinking. I smoked heavily back in the pulp days. I kept an ashtray next to my typewriter and a bottle in the kitchen. I thought drinking would help free up my creativity. It seemed to at the time, but upon reading what I wrote the next day, I usually tore it up. Some drinking may help, but it quickly reaches a point where it hurts the creative process. I've only been roaring drunk a few times in my life. I don't drink much now because if I have one, my inhibition goes to hell and I might drink four or five."

Reflecting on his life

"I've always had a yen to go places and do things. It's why I bought an old run-down coffee plantation in Jamaica's Blue Mountains and spent some 15 years restoring it. I never stopped writing, though, even while planting coffee. I spent part of every day and almost every evening writing books, or short stories for the slicks, in the hope of one day retiring there on Arntully Highlands."

His beliefs

You begin by being born and end by wondering why.[22]

"I keep an open mind about the hereafter. It's not very comforting to think there may not be anything after this life. I enjoy watching shows about miracles, sightings, and so forth, but I'm not sure I believe or don't believe any of it. I envy people who have the faith that there is something beyond life."

"I don't like funerals. I sat in the choir at a lot of funerals as a boy, sitting in the loft and looking down at the coffin at the foot of the chancel. Looking at dead people lying in coffins is not my idea of how to say good-bye to someone. I would prefer to think of them like the last time I enjoyed their company, talked to them, had fun with them.

"I plan to be cremated when I die. My mother was also sold on cremation. She cut an article out of *Reader's Digest,* which I still have today, 'Light Like the Sun.' It's the description of a woman who went to see her husband cremated and she could watch everything through a glass door. She was impressed with its brilliance, which gave the piece its title. That was early in the game; nobody knew much about cremation then."

"Mother wasn't overly religious, but went to church each Sunday. She didn't talk about religion though. Both of my parents belonged to the Church of England. Margaret and I didn't go to church as much. She was a Congregationalist and we were married in a Congregationalist church at the foot of College Hill in Providence. We took our kids to church and Sunday School at East Greenwich Presbyterian Church."

"Out in Washington, Peg and I became involved with a group through my doctor after telling him that we had tried several churches with no luck. The people in this group were all perpetual missionaries who didn't have any personal homes or possessions. They followed the pattern of the first disciples, preaching the Gospel, but not accepting any money for their effort. We met with them for a while and that's the closest we have come to religion."

"There are many unanswered questions in the Bible. For instance, who was Cain's wife? Adam and Eve were the first people and had two sons, so where did she come from? Scholars say these stories came from many other religions, and the people at fault for making these mistakes were the editors of the Bible. The story of Adam and Eve itself has two versions, one says God created man and woman, the other says woman was created from man's rib. It was just bad editing."

"Religious beliefs are very personal, and I think the world would be a much better place if everyone simply respected each other's beliefs. Barry Clinton, the white missionary in *The Cross on the Drum,* best reflects that view in a conversation with Catus Laroche, his black voodoo priest:

> 'Remember this: no man has ever actually solved the mystery of life, Catus. No man can tell you who you are, or who I am, or why we are here. All religions, yours, mine, all the others, are simply a search for truth. Look for it in darkness and you're going to find only dark and frightening answers. Search in the light and you'll lift yourself up to the light.' "[15]

"A Writer's Ten Commandments," according to Hugh B. Cave

1. Try not to imitate any other writer; be an individual.

2. Avoid the gimmickry, garbage language and deliberate obscurity that has invaded so much of what is published today. It's a fad and a bad one; the writers doing it won't be remembered as good writers.

3. If you drink, don't drink while writing. If you do, you'll probably throw away what you've written when you sober up and read it.

4. Remember this: If you specialize in one kind of writing—one "genre"—you'll become well-known a lot sooner, but only as "*that* kind of writer." Becoming a well-known mainstream writer may take longer, but it will pay off better in both reputation and dollars. (Critics have written that if Hugh B. Cave had stuck to "supernatural" fiction, he might have become as popular as H.P. Lovecraft. That may be true, but he wouldn't have sold 43 stories to *Saturday Evening Post* or written travel books and war books as well as mainstream novels.)

5. If you're going to be a writer you must glue your butt to a chair and write, not just talk about it.

6. Read—and I don't mean just what's on today's best-seller list. Read the old masters; they are remembered for a reason.

7. Learn to type. You *can* write in longhand, but it takes too long, and as you become a better writer your thoughts will out-

race your fingers. If at all possible, use a computer. The keys are quiet enough not to intrude upon your thinking. Also, editing on a computer is so much easier. You don't have to retype a whole page to correct a couple of mistakes.

8. Go places and do things. Reading is good, but a writer who has been to the Congo will write more interestingly about it than one who has merely read some books about it. When you're a writer, *everything* you do becomes part of you, to be drawn upon when needed.

9. Keep a notebook. If you don't, you'll forget things that may later be important. Part of keeping a notebook is the way it disciplines you to stay alert at all times for story ideas, bits of description, etc. Your mind will be an open container always ready for something good to come along and fall into it.

10. Ignore these 10 rules and make up your own!

And finally . . .

On September 22, 1972, Hugh B. Cave wrote a letter to Robert Kenneth Jones in answer to Jones' request for biographical information to include in his forthcoming book, *The Shudder Pulps*. The short, one-page letter ended with this paragraph:

> Wish I could offer you something a little more colorful, but, honestly, nothing of that sort ever happened to me.[2]

Fortunately, we now know that Mr. Cave was being painfully modest.

APPENDIX

Cave on Cave

Following are Hugh Cave's own comments, reflections and criticisms about selected stories (the stories can be referenced under Bibliography):

"Alike Under the Skin" This is good South Seas jungle stuff, and it won some sort of prize for stories against racial prejudice.

"But the Kill Was Cold" There are too many characters, and while the story is fairly well-written, these other characters don't come to life as they ought to.

"The Curse of the Grinning Skulls" A simple plot, really, but a story with lots of South Seas color. This was written when I was 23, long before I saw the South Seas first-hand, so I must have done some pretty good research, even ferreting out some native phrases.

"Dyak Torture" This is a well-written jungle story but so grim that Peg asked me to stop reading it to her at bedtime, saying she wouldn't be able to sleep.

"Ladies In Waiting" I wrote it while alone on my Jamaican plantation house on a dark rainy night in 1974, all 4,000 words in one sitting. My housekeeper had gone home and no one was there. The diesel power plant chugged to provide light. I wanted to see if I could still do it after all these years. I was tired of writing for *Good Housekeeping,* where I had done 36 stories in all. After Stuart Schiff bought the story and said it was vintage Cave, I started my first horror novel and never did another story for *Good Housekeeping,* which was my last slick market.

"The Missing Mr. Lee" This is a one-of-a-kind story—I don't believe I ever wrote another such—and it's a good one, well written, with an unexpected ending.

"No Detour" This is one of my best short stories, colorful writing, great theme, really gripping.

"Readin', Writin' and Rough Stuff" The sheriff can't spell, and when he puts up a notice about the town bank's being robbed, half the words are spelled wrong. Then the robber leaves a note and—oh, hell, forget it. This is probably the worst Western I ever wrote.

"Bannigan's War" In one of the best adventure yarns I ever wrote, Bannigan, an American, saves the country of San Nicholas. A '10' if ever I wrote one.

"Chernik" A first-rate voodoo horror story.

"Cult of the White Ape" Douglas Dold provided the idea and background notes for this story and it has a great ring of authenticity (he had explored the Congo). A well-written, taut, creepy story of African magic.

"Damballah's Slough" It's voodoo, of course, but it's a first-rate spooky story.

"Danger By Night" (Reprinted as "The Prowler") A couple on the verge of divorce, in Haiti where he works for the U.S. Embassy, are threatened by an intruder who slits the screen of their bedroom window at night and may come back. While waiting for his return, they find each other again. First-rate story done on TV with David Niven.

"Ding Dong Belle" A first-rate Peter Kane story about a young woman who is murdered while playing Ping Pong at midnight in a bathing suit. There is some really sharp writing in this and the story is good fun.

"Inn of the Shadow Creatures" The plot here isn't any crazier than other Dime Mystery plots, but the writing is wildly unrestrained, using every adjective in the dictionary, making this story perhaps the worst piece of pulp fiction I ever wrote.

"Invasion from Inferno" It's one the best shudder stories I've written. It's exciting, different, and full of surprises.

"Complete Rifles at Dawn" A dramatic novel of an American secret agent who must pit his wits against the master minds of political greed. This is a well-written thriller full of action, plot twists, good characters, all based on a good, solid theme. At 39,000 words, one of the best long pulp stories I ever turned out.

"Satan's Altar" This may be the worst story I have ever written.

"So Long Sister" Despite its plot, this story contains some of the most vivid writing I've ever come up with.

FOOTNOTES

1. From Hugh B. Cave personal papers and clippings.

2. Robert Kenneth Jones, *The Shudder Pulps,* copyright 1975, FAX Collector's Editions, Inc., West Linn, OR.

3. "The Sins of the Fool," by Hugh B. Cave, *The Dagger of Tsiang,* copyright 1997, by Tattered Pages Press, Chicago, IL.

4. Website: *vintagelibrary.com.*

5. "Stragella," by Hugh B. Cave, copyright June 1932, *Strange Tales.*

6. "Murgunstrumm," by Hugh B. Cave, from *Murgunstrumm and Others,* copyright 1977, Carcosa.

7. *Magazines I Remember,* by Hugh B. Cave, copyright 1994, Tattered Pages Press.

8. "The Corpse-Maker," by Hugh B. Cave, *The Corpse Maker,* copyright 1988, Starmont House, Inc.

9. "The Prophecy," by Hugh B. Cave, from *Murgunstrumm and Others,* copyright 1977, Carcosa.

10. "The Eel Slips Through," by Hugh B. Cave, *Escapades of the Eel,* copyright 1997, Tattered Pages Press, Chicago, IL.

11. "Eel Trap," by Hugh B. Cave, *Escapades of the Eel,* copy-

right 1997, Tattered Pages Press, Chicago, IL.

12. "The Pulp File" by Don Hutchison, *Wordsmith,* copyright 1986, Renegade Press, North Hollywood, CA.

13. *Haiti: High Road to Adventure,* by Hugh B. Cave, copyright 1952, Henry Holt and Company.

14. *Legion of the Dead,* by Hugh B. Cave, copyright 1979, Avon Books.

15. *The Cross on the Drum,* by Hugh B. Cave, copyright 1958, Doubleday & Company Inc.

16. *Black Sun* by Hugh B. Cave, copyright 1960, Doubleday & Company Inc.

17. "The Mission," by Hugh B. Cave, copyright 1959, the *Saturday Evening Post.*

18. *Four Paths to Paradise: A Book About Jamaica,* by Hugh B. Cave, copyright 1961, Doubleday & Company, Inc.

19. *Lucifer's Eye,* by Hugh B. Cave, copyright 1991, Tor Books.

20. *Pulp Man's Odyssey,* by Audrey Parente, copyright 1988, Starmount House, Inc.

21. "Hugh B. Cave: An Appreciation," by Don Hutchinson, copyright 1987, *Borderland* (convention issue).

22. "Kane's Old Man," by Hugh B. Cave, *Dime Detective,* April 1, 1935.

23. "Southern New England Tropical Storms and Hurricanes, A Ninety-Eight Year Summary, 1909-1997," by David R. Vallee and Michael R. Dion, National Weather Service, Taunton, MA.

BIBLIOGRAPHY:

First Edition Hardcover/Paperback Books

Fishermen Four, New York, Dodd Mead & Co., 1942

Long Were the Nights, New York, Dodd Mead & Co., 1943

The Fightin'est Ship, New York, Dodd Mead & Co., 1944

We Build, We Fight, New York, Harper & Brothers, 1944

I Took the Sky Road, New York, Dodd Mead & Co., 1945

Wings Across the World, New York, Dodd Mead & Co., 1945

Haiti: High Road to Adventure, New York, Henry Holt & Co., 1952

Drums of Revolt, London, Robert Hale Ltd., 1957

The Cross on the Drum, Garden City, Doubleday, 1959

Black Sun, Garden City New York, Doubleday, 1960

Four Paths to Paradise, Garden City, Doubleday, 1961

The Witching Lands, Garden City, Doubleday, 1962

Run, Shadow, Run, London, Robert Hale Ltd., 1968

Larks Will Sing, London, Robert Hale Ltd., 1969

Murgunstrumm & Others, Chapel Hill, Carcosa, 1977

Legion of the Dead, New York, Avon, 1979

The Nebulon Horror, New York, Dell Publishing, 1980

A Summer Romance and Other Short Stories, London, Longman Group Ltd., 1980

The Evil, New York, Ace Charter, 1981

Shades of Evil, New York, Ace Charter, 1982
Disciples of Dread, New York, Tor Books, 1988
The Voyage, New York, Macmillan, 1988
The Corpse Maker, Mercer Island, Starmount House, Inc., 1988
Conquering Kilmarnie, New York, Macmillan, 1989
The Lower Deep, New York, Tor Books, 1990
Lucifer's Eye, New York, Tor Books, 1991
Magazines I Remember, Chicago, Tattered Pages Press, 1994
Death Stalks the Night, Minneapolis, Fedogan & Bremer, 1995
Bitter/Sweet, West Warwick, Necronomicon Press, 1996 (chapbook)
The Dagger of Tsiang, Chicago, Tattered Pages Press, 1996
The Door Below, Minneapolis, Fedogan & Bremer, 1997
Escapades of the Eel, Chicago, Tattered Pages Press, 1997
The Death-Head's March and Others, Bloomington, Black Dog Books, 1998 (chapbook)
White Star of Egypt, Bloomington, Black Dog Books, 1999 (chapbook)
The Desert Host, Bloomington, Black Dog Books, 1999 (chapbook)
Isle of the Whisperers, Nottingham, Pumpkin Books, 1999
The Lady Wore Black and Other Weird Cat Tales, Ashcroft BC, Ash Tree Press, 2000
Bottled in Blond, Minneapolis, Fedogan & Bremer, 2000
Long Live the Dead & Other Black Mask Stories, Norfolk, Crippen & Landru, 2000
The Dawning, New York, Leisure Books/Dorchester, 2000
Officer Coffey Stories, Burton, Subterranean Press, 2000 (chapbook)
Dark Doors of Doom, Bloomington, Black Dog Books, 2000 (chapbook)
The Evil Returns, New York, Leisure Books/Dorchester, 2001
Loose Loot, Sebastian, Sidecar Preservation Society, 2001 (chapbook)
The Restless Dead, New York, Leisure Books/Dorchester, 2003

BIBLIOGRAPHY:

Short Fiction Anthology Originals

Alphabetically by magazine/book, story title, chronologically

Whispers I, Ladies In Waiting, 1975
Whispers II, From the Lower Deep, 1979
Whispers III, The Door Below, 1981
Death, Always Together (Allen Beck), 1982
Whispers IV, What Say the Frogs Now, Jenny? 1983
World Fantasy Convention Program Book, To Chicago, 1983
Whispers V, Footprints In Perdu, 1985
Lovecraft's Legacy, The Blade and the Claw, 1990
Psycho-Paths, Red Devils, 1991
Ghosttide, The Mountains of Time, 1993
Journeys To The Twilight Zone, Another Kind of Enchanted Cottage, 1993
Mammoth Book Of Zombies, Mission To Margal, 1993
Northern Frights II, Vanishing Point, 1993
Dark Voices VI, Just Another HPL Horror Story, 1994
The Earth Strikes Back, Genesis II, 1994
Fred Olen Ray's Weird Menace, 1994
Don't Open the Door
The Kutting Edge
Journeys To The Twilight Zone II, Gordie's Pets, 1994
Ancient Enchantresses, A Dying At Blackwater, 1995

100 Vicious Little Vampire Stories, 1995
First Love
The Law
Werewolves, Nights In the Mountains of Haiti, 1995
100 Astounding Little Alien Stories, A Stranger From Atlanta, 1996
Dark Dixie, The Coming, 1997
World Fantasy Convention Program Book, Noble Warrior, 1997
Dancing With the Dark, Haitian Mysteres, 1998
Mammoth Book Of Dracula, The Second Time Around, 1998
365 Scary Stories, 1998
Encore
Green Fingers
One Way
Teacher's Pets
Unfinished Journey
Imagination Fully Dilated, Lady From Hell, 1999
New Mythos Legends, The Govi, 1998
Northern Frights 5, A Voice in the Wild, 2000
October Dreams: A Celebration Of Halloween, Zombies, 2000
100 Crafty Little Cat Crimes, Joey, 2000
Shadows And Silence, Littler, 2001
Song of Cthulhu, Intruders, 2001
Tooth & Claw, Mighty In Battle, 2002

BIBLIOGRAPHY:
Short Fiction by Publication

A Summer Romance & Other Short Stories
London, Longman Group Ltd, 1980
A Home for Life
No Complaints
Summer Music

Abbott's Monthly
Title Unknown, mo. Unknown-1933

Ace G-Man Stories
Federal Trails to Glory, 11/12-1938

Ace High Magazine
The Curse of the Grinning Skulls, 12-1933
Sons of Shadow, 8-1934
Heads Up in Hell, 9-1934
Nigger Jarl, Slaver, 10-1934

Ace High Western
The Mumbler Rides Again, 2-1934

Ace High Mystery
The Horde of Silent Men, 5-1936

Action Stories

The Price of Vengeance, 8-1929 (reprinted as "The Red Trail to Zanzibar" in Jungle Stories, Winter-1938)

Jungle Loot, 10-1929 (reprinted as Black Bondage, Shock:The New Mystery Magazine, 7-1939)

Wolf Breed, 11-1929

Adventure

Derelict, 4-1937

Swamp Trap, 6-1942

Tomorrow is Forever, 9-1943

A Man to Gun For, 6-1953

Alfred Hitchcock's Mystery Magazine

The Catbird Nest, 8-1965

Isle of Truth, 10-1983 (cover)

The Lady Wore Black, 3-1984

Appointment With Yesterday, 6-1984 (not same story as Detective Fiction Weekly yarn)

Mistress of Shadows, 2-1985 (novelette)

The Hard Luck Kid, 11-1992 (as Geoffrey Vace)

The Caller, 11-1993

All Detective

The Black Brotherhood, 11-1932

Hands Down, 2-1934

Sign of the Serpent, 1-1935 (cover)

Amazing Detective Stories

Four Minutes After Midnight, 4-1931 (AKA Four Past Midnight, by Geoffrey Cave)

American Boy

The Warning on the Wall, 11-1932

The Golden God, 7-1934

American Magazine

The Road Ahead, 8-1942

Wedding in Haiti, 4-1952

Hurricane, 11-1952

The Devil's Pit, 7-1953

Terror Mountain, 8-1953 (retitled:The Mountains of Fear, *The Witching Lands,* Doubleday, 1962)

Fortress of Fear, 4-1955

Argosy

Steal a Dog's Bone, 7-18-1931
In the Bag, 5-22-1937 (as Carey Barnett)
Boomerang, 6-10-1939
No Detour, 1-1947
The Secret of Trinity's Island, 11-1947
The Man Who Couldn't Die, 2-1948
Pete Hindley's Gold Machine, 5-1948
Payoff at Palembang, 12-1950
Vengeance Island, 8-1953
Island Feud, 12-1953

Astounding Stories

The Corpse on the Grating, 2-1930
The Murder Machine, 9-1930

Author and Journalist

Too Much Imagination, 1-1932

Bitter/Sweet

Necronomicon Press, West Warwick, 1996 (chapbook)
Aiyana and the Gallant Rider
By Heaven

Black Book Detective

The Grisly Death, 8-1934
The Prophecy, 10-1934
Maxon's Mistress, 2-1935

Black Mask

Too Many women, 5-1934
Dead Dog, 3-1937
Shadow, 4-1937
Curtain Call, 11-1938
Smoke in Your Eyes, 12-1938
Long Live the Dead, 12-1938 (as Allen Beck)
Lost—and Found, 4-1940
The Missing Mr. Lee, 11-1940
Front Page Frame Up, 2-1941
Stranger in Town, 4-1941

Blue Book

New Guinea Manhunt, 10-1951

Borderland (Can.)

Of Time and Space, 1985 (Volume 1, #2)
The Back of the Mirror, 10-1987 (Mini-issue for 13th World Fantasy Convention)

Boston Globe

Retribution, 1925 (first published story)
Great and Small, 1926

Boston Globe Sunday Magazine

The Last Guess, 1-16-1938
One Eye Blind, 1947 (mo. unk.)

Boy's Life

Worth Fighting For, 4-1944
Midget Sluggers, 7-1944
PT Boat Missing, 3-1945 (or 1946)
Just Fishing Isn't Fishing Enough, 5-1947
The Test, 4-1948
River to Nowhere, 5-1948
Treasure Deep, 6-1950
The Spectre in the Pool, 5-1952
Trapped in the Tomb, 9-1953
The Phantom Moth, 8-1954
Flight of the Jungle Bird, 2-1956
Terror in the Temple, 4-1957
Troubled Waters, 11-1957
Voodoo Village, 6-1959
The Wailing Waters, 2-1960
Peril at the Gorge, 10-1961
The Unwanted, 4-1962
Cavern of the Lost, 5-1964
Peril at the Bridge, 7-1965
The River of Voices, 1965 (mo. unk.)

Brief Stories

Island Ordeal, 7-1929 (first pulp sale)
The Pool of Death, 8-1929
The Fight for Red Angel, 1-1930
Condemned to a Living Tomb, 4-1930

Canada Wide Feature Service Ltd.

You Could Hold My Hand, 1946 (mo. unk.)

Canadian Magazine

Improper Lady, 5-1932
Ordeal by Battle, 11-1932
Prelude to a Love Affair, 6-1933
Road Map, 7-1933
Might of Men, 10-1933
Cracked Up, 11-1933
The Evil Eye, 2-1934
Red, 4-1934
Sold Out, 7-1934
The Red Road Up, 8-1934 (as Geoffrey Vace)
Fool Woman, 2-1935
The Last Guess, 2-1935 (as Geoffrey Vace)
Black Heart, 6-1935
The Tougher You Are, 8-1935
Candle Woman, 10-1935
Love Laughs Last, 1-1937
No Charge for Admission, 2-1937
Extra Woman, 4-1937 (as Justin Case)
Pilot Beware, 8-1937

Candid Detective

Something for Nothing, 1-1939

Cemetery Dance

Five to Get Ready, Two to Go, 4-1996
Halleluja, 10-1996
The Halleluja Horrors, 2-1997
Mr. Mowry Goes to War, 4-2002

Chatelaine (Canada)

Big Medicine, 1933 (mo. unk.)
Strange Antidote, 7-1933
Night Wind, 3-1934

Christian Herald

David, 6-1947
Night Wind 6-1947
Bus to Town, 10-1947
Goodnight, Sweetheart, 11-1947
Full Circle, (date unk., 1940s-1960s)
The Pied Piper of Asangai, (date unk., 1940s-1960s)
Pursuit of Happiness, 10-1950

All Through the Night, 11-1954
One Friday Morning, 7-1956
Left Out, 12-1959
A Place to Hide, 8-1961
Bonaime, 7-1963
The Gift, 10-1965
The Bell, 1965 (mo. unk.)
Big Day Tomorrow, 10-1966

Clues Detective Stories

Seven to Be Slain, 10-1936
The Dead Speak Softly, 11-1936
Dance Macabre, 4-1937

Collier's

Navy Man, 1-6-1945
Serpent in the Sun, 6-10-1955

Complete Detective

The Devil Has Flaming Eyes, 8-1938

Cosmopolitan

The Spectre in the Jungle, 8-1953
Spell of a Stranger, 1-1960
Island Girl, 10-1961

Country Gentleman

The Crucible, 10-1948
The Man From Heaven, 5-1949
The Ship of God, 6-7-8-9-1950 (four-part serial)
The Way Back, 1-1951
The Last Accounting, 9-1952
Wave of Terror, 3-1954

Cowboy Stories

Tame Wildcat, 11-1933

Crypt of Cthulhu

Just the Two of Us, 1984
And When We Sleep, 1986

D.C. Thompson (England)

The Journey, (date unk. 1950s-1960s; retitled as One to Chicago, WFC program, 1983)

Detective Fiction Weekly

The Infernal Web, 3-21-1936
No Way Out, 5-9-1936 (reprinted as "The Chair")
You Just Can't Lose, 6-13-1936
Nuts About Mutts, 10-17-1936
Trail of the Torch, 12-19-1936 (cover)
Queer Street, 4-10-1937
The Smoke of Vengence, 5-22-1937
Deadline, 11-13-1937
You Could Be Next, 1-15-1938
Match Ya for It, 4-9-1938
Murder Makes a Frame, 4-30-1938
Joker in the Deck, 6-18-1938
Desperate Character, 7-9-1938
Scandal Sheet, 9-17-1938
Murder at Hand, 10-1-1938
I Am the Law, 11-12-1938
No Trial By Jury, 11-19-1938
Death Writes a Policy, 12-10, 12-17,12-24,12-31-1938 (serial)
Cops Are Not Heroes, 1-7-1939
The Pushover, 1-14-1939 (reprinted as Guilt Frame in 15-Story Detective 2-1951)
John Bum's Body, 3-4-1939
Red for Rebellion, 4-1-1939
According to Hoyle, 4-8-1939
Death Comes for a Diva, 4-15-1939
The Mystery of the Maudlin Mermaid, 4-22-1939
The Head of J. James, 4-29-1939
Hideout, 5-6-1939
Seven Dirty Dollars, 5-13-1939
Wit's End, 5-27-1939
Time for Murder, 6-17-1939
And Sudden Death, 7-1-1939
Footprint, 7-8-1939
Treadmill, 7-22-1939
Mister Petrie Ties a Fly, 7-29-1939
Beards Grow Slowly, 8-05-1939 (cover illustrated)
But the Kill Was Cold, 8-12-1939
Symphony in Shrouds, 8-26-1939
A Den for Daniel, 9-2-1939
Seven Into Murder, 9-9-1939
Come Into My Parlor, 9-16-1939
But Few Are Chosen, 10-21-1939

My Old Man, 11-11-1939
So Long, Slicker, 11-25-1939
Laugh, Clown, 12-9-1939
The Barricade, 12-23-1939
The Signature of Murder, 1-13-1940
Phantom Trap, 2-3-1940
Big City Blackout, 2-10-1940
Certainly, Sister, 4-20-1940
Weak Sister Act, 6-29-1940
Coffin Cargo, 7-20-1940
A Picture of Guilt, 8-3-1940
Prowl By Night, 9-14-1940
Easy to Kill, 10-18-1940
Murder Off Key, 11-2-1940
Terror's Twin, 3-1-1941
Appointment With Yesterday, 5-24-1941 (as Geoffrey Vace)
Shadow Man, 5-31, 6-7, 6-14, 6-21, 6-28-1941 (5-part serial)
Two Kinds of Snake, 7-5-1941
Photo Finish, 9-17-1941
Homocide Highway, 11-19-1941
Faith For Rent, 12-27-1941

Detective Short Stories

Black Fury, 8-1937
The Careless Cadaver, 1-1939
Murder in Their Eyes, date unk.

Detective Story Annual

Seven to be Slain, 1944
As Does the Spider, 1946

Detective Story

You Forgot Something, 2-25-1934
Tiger Face, 10(?)-1936
Necktie Party, 3(?)-1938
Two Can Fight, 4(?)-1938
Too Tight the Grave, 8(?)-1940
The Albino Butterbugs, 1-1941
Monkey See Murder, 3-1943
Steve Takes a Hand, 1-1944
Southbound Special, 3-1944

Detective Tales

Murder—The Matchmaker, 8-1937

Odds to Die for, 2-1938
Neither Gold Nor Glory, 6-1939
A Gun for Galahad, 3-40
The Cat and the Killer, 6-1941 (reprinted as The Richest Cat in Town, 2-1951)

Detective Yarns

Satan Wears a Mask, 12-1938

Dime Detective Magazine

The Late Mr. Smythe, 8-1-1934
Hell on Hume Street, 11-1-1934
Bottled in Blond, 1-1-1935
The Man Who Looked Sick, 4-1-1935
Kane's Old Man, 4-1-1935 ("biography" of Peter Kane, written as editorial, in article about HBC)
The Screaming Phantom, 5-1-1935
The Brand of Kane, 6-15-1935
The House of Sudden Sleep, 12-1935
The Lady Who Left Her Coffin, 6-1936
Footsteps to a Finish, 8-1937
Twenty After Murder, 11-1937
Deal From the Bottom, 8-1939
Farewell With Trumpets, 1-1940
Loose Loot, 4-1940
He Didn't Know Nothin', 7-1940
Ding Dong Belle, 8-1941
The Dead Don't Swim, 11-1941
Death Drains the Well, 1-1942
No Place to Hide, 2-1942
The Fugitive Face, 9-1942
This Is the Way We Bake Our Dead, 6-1943

Dime Mystery Magazine

The Graveless Dead, 10-1933
The Corpse Maker, 11-1933 (cover)
The House of Evil, 11-1933 (cover-as Geoffrey Vace)
They Feed at Midnight, 12-1933
Dark Slaughter, 1-1934
Devils in the Dark, 2-1934
Unholy Night, 4-1934
Death in the Dark, 6-1934
House of Lost Souls, 9-1934
The Pain Room, 10-34

Terror From the Deep, 11-1934 (cover)
Inn of the Shadow Creatures, 12-1934
Dark Bondage, 1-1935 (cover)
House of the Restless Dead, 5-1935
Satan's Mistress, 6-1935
Mistress of the Dead, 10-35
Daughters of Dark Desire, 12-1935
Death Holds for Ransom, 2-1936
Modern Nero, 8-1936

Double Action Detective

Ticket to Trouble, 10-1938

Double Detective

Crazy Guy, 1-1938
There's Always a Way Back, 4-1938
Worth Fighting for, 5-1938
In This Corner—Death, 6-1938
Rifles at Dawn, 7-1938
The Forgotten Man-Killer, 8-1938
The Education of a Killer, 9-1938
Three Rats, One Hole, 10-38
Counsel for the Damned, 12-1938
Special Delivery, 1-1939
Time Out, 2-1939
Payroll Heist, 9-1939
The Melancholy Mask of M. Montreau, 10-1939
No Errors, 2-1940
Murder Me Him, 5-1940
Not Dead But Sleeping, 9-1940
The Guardian Angel, 10-1941

Elks Magazine

Give 'Em a Little Corn, 2-1946
It's You I Want, 5-1946
Hell on the Half Shell, 4-1947 (reprinted as Trouble on the Half Shell, *Toronto Star Weekly,* 7-47)
Thanks for Everything, 10-1947 (reprinted as The Hand of Kajo, *Boys Own Paper,* Eng. 4-55)
White Lightning, 1-1948
It's the Fight, 3-1950
River of Fear, 1952 (mo. unk.)
Hour of Violence, 4-1953 (reprinted as Treasure of the Grotto, *Toronto Star Weekly,* 8-53)

Slow Boat to Danger, 8-1953
Phantom Warning, 11-1957
The Impossible Thief, 7-1958
High Man on the Mountain, 12-1959
A Slight Official Error, 1960 (mo. Unk.-reprinted as Double or Quit, *Argosy England,* 2-61)
San Marlo Revolution, 5-1961
A Touch of Magic, 10-1974

Ellery Queen's Mystery Magazine

Alike Under the Skin, 5-1955
Naked in Darkness, 8-1965
The Course of Justice, 10-1965
Many Happy Returns, 4-1966 (as Justin Case)

Esquire

The Forbidden Island, 4-1953

Everybody's Australia

This Side of the Wall, 1963 (short short version, long version in *Toronto Star Weekly,* 2-65)

Everywoman (Eng.)

Mysterious Disappearance of Henry Warburton, 1957 (mo. Unk.)

Exciting Detective

The Silken Snakes, 7-1941

Extension

The Beautiful Horses, 12-1943
Brother Sam, 8-1944
Situation in Hand, 7-1945
Manila—City of Sorrow, 10-1945
Thank You, Mr. Joe, 10-1945
He Trod the Mine Field, 11-1945
Your Missing Boy May Yet Return, 12-1945
Well Anyway, It's Almost Home, 1-1946
It's Your Pacific, 2-1946
Night Call, 8-1947 (reprinted as A Swift Triumph, *Toronto Star Weekly,* 9-47)
Youth Song, 10-1947
A Touch of Integrity, 3-1948
Love, Love, Love, 3-1950

The Exile, 4-51
The Man Who Wouldn't Quit, 2-1955
Dangerous Passenger, 6-1955
Father Denny and the Devil, 1958 (mo. Unk.)
Forbidden Ground, 11-1959
Valley of the Drums, 6-1960
Old Love, New Love, 10-1965

F.O Ray's Weird Menace

Don't Open the Door, 1994

Family Circle

The Kweilin Express, 3-1947
The Dragon, 8-1947
Big People, 1947 (mo. unk.)
What Every Young Woman Should Know—About Fishing, 5-1948

Family Herald & Weekly Star (Can.)

The Beaten Path, 5-19-1943
Rendezvous at the River, 6-15-1943
Lady's Luck, 8-18-1943
So Little Time, 1-5-1944
Wire—Special Delivery, 3-14-45
Second Growth, 7-4-1945
Three A.M., 11-14-45
The Girl From Toronto, 6-30-1948
Beginner's Luck, 12-9-1965

Fantasy Tales (Eng.)

A Place of No Return, 7-1981
After the Funeral, 12-1986

Far East Adventure Stories

Sing Lee, Weaver of Mats, 1-1931
That Monkey of Simms, 1-1931 (as Jack D'Arcy)
Rigler's Third Round, 4-1931
Kuching Cunning, 7-1931
The Stinging N'Ting, 9-1931 (as Geoffrey Vace)
The Midnight Horde, 9-1931, 11-1931, 12-1932 (serial-final installment not published, magazine folded)
Up-River From Sandakan, 12-1931 (as Geoffrey Vace)

Federal Agent

Killer's Exit, 3-1937 (reprinted as The Hostage in *The Door Below,* Fedogan & Bremer 1997)
Wings of Death, 5-1937
Holidays in Hell, 7-1937
The Dead Talk Back, 9-1937

Flynn's Detective Fiction

Blackguard's Book, 12-1942

Ghost Stories

The Strange Case of No. 7, 1-1931
The Affair of the Clutching Hand, 5-1931

Gioia (Italy)

Two Small Feet, 1965 (mo. unk.)

G-Men Detective

Death on the Program, 1-1941

Good Housekeeping

Wake Up, Mr. Bardwell, 4-1962
A Dark and Tender Street, 6-1962
The Perfect Gift, 12-1962
In Your Own Backyard, 5-1963
Love is Never Forgotten, 6-1963
After the Wedding, 1-1964
Listen, I Love You, 3-1964
I'll Walk You Home, 4-1964
End of the Road, 3-1965
To Trust in Andy, 4-1965
Double Wedding, 7-1965
He Loves Me, 10-1965
When the Real Thing Comes Along, 1965 (mo. unk.)
Something Wonderful, 1965 (mo. unk.)
My Brand New Mother-In-Law, 3-1966
Second Baby, 4-1966
Summer Serenade, 7-1967
Island of Eve, 10-1967
Come Live With Me, 3-1968
The Girl in Apartment 3-A, 1-1969
Believe in Me, 3-1969
The Search for Little Mary, 6-1969

A Forever Kind of Thing, 8-1969
Two Very Special People, 4-1970
All About Love and Marriage, 5-1970
Small Town Girl, 1-1971
The Secret Treasure, 2-1971
One Touch of Magic, 9-1971
People You Can Count On, 4-1972
Someone For David, 8-1972
In Dangerous Courtship, 9-1972
A Summer Romance, 7-1973
The Wedding of Jennifer, 10-1973
Remember Island, 8-1974
Portrait of Love, 11-1975

Green Ghost Detective

An Eye for the Future, 4-1941

High Spot Magazine/Over the Top

Black Spots On White, 9-1930

Home Life

What Can We Do With Mother? 1964 (mo. unk.)

Horror Stories

By Night They Creep, 2-1935
Mate for a Monster, 3-1935 (cover)
Brides for the Dead, 8-1935
Death Calls From the Madhouse, 9-1935 (cover)
Imp of Satan, 10-1935
Disturb Not the Dead, 10-11-1936

Holland's

The Lonesome Road, 8-1947

Household Magazine

Scarecrow in Scarlet, 10-1933 (cover)

Ladies Home Journal

The Wild One, 5-1961
Creatures of the Night, 9-1963

Liberty Magazine

Okay, Mary, 9-1949
Title Unknown, date unk., in the 40s

Liguorian Magazine

Planned Encounter, 2-1995 (as Judy Case)
Hold On There Just a Minute, Mr. Carlyle, 1998
Silence is Not Always Golden, 4-1999 (as Judy Case)

London Evening News

Water Girl, date unk., prob. 1975

MacLean's

The Key, 7-1-1948
Swamp Justice, 10-1-1948
Lord of Roanonga, 1-1-1949

Magalog (Can.)

A Matter of Timing, 1998

Man Stories

The Red Swede Goes Mad, 2-1931
Fever Laugh, 3/4-1931
The Dead Face Grinned Twice, 5-1931
Jailuki Jaws, 6-1931 (as Allen Beck)

Mike Shayne Mystery Magazine

The Woman at the Pond, 2-1965
Run for Your Life, 10-1984

Modern Romances

Reluctant to Love, 2-1947
Rebound, 4-1947

Montreal Standard

No-Account, 7-19-1947

Mystery Novels Magazine

Death Stalks the Campus, 4-1936

Mystic

Title Unk., date unk., probably 1928
Title Unk., date unk., probably 1930

National Home Monthly (Can.)

Ill Wind, 3-1934
Big Guy, 10-1934

New Detective Magazine

Passport to Hell, 3-1943

New Mystery Adventures

The Flame Fiend, 4-1935

Nickel Western

One on You, Zeus, 4-1933 (cover)

Night Terror

Right of Way, 6-1998

Oriental Stories

Four Doomed Men, 7-1931 (written by Geoffrey Cave)
The Death-Head's March, 10-1931 (written by Geoffrey Cave)

Outlaws of the West

Isinglass, 8-1930
Title Unk., 8-1931
Fourth Floor Front, 3/4-1932

Pete Rice Adventure Westerns

Two Fools and a Fiddle, 9-1935
The Man From Laramie, 10-1935

Phantasm

Chernik, 1994 (first and last issue)

Pirate Writings

And Out, 1997

Pocket Book (Aust.)

Phantom Valley, 10-13-1956 (reprinted as The Mountains of Time in *Ghosttide* Anthology, 1993)

Pocket Detective Magazine

Sense of Humor, 12-1936
The Hidden Eye, 2-1937
The Dead Samaritan, 7-1937

Popular Detective

Marked for Murder, 7-1935
The Silent Men, 3-1936
Greetings to You, 1-1937

Popular Fiction

The Flaming Skull, 11-1931
Texas Bred, 12-1931
The Fool Fetish, 3-1932

Private Detective Stories

Dizzy Dame, 10- (or 11-)1937 (as Justin Case)
Design for Death, 1-1938 (as Justin Case)
She Slept Too Long, 6-1938 (as Justin Case)
Bad Water, 11-1943 (as Justin Case)
Hangman's Chain, 12-1943
P.D. File 213, 3-1944 (as Justin Case)

Public Enemy

Dig the Grave Deeper, 2-1936
The Red Butcher, 3-1936

Publication Unknown

Title Unknown, 1926 (mo.unk.—first paid sale, D.C. Cook Company)

Reader's Digest

Title Unknown, 4-1960

Real Confessions

Something to Live For, 5-1943

Real Romances

Lover's Hideaway, 4-1947

Red Star Adventures

Deadfall by Night, 10-1940

Red Star Detective

Copper's Exit, 8-1940

Redbook

The Woman at the Shrine, 2-1957 (cover)
Lifeline, 11-1957
Forbidden Love, 1-1958
Lonely Journey, 9-1958
Second Wife, 12-1958
The Question, date unk. (in 1950's or 1960's)
End of Summer, 9-1960

Reveille (Eng.)

A Very Vital Statistic, 1964 (mo. unk.)
The Intruder, 1964 (mo. unk.)
The Dart Game, 10-1965 (reprinted as To The Point, *Tall Tales & Short Stories,* 8/9-1993)
Nightmare on Wheels, 1965 (mo. unk.)

Risque Stories

Erzulie, 10-1984
Sixgun Hellcats From Black River, 10-1986 (written with Charles Hoffman & Marc A. Cerasini)

Robert Price's 'Pulp' Magazine

Anti, 3-1989

Romantic Detective

The Gorilla Will Get You, 12-1938

Sacred Heart Messenger

Trapped, 9-1955
The Intruder, 10-1955
In the Groove, 6-1958
The Well-Planned Trip, 1958 (mo. unk.)
Footsteps in the Night, 1962 (mo. unk.)
Time of Truth, 1963 (mo. unk.)
To Save a Life, 1963 (mo. unk.)
Father Knows Best, 2-1965
The Common Ground, 6-1965
What Have You Been Reading Lately, Mr. Follansbee, 7-1965
By Lamplight, 1965 (mo. unk.)
Something Else to Fix, 1-1966
Agatha's House, 2-1966

Saturday Evening Post

Angry Little Sister, 11-25-1944
Fool's Courage, 6-18-1949
The Woman Who Wouldn't Run, 10-22-1949
The Unapproachable Woman, 2-4-1950
The Ardent Woodsman, 2-18-1950
The Lady in the Jungle, 10-16-1950
The Doctor's Wife, 2-24-1951
The Troublesome Taxi, 3-31-51
The Silent Horror, 4-28-1951
Murder Island, 4-19-1952

Betrayal, 8-9-1952
River of Death, 11-22-1952
The Jungle That Couldn't Be Tamed, 5-9-1953
The Madman of the Mountain, 6-12-1954
The Woman at Fog Point, 10-16-1954
Death Dive, 6-14-1955
Girl Shy, 8-14-1955
The Girl Who Swam at Night, 10-19-1955
Senorita of Minnesota, 12-3-1955
Extra Girl, 2-25-1956
The Hunter and the Hunted, 3-31-1956
Bait for a Bachelor, 6-9-1956
San Marlo Incident, 10-6-1956 (reprinted as The Angel of Bel Air)
The Too Proper Young Man, 11-17-1956
The Unwelcome Tourists, 1-5-1957
The Lovable Liar, 5-25-1957
Secret of Happiness, 9-7-1957
Wild Ride, 5-17-1958
The Girl Who Did Everything Wrong, 7-19-1958
Mob Victim, 8-23-1958
The Girl on the Road, 1-31-1959
The Mission, 3-14-1959
Terror in the Town, 4-25-1959
Prowler in the House, 7-11-1959 (reprinted as Three's a Family)
The Gang in Black Jackets, 8-22-1959
Strange Awakening, 1-9-1960
His Sister's Keeper, 4-23-60
Hard of Heart, 6-11-60 (reprinted as The Brats, *The Witching Lands*, Doubleday, 1962)
Bannigan's War, 8-6-1960
Little Girl in Black Stockings, 10-22-1960
Jamaica Storm, 10-28-1961

Scholastic Magazine

Two Were Left, 1942, (mo. unk.—reprinted as Marooned on an Island, *This Week*, 12-11-1949)

Secret Agent X Detective Magazine

Killer's Test, 6-1935

Short Stories

The Shadow of Tsiang, 10-25-1929

Captain Murder, 1-25-1930
The Sins of the Fool, 2-10-1930
Cry Wolf, 3-10-1930
A White Man Dies, 5-15-1930
Hamadryad, 6-25-1930
The Green Eyes of Confucius, 8-10-1930
Ten Paces, 8-25-1930
Borneo Brag, 9-10-1930 (plagiarized in Popular Fiction 12-1931 as "Young Courage")
Bring Me His Blood, 11-25-1930
The Spider of Kuching, 12-25-1930 (same as The Fingers That Fraim Forgot, date unk.)
Six-Leg Nerve, 1-25-1931
Hypocrite House, 2-25-1931
The Thirty Swords, 5-10-1931
Hell Hole Hate, 9-25-1931
The Silent Joker, 11-10-1931
The Reformation of Private Blake, 6-25-1932
The Mouth of Mao-Heng, 7-10-1932
Sleep Baby Sleep, 8-10-1932 (as Justin Case)
Pawn of Circumstance, 4-25-1933
Suicide Trail, 5-10-1933
Sheriff Pop Plays Possum, 11-10-1933
According to Hoily, 3-25-1934
The White Claw, 4-25-1935
Merely McHenry, 8-25-1937
Free Frenchman, 11-10-1941
A Man's Mark, 10-10-1942
One Man's River, 3-10-1943
A Man's Mark, 8-1-1943
The Bribe, 8-25-1943
This Lasting Light, 2-10-1945
Two Make a Team, 2-25-1947
Hideout, 9-10-1947
The Flame, 7-10-1948
The Surangani Affair, 11-10-1948
The Treasure, 4-1949 (now a monthly)
Number One Magic, 10-1949

Shudder Stories

The Room Above the Top, 6-1984
Brides of the Bloody Fields From Hell, 12-1984
Damsels for the Damned, 4-1985

Sinister Stories

School Mistress for the Mad, 5-1940

Sir

Crykes, date unk.
Tomorrow's Hymn, 1-1943
Prussian Lullaby, 9-1943
No Moss on Lacey, 9-1946
The Dilemma of Herbert Roddy, 2-1965

The Skipper

Doll of Death, 4-1937

Southern Agriculturist

Mission at Dawn, 5-1946
The Heavenly Fire, 1-1947
Star Performance, 10-1947
The Last Word, 2-1948

Speed Adventure Stories

Comeback in Redling, 3-1944 (as Justin Case)
He Knew the Enemy, 3-1944
So Long, Sister, 5-1944
Donovan's Island, 7-1944
The General Comes to Town, 7-1944 (as Justin Case)
No Man's Island, 1-1945

Speed Mystery

Dark Doors of Doom, 2-1943 (as Justin Case)

Spicy Adventure Stories (all as Justin Case)

The Crawling Ones, 2-1936 (reprinted as Death Box, 2-1942 by Paul Hanna)
In the Dragon's Lair, 3-1936
Eel Trap, 6-1936
The Yellow Horde, 7-1936
Dark Temple of Torment, 1-1937
River of Blood, 4-1937
Shotgun Ceremony, 6-1937 (reprinted as For Keeps, by R. T. Maynard, 12-42)
Secret of Lost City, 8-1937
The Eel Slips Through, 12-1937
Hell Hole, 1-1938
Eel Bait, 2-1938

The Black Cat of Joe Ming, 3-1938
Prisoner of Tituan, 4-1938
Tomorrow You Die, 9-1938 (reprinted as Dark Outlaw, by Wm Decatur, 10-42)
Prey of the Prowler, 10-1940
Hurricane Tramp, 3-1941 (cover)
The Second Slug, 7-1941(reprinted as Bullet to Spare, *Private Detective Stories,* 6-47)
The Vanishing Dead, 5-1942
White Star of Egypt, 11-1942 (cover)

Spicy Detective Stories (all as Justin Case)

I See by the Papers, 5-1936 (reprinted as Headline Bait, *Private Detective Stories,* 3-38)
Women are Damned Fools, 9-1936
Death to Cops, 1-1937
Eel Poison, 8-1937
Death Wears No Robe, 10-1937
Prison Pay-Off, 8-1938
Eel's Errand, 8-1940
The Widow Wears Scarlet, 10-1940
The Lady's Last Laugh, 12-1940
Annie Any More, 3-1941
On Ice, 4-1941
Death Has Green Eyes, 6-1941
Krock's Wife, 10-1941
A Pile of Publicity, 1-1942
Eel's Eve, 4-1942

Spicy Mystery Stories (all by Justin Case)

Dark Night of Doom, 1-1936
Doom Door, 3-1936
Mistress of Vengeance, 6-1936 (reprinted as Canyon of Fear by Max Neilson, 1-43)
She From Beyond, 7-1936
The Evil Flame, 8-1936
Prey of the Nightborn, 9-1936
Cult of the Corpse, 10-1936 (reprinted as Voodoo Madness by John Wayne 12/42)
Hurricane Woman, 2-1937
The Strange Death of Ivan Gromleigh, 3-1937
Cavern of the Damned, 5-1937
Tomb for the Living, 6-1937
Satan's Altar, 1-1938

Six Were Slain, 2-1938
The House of the Deathless Shadows, 4-1938
Death's Fiery Serpents, 5-1938
Zannini's Puppets, 8-1938
Servant of Satan, 9-1938
Sabali Madness, 10-1938
Song of the Lash, 12-1938
Beneath the Vapor Veil, 1-1941
The Monster Fringe, 5-1941
The Thing From the Swamp, 2-1942
Purr of a Cat, 3-1942
The Whisperers, 4-1942
The Caverns of Time, 5-1942
Satan's Slough, 9-1942
Calavan, 12-1942

St. Anthony Messenger

Time of Truth, 1963 (mo. unk.)
A Thing of Beauty, 1964 (mo. unk.)
Don't Feel Sorry for Me, 1965 (mo. unk.)

St. Joseph Magazine

Night Out, 8-1946
Your Land, My Land, 2-1947
A Little Bit of Habit, 8-1947

Star Detective Magazine

Death Stalks the Night, 8-1935 (cover)
Title Unk., 12-1935

Star Novels Magazine

Jungle Justice, 2-1931

Strange Detective Mysteries (Can.)

The Crystal Doll Killings, 5/6-1939
Satan's Red Mist, 5-1941
The Guardian Angel, 11-1943 (cover)

Strange Detective Stories

Halfway to Hell, 12-1933

Strange Tales

The Door of Doom, 1-1932
Stragella, 6-1932 (cover)

The Infernal Shadow, 10-1932
Murgunstrumm, 1-1933 (cover)

Super Detective Stories

Terror Island, 6-1934 (different than *Terror Tales* story)
The Corpse Crypt, 9-1934
Vale of Inferno, 12-1934
Fall Guy, 2-1944

Super Sports

The Big If, 10-1941

Ten Detective Aces

Sinister Street, 7-1937

Ten Story Gang

Stand in for Death, 11-1938

Terror Tales

Terror Island, 9-1934 (first issue of magazine)
Death's Loving Arms, 10-1934 (cover)
Enslaved to Satan, 2-1935
Satan's Sepulcher, 4-1935
The Scarlet Widow, 6-1935
Death Tolls the Bell, 7-1935 (cover)
The Dolls of Doom, 9-1935
Buyer of Souls, 10-1935
Daughter of the Plague, 1-1936
House in Hell's Forest, 7/8-1936
My Pupil, the Idiot, 9/10-1937 (cover)
The Thirsty Thing, 1-1941
The Beast of Little Black, 3-1941

The Feds

Death Hogs the Highways, 2-1937
Blood in His Eyes, 10-1937

The Home Magazine

Behind the Mask, 1933 (mo. unk.)

The Illustrated Love Magazine

Title Unk., 1932 (mo. unk.—first original slick sale)

The Lamp

Take a Chance, Johnny, 11-1954

The Magic Carpet

Step Softly, Sahib, 1-1933 (as Geoffrey Vace)

The Desert Host, 4-1933

The Jumping Well, 7-1933 (as Geoffrey Vace, actually written by Geoffrey Cave)

Red Rendezvous, probably 1933 (as Geoffrey Vace, actually written by Geoffrey Cave)

The Pulpster

The Case of the Disappearing Paintings, 1998

The Sign

The Answer, 6-1946

Day of Decision, 2-1947

Goodbye, Katie, 6-1947

All the Answers, 9-1947

The Song, 2-1948

Golden Bird, 3-1948

Take My Hand, 9-1948

All-American, 1948 (mo. unk.—reprint of *This Week* story purchased but never published)

Look at Me, 2-1949

With Love, 5-1949

The Squealer, 11-1949

Isle of No Escape, 2-1950

Something Big, 8-1950

Listen to the Lonesome Drum, 2-1951

Slam the Door , 9-1951

Golden Girl, 1-1952

Light in Darkness, 5-1952 (reprinted as Off Course, Lost, in *John Bull* (Eng.) 11-1952

Mountain Girl, 7-1952

The Fortune Hunter, 1-1953

The Silent Partner, 1-1954

Voice of the Drums, 6-1954

Mountain Magic, 10-1954

The Treasure Box, 7-1955

Goblins on the Hearth, 4-1957

Deadly Enemies, 8-1958

Farewell, Miss Katy, 11-1964

The Numbers Game, 11-1965

A Lesson in Love, date unk., 1940's-1960's

The Skipper

Doll of Death, 4-1937

The Tome

Long Live the Queen, 11-1991

The Urbanite

The Skeptic, 1993
Puss-Puss, 1994
Forever is a Long, Long Time, 1995
Killing Time, 1997
Total Reality, 1998
Quiet Zone, 2000

The Victorian

His Son's Teacher, 3-1947
Optical Illusion, 4-1948

The Vincentian

Some People Have Everything, date unk. (1940's-1960's)

The War Cry—Salvation Army

And Ye Shall See Him, 4-1948

This Week

Brother to the Hawk, 10-26-1941
Beyond Price, 11-9-1941
Swamp Terror, 4-12-1942
Some Drift Forever, 3-7-1943
Softly—With Feeling, 7-18-1943 (reprinted as Say it with Music, *Tid Bits,* Eng., 1943)
Magic in the Hat, 8-22-1943
There Goes Henderson, 11-7-1943
For Marianne, 11-14-1943
Why Did You Do It?, 2-20-1944
Jonah, 3-12-1944
Why Pete Came Back Home, 4-1-1945
Sealed Orders, 4-19-1945
Missing Item, 9-9-1945
Hero's Brother, 10-7-1945
Women Must Wait, 10-20-1946
The Pampered Little Punk, 12-8-1946

Love Affair of a Homely Girl, 1-12-1947
Rope Enough, 8-3-1947
Peril of the River, 10-24-1948
Phantom Fortune, 11-14-1948
Footsteps, 9-26-1965 (as Justin Case)

Thrilling Adventures

The Preying Hands, 4-1932
The Stump of Mahakan, 5-1932 (as Ace Williams)
Dyak Torture, 3-1934
Crimson Trails, 7-1934
Holocaust House, 1-1936
The Sandakan Stiff, 4-1936
The Spider of K'ruga, 7-1937
Lair of the Pythons, 9-1937
Incident at the Border, 4-1939
Crocodile, 2-1942

Thrilling Detective

Rendezvous, 12-1934
Murder Backfire, 11-1936 (cover)
One Way—Dangerous, 2-1938

Thrilling Mysteries

Horror in Wax, 4-1935
Hell's Darkest Halls, 2-1937

Thrilling Mystery

The Twisted Men, 3-1936 (cover)
Blood in the House, 6-1936
Everglades Horror, 1-1937
Death Plays Host, 4-1937
Invasion from Inferno, 5-1937 (cover)
The Infernal Box, 6-1937
Blood for the Wolf Pack, 5-1938
Titans of Torture, 11-1938

Today's Family

The Quiet Man, 11-1964

Today's Woman

The Huntress, 11-1951
Danger by Night, 4-1954 (Retitled "The Prowler" for *The Witching Lands*)

Top Notch

The Thin Flame of Courage, 11-1-1931
The Green Gorgon, 10-1935
Seven Steps to Doom, 10-1936
Creighton Sees It Through, date unk., 1930's

Top Notch Detective

By the Neck Until Dead, 3-1939

Toronto Star Weekly

Slow to Anger, 8-8-1942
Who'll Wear My Roses?, 1-30-1943
Leap My Lovely, 3-6-1943
Margin of Victory, 6-5-1943
Most Treasures Buried Deep, 1-15-1944
The Light in the Fog, 2-26-1944
I Love You, Laura, 3-25-1944
With This Ring, 4-1-1944
No More Mail, 4-8-1944
Don't Be Afraid, 4-29-1944
House for Sale, 3-10-1945
Other Man's Pizen, 1-5-1946
It's My Life, 1-5-1947
The Goblins and the Golden Voice, 9-6-1947
Deep Waters, 4-10-1948
The Long Wait, 5-22-1948
On the Trail of an Angel, 7-7-1948
Lost Man Island, 10-2-1948
The Stone Flower, 1-15-1949
Phantom Footprints, 2-19-1949
The Secret Place, 6-11-1949
The Hanging Rope, 11-5-1949
Defence in Depth, 1-7-1950 (reprinted as A Wonderful Life, *John Bull,* 1950)
A Night Ordeal, 10-14-1950
Perilous Journey, 9-15-1951
Revolt on the River, 1-9-1952
The Flame in the Jungle, 7-18-1953
Stubborn Old Fool, 1953 (mo.unk.)
The Diplomat's Dancing Daughter, 5-29-1954
Hard to Kill, 8-21-1954
No Substitute, 10-2-1054
The Mountain of the Lost, 11-20-1954
The Girl He Lost, 11-26-1955

Drums of Revolt, 12-31-1955
The Other Side of Silence, 3-3-1956
The Trail to Everywhere, 3-31-1956
The Frightened Bride, 2-3-1957
Ah, the Simple Life, 7-27-1957
Papa Was Nobody, 8-31-1957
After You, Admiral, 1-4-1958
Mr. Mowry Slept Here, 8-1-1959
Miracle of the Mud Hut, 8-15-1959
Stubborn Woman, 8-22-1959
The Eldred Sisters, 2-20-1960
Stranger Go Home, 1961 (mo. unk.)
The Hunted, 1-20-1962
The Child Who Did Not Exist, 10-13-1962
The Girl in San Marlo, 2-2-1963
Stars in His Eyes, 5-4-1963
A Walk in the River, 10-12-1963
A Smile From the Princess, 11-16-1963
Long Way Home, 11-30-1963
Love Me Simple, Love Me Strong, 8-22-1964
The Empty House, 1964, (mo. unk.)
Grandfather and the Wondrous Beast, 1-9-1965
This Side of the Wall, 2-13-1965
A Mountain to Cross, 6-5-1965
The Broken Sword, 5-28-1966
Forsythe's Devil, 7-23-1966
Time Out For Love, 9-10-1966
Outcast Island, date unk., 1940's-1960's
The Fourth Excursion, date unk., 1940's-1960's
The Reluctant Tourist, date unk., 1950's-1960's
A House for Grandpa, date unknown, 1960's
Never Trust a Man, date unk., 1960's

Triple-X Western

The Poison Sears, 5-1930
Three Doomed Men, 1-1931 (sold as The Terrible three B'Ruga)

True Experiences

Love's an Easy Thing, 1947 (mo. unk.)
Dennison's Wife, 2-1948

True Gangster Stories

Headstone for a Heel, 2-1942
This Way to Death, 6-1942

Twenty Story Magazine

Watch Your Slip, 1932 (mo. unk.)

Two Gun Western

Holy Voice, 7-1931
Border Shanty, 8-1931
War Cry (Salvation Army magazine)
And Ye Shall See Him, 4-1948

Weird Menace

The Kutting Edge, 1994 (as Justin Case)

Weird Tales

The Brotherhood of Blood, 5-1932
The Ghoul Gallery, 6-1932
The City of Crawling Death, 7-1932
Spawn of Inferno, 10-1932
The Cult of the White Ape, 2-1933
Dead Man's Belt, 5-1933
The Crawling Curse, 6-1933
The Watcher in the Green Room, 9-1933
The Black Gargoyle, 3-1934 (cover)
The Isle of Dark Magic, 8-1934
The Death Watch, 10-1939
A Honeymoon to Remember, 4-1994
Inside the Earth, Under the Sea, 1999

Western Action Stories

Torment Trail, date unk.

Western Family Magazine

Word From Davey, 7-22-1943

Western Story Magazine

Rustling on Dishpan Range, 9-14-1932
The Arizona Kid, 12-17-1932 (mo. unk.)
Branded, 1932 (mo. unk.)
The Debt, 1932 (mo. unk.)
Lonesome Rides Again, 1932 (mo. unk.)
Temper and Fists, 1932 (mo. unk.)
Wildcat and Range Wolf, 1-28-1933
Notched Guns, 2-18-1933
Lost Lode Bad Men, 3-4-1933
The Star K Holdup, 4-22-1933

Readin' Writin' & Rough Stuff, 6-10-1933
Plumb Scared, 9-2-1933
Red River Roundup, 11-18-1933
Bad Man, 1-13-1934
Wildcat Breed, 5-18-1934
Showdown on Squaw Mountain, 8-9-1941
White Water Run, 2-14-1942
Frame Trap, 4-25-1942
Hangman's Swamp, 5-16-1942
Blizzard Pasear, 8-1-1942
Payoff for a Polecat, 8-29-1942
Timber Treachery, 9-26-1942

Western Trails

Blood Brand, 3-1932

Whispers

Take Me, for Instance, 11-1974
Ladies in Waiting, 6-1975
Final Game, 10-1983
Dambella's Slough, 12-1984
No Flowers for Henry, 11-1987 (as Carl Hughes)

Wild World Adventures

The Dagger of Tsiang, 5-1930

Wild West Weekly

The Coming of Senor Bravo, 6-28-1941
Trouble Tamin' Tumbleweed, 7-19-1941
Lynx Sign, 8-16-1941
Cure for Coyotes, 8-30-1941
Ghost Town Gamble, 9-13-1941
Double Doom, 11-8-1941

Woman (Eng.)

You're Likely to End Up Married, date unk., 1950's-1970's

Woman's Day

Leave My Girl Alone, 9-1956
Change of Heart, 4-1959
The Girl From Nowhere, 1960 (mo. unk.)

Woman's Day (Aust.)

The Woman He Wanted, 1953 (mo. unk.)

A Kind of Pickup, 1964 (mo. unk.)
A Tree Is for Growing, date unk., 1950's-1970's

Woman's Home Companion
The Seventy-fifth Baby, 3-1945 (as C.H. Barnett)

Woman's Home Journal (Eng.)
Journey Down an Unknown River, 10-1967

Woman's Own (Eng.)
The Artful Imp, 1968 (mo. unk.)

Women's Weekly (Aust.)
The Ladies of Cantwell, 1965 (mo. unk.)

Your Life
More Than a Loaf of Bread, 4-1949

BIBLIOGRAPHY:

Short Non-Fiction by Publication

Adventure

A Few Tons of Plywood, 11-1943 (excerpt from *Long Were the Nights*)

Americas

Haitian Hinterland, 2-1956
Port-au-Prince, 12-1956
Take to the Haitian By-Roads, 1-1957
A Walk to the City, 4-1957

Author and Journalist

Onomatology & Onomatopoeia, 12-29-1928
Confessions of a Vanity Publisher's Assistant, 1928 (mo. unk.)

Boston Post

Bell Hopping Is Hopping Plenty, 1928 (mo.unk.)
Miscellaneous poems, 1927-1928

Boston Post Sunday Magazine

Real Voodoo Uncanny, 1950's (date unk.)

Boy's Life

Just Fishing Isn't Fishing Enough, 5-1947
Table Tennis Tips, 11-1952

Bozart Poetry Magazine

Description, 1/2-1929

Buick Magazine

Tent Town Democracy, date unk. (1950's-1970's)

Elks Magazine

It's Not Funny, 9-1946 (reprinted as Sadism in the US Navy in *Everybody's Digest, 2-47)*

Ford Times

Bake Today! 7-1948
Crabbin' the Blues, 8-1948

Granite

Miscellaneous Poems, 1927-1928

Justice, Inc., New York, Hero Games, 1983

Adventures in the Pulps (foreword)

Latin American Report

The New Voodoo, 9-1956
Sportsman's Paradise in Haiti, 7-1957

Liberty Magazine

I Took the Sky Road, 8-25-1945 (condensation of the book)

Life Can Be Beautiful Magazine

Do We Want Too Much? 4-1949

Los Angeles Times

Forget? 1928 (mo. unk.)

Monsters and Other Stories

Burton MI, Subterranean Press, 1998

Afterword

Necrofile

A Ride on the GG&O, 1993

Pawtucket Times

Miscellaneous poems, 1927-1928

Phanton Perfumes: Memories of Ghost Stories Magazine, BC Canada, Ash Tree Press, 2000

Foreword

Presbyterian Advance

Miscellaneous poems, 1927-1928
Life, 7-19-1928 (poem)

Providence Evening Bulletin

Miscellaneous poems,1927-1928

Providence Journal

Miscellaneous poems, 1927-1928
Love Letter to Warwick, 10-5-1952
A Rhode Islander Writes About Haiti, 1952 (mo. unk.)

Pulpster (for Pulpcon)

Monikers, 1996

Pulp Vault

Magazines I Remember, 1992 (Issue #10), 1993 (Issue #11)

Report to Writers

Let's Write Better Stories, 1953 (mo. unk.)

Saturday Evening Post

I Saw the Helena Go Down, 1-22-1944 (excerpt from *The Fightin'est Ship*)
Bluefins are Bedlam, 12-20-1947

Shudder Stories #4

On Voodoo, 3-1986

The Sign

A Boy and His Camera, 3-1949
The Sportlight—Grantland Rice
Chains, date unk. (1927-1928, poem)

Sunset Magazine

Men, 1930 (mo. unk., poem, later used as lyrics to song of the same name, *Oliver Ditson Co.*)

The US Navy in WWII, New York, Wm Morrow & Co., 1966 (Book-of-the-Month Club selection)
First Strike on Iwo (exerpt from *I Took the Sky Road*)
Kula Gulf (exerpt from *The Fight'nest Ship*)
Thunder Mug at Apamama (Excerpt from *I Took the Sky Road*)

The Vampire Master and Other Tales of Terror
Royal Oak Michigan, Haffner Press, 2000
Introduction

The Writer
Your Debt to the Reader, 12-1953
The Use of Background, 8-1957

This Is the Navy, New York
Penguin Books, 1944
Long Was the Night (excerpt from *Long Were the Nights*)
Take the Big Ones First (exerpt from *The Fightin'est Ship*)

This Week Magazine
Sealed Orders, 4-29-1945

Travel Magazine
Tortuga, Pirate Paradise, 5-1958

True Magazine
Saga of the Transports, 12-1944 (excerpt from *Wings Across the World*)
Long Were the Nights, 6-1944 (condensation of the book)

Vampire Master & Other Tales of Horror
Royal Oak, Michigan, Haffner Press, 2000
Foreword

Yachting Magazine
Squadron X, 11-1943 (excerpt from *Long Were the Nights*)

YMCA News
"Ah Foo" Sayings, Miscellaneous poems, 1927-1928

Your Life
Warm Hearts Share Their Glow, 4-1947
Put A Polish On Dull Moments, 10-1947

INDEX

Two thousand five hundred copies of this book have been printed by the Vail-Ballou Mfg. Grp., Binghamton, NY using Sabon typeface on 55# Bright White Tradebook paper. The binding cloth is Roxite C grade. Typesetting by The Composing Room, Inc., Kimberly, WI.